BARRIOS ARES

LATINO URBANISM NO "NEW"

"NEW URBANISM" : EXCULSIONARY, ALSO.

STUPID SUBURBIA
    ARCHITECTURE OF :

· COMERCIAL/ RESIDENTIAL
· LIVE/WALK SPACE
· RECYCLING
· FOOD SOVERNIGHTY
· PUBLIC/TRANSIT
· WALKING
    ECONOMIC/ ART & CULTURE

SOCIAL KNOWLEDGE : COMPACT DEVELOPMENT
    → MORE INTERACTION

    LIVE/WORK/SPACE
        ENVIORNMENTALIST → EURO-CENTRIC
    ENVIORNMENTAL JUSTICE → ACKNOWLEDGING
    LATINO

                    I. CRITISIZE

RENT STRIKES
    OPPOSITION OF FREEWAYS

MW01039682

Latino Urbanism

The Politics of Planning, Policy, and Redevelopment

EDITED BY
David R. Diaz and Rodolfo D. Torres

NEW YORK UNIVERSITY PRESS
New York and London

NEW YORK UNIVERSITY PRESS
New York and London
www.nyupress.org

© 2012 by New York University
All rights reserved

References to Internet websites (URLs) were accurate at the time of writing.
Neither the author nor New York University Press is responsible for URLs
that may have expired or changed since the manuscript was prepared.

Library of Congress Cataloging-in-Publication Data
Latino urbanism : the politics of planning, policy, and redevelopment / edited by David R. Diaz and Rodolfo
D. Torres.
p. cm.
Includes bibliographical references and index.
ISBN 978-0-8147-8404-4 (cl : alk. paper)
ISBN 978-0-8147-8405-1 (pb : alk. paper)
ISBN 978-0-8147-2470-5 (ebook)
ISBN 978-0-8147-2483-5 (ebook)
1. Hispanic Americans—Social conditions. 2. City planning—United States. 3. Hispanic American
neighborhoods. I. Diaz, David R., 1951- II. Torres, Rodolfo D., 1949-
E184.S75L3649 2012
305.86'8073—dc23
2012018749

New York University Press books are printed on acid-free paper,
and their binding materials are chosen for strength and durability.
We strive to use environmentally responsible suppliers and materials
to the greatest extent possible in publishing our books.

Manufactured in the United States of America
c 10 9 8 7 6 5 4 3 2 1
p 10 9 8 7 6 5 4 3 2 1

CONTENTS

DEDICATION

Francine Marie Diaz, "Your eclectic spirit, fearless politica and lust for life remains powerful in the young Third World, aspiring attorney's at Boalt Hall in Berkeley who all vie to follow your courageous leadership."

Por me especial Tias, Latinas who inspired my life, who were raised in the apartheid era.

Tia Minnie Levy and Tia Rita Montez, Familia Galarze de Joyo Maravilla. Tia Rita your smile and affection always brighten my spirit. Tia Mini, you encouragement and support throughout my tumulus young adulthood was critical to who I am.

Tia Irene Biolley, East Los Angeles and La Puente. Tia Irene your strength, positive vibes, love, along with my dear Tio James, have constantly sustained me.

Tia Irene Biolley, East Los Angeles and Goleta. Tia Irene, at an early period in my intellectual development you showed what an intelligent, inquisitive and opinionated Chicana was all about.

David R. Diaz

ACKNOWLEDGMENTS

We wish to express our gratitude to all the contributors to this volume as well the external reviewers. It's been a wonderful experience working alongside our contributors, who are all in their unique way forging new intellectual spaces for a critical engagement with cities across the United States. A special thank you to both Ilene Kalish and Aiden Amos of NYU Press for their patience and their support of this project.

There was no defined division of labor on the project; thus the names appear in alphabetical order and have no editorial significance.

Introduction

David R. Diaz and Rodolfo D. Torres

The last three decades of the twentieth century marked the beginning of epochal socioeconomic transformation of U.S. society. The economic reverberations of these changes have continued through the first decade of the twenty-first century as the income and wealth gap continues to widen. Nowhere is this more obvious than in U.S. cities and surrounding metropolitan areas, where the damaging effects of the deep recession on the living standards of working-class, lower-class, and middle-class American workers and their families are felt the most.

In addition to macroeconomic trends, immigration and population shifts have had a tremendous economic impact on U.S. cities. Recent protests in major cities across the United States against several proposed changes in U.S. immigration policy and citizenship status have once again brought attention to big cities, where much of the precipitous growth of immigrant populations has occurred.

According to the U.S. Census Bureau (2011), as of April 1, 2010, an estimated 50.5 million Latinos lived in the United States, making people of "Latino origin" the nation's largest ethnic minority group. Latinos constituted 16.3 percent of the nation's total population of nearly 308.7 million. It was projected that this population would grow to nearly 132.8 million by July 1, 2050, and that Latino men, women, and children would then constitute 30 percent of the nation's population. The Mexican American population constituted 63 percent of the nation's current 50.5 million Latinos, with Puerto Ricans another 9.2 percent, Cubans 3.5 percent, and Salvadorans 3.2 percent. The remainder were of some other Central American, South American, or other Hispanic or Latino origin.

William H. Frey (2001), in a recent publication of the Brookings Institute, asserts that over half of America's cities are now majority nonwhite. Primary cities in fifty-eight metropolitan areas were "majority minority" in 2010, up from forty-three in 2000. Cities lost only about half as many whites in the 2000s as in the 1990s, but "black flight" from cities such as Atlanta, Chicago, Dallas, and Detroit accelerated in the 2000s.

Frey also reports that ethnic minorities represent 35 percent of suburban residents, a proportion similar to their share of the overall U.S. population. Among the hundred largest metro areas, thirty-six feature "melting pot" suburbs where at least 35 percent of residents are nonwhite. The suburbs of Houston, Las Vegas, San Francisco, and Washington, D.C., became majority minority in the 2000s.

More important than the sheer numbers is the fact that Latina/o men and women and their families are a growing sector of the U.S. working class and a fragile first-generation middle class. Equally significant, they are increasingly concentrated in the very industries that have been most influenced by the economic restructuring of the United States. They are trapped in low-wage jobs in an economy that is producing far too few living-wage jobs to accommodate the increasing number of workers entering the labor market and to sustain a robust and democratic economy.

Principles of critical urbanism will guide the reader through this volume, which examines Latinos within the context of the changing role of cities in a market-driven and racialized environment. A growing portion of the world's population lives and works in cities, thus the knowledge of how cities develop and function is a critical component of a planner's intellectual tool kit. Applying an understanding of the effects of socioeconomic change on cities to other major areas of urban theory will enhance planners' ability to develop appropriate policy measures. In addition, the dramatic social changes that are reshaping the terrain of planning politics are predominantly an urban phenomenon. The characteristics of contemporary cities—increasing diversity, globalization of production and consumption, new sources of inequality, and uneven development—are creating different terrains for the policy actions that are the primary focus of the urban studies under late capitalism.

The contributors to this book represent a diverse group of scholars attempting to link their own unique theoretical interpretations and approaches to political and policy interventions in the spaces and cultures of Latino everyday life. It matters how cities are theorized, as this underpins the ideological and political designs and the policy frameworks adopted. Given the gaps between explanatory and normative concepts underlying urban planning and the radical changes in the United States, as well as globally, regarding economies, political systems, and information technologies, many subject areas must be considered experimentally.

On a range of levels, urban environmental crises are traceable to racism and market-driven forces. But the approach called New Urbanism or Smart Growth, which claims to address the latest iteration of urban crisis, fails to adequately analyze and address these factors. When Bullard, Johnson, and Torres (2000) denounced planning's main production in the modern era, sprawl, as "stupid growth," they implicitly exposed the profession's dubious history of complicity in creating a failed suburbia (Diaz 2005). The current race to envelop planning practice in a new ideology is a shallow and intellectually dishonest evasion of the task of thoroughly and painfully acknowledging planning's institutional and intellectual failure. Eurocentrists, who continue to control the educational and administrative functions of planning, are reluctant to give credit where credit is due, especially in the necessary discourse over why the suburban model and the programs promising federally funded revitalization in the post–World War II era have been characterized by systemic irrationalities with regard to planning, public policy, and the environment.

The class and racial hierarchy that persists in the planning profession is not "new," nor will the construction of a "new" ideology undo a history of failed urban policy. On a multitude of levels, uncritically adopted rational-functional principles have been reified by an elitist, Eurocentric planning profession that has proven resistant to critique from ethnic communities (Taylor 1998). Innumerable planning graduate programs maintain only token minority representation, with the University of California system being among the worst. One of the editors of this volume is one such token faculty member in a planning department. Power in the profession, whether in the public or the private sector, remains concentrated among a cloistered Euro-American elite. Yet when this system of dominance is challenged, the tried-and-true class-based defense emerges, asserting technical knowledge, professional experience, managerial proficiency, bureaucratic power relations, and/or privileged educational attainment over public ignorance.

The structural economic, psychological, and environmental crises of suburbia that now confront planning were created and defended by this very hierarchy (Beatley 2000; Deleage 1994; Barry 2005; Booth 2004). Current planning discourse, despite its claims to novelty, is still rife with contradictions and irrationalities that are evidence of the fundamental failure of Eurocentric control over planning education and practice for over two generations. Thus, any claim to enlightened discourse will be initiated only by addressing who was (and is) most responsible for the failures of planning into the current era. This analysis, which must incorporate the voices of excluded ethnic others, will necessarily confront a legacy of racism in planning on multiple levels: in planning education, in the training of students, in private and public sector practice, and in the blatant manipulation of redistributive federal programs and planning ideology. Only then will planning create the potential space for meaningful transformations and potentially egalitarian transitions in both practice and urban social change. Specifically, this historical and critical approach is a necessary initial stage for restructuring an urban planning strategy that is based on barrio urbanism and that includes and engages Latina/o community leaders. Latino scholarship on the urban condition must also be included: for example, the urban writings of Ernesto Galarza, a progressive public intellectual and prominent in Mexican American community activist whose wide-ranging and groundbreaking work in urban politics and human geography has been largely neglected by the planning community as well as by urban scholars.

Situating "El Barrio" in Planning Discourse: Lessons from the Front Line

Though barrios were historically created and maintained by segregation and discrimination, their everyday life has kept a vitality and sense of place that validate the importance of the urban in the midst of the logic of decentralized sprawl that permeates planning. The power of Latina/o culture is a fundamental characteristic of barrio urbanism, a symbolic resistance to racism and a celebration of culturally situated social practices. Interwoven into this urban milieu is an internally defended concept of the importance of the social, testifying that the significance of what Alain Touraine (1988) described as "the social actor" persists, despite its loss in academic discourse in the rush to a postmodern explanation for all things urban. Without the reconstruction of the art of the social that barrio communities vividly exemplify, sustainable urbanism is unlikely to succeed in this consumption-obsessed society.

The concept of the *ciudadano,* the citizen situated in everyday life and urban culture, is linked to the most mundane and fundamental act, the act of walking. Walking makes possible the evolution of a cultural community over time through shared experiences on the human scale of relationships. Visually, walking in the neighborhood lends itself to an appreciation of *jardines, color, calles, árboles, tiendas, arte publico, y la vida de la calle.* Culturally, it has offered a historic respite from a repressive, discriminatory society that has traditionally marginalized everyday life as much as ethnic difference. The art of traversing through a neighborhood, both practical and pleasurable, is part of an aesthetic that planning has only recently and lamely attempted to reclaim.

Historically, environmental sustainability is fundamental to spatial relations within *el barrio*. The defense and utilization of *la tierra* for food production in collective gardens and farms, watershed management, communal celebrations, and the protection of nature have all been normative in the barrio; these practices predate European immigration to the Western Hemisphere. Other essential features of barrio life, such as mixed use, reliance on public transportation, recycling and adaptive reuse, collective sharing of space, and eclectic reproduction of the urban landscape through public art, have only recently been rediscovered as important reforms to past planning practice.

Because of discriminatory redistribution of public funds, barrios have received little in the way of formally recognized public spaces such as parks and recreational facilities, but they have developed numerous ways of maximizing the utilization of space for the community and particularly for children. *La tierra es par los niños*, even when the spaces available are merely neighbors' side or front yards, streets, and vacant lots. Even private spaces may be turned into civic resources and made inviting (Gámez 2002; Rojas 1999). Most barrio residents would be amused to learn that in trendy architectural discourse front porches are a "must amenity."

Further, everyday life in barrios has always involved recycling. Responding to economic marginalization and necessity, barrio residents have actively recycled a wide range of materials (Peña 2005). *Ropa, madera, pipas, ventanas, puertas, ladrillos, y tinas* have been adaptively reused for personal use, landscape design, structures, and/or art. In fact, no other social sector has been more directly engaged in active recycling throughout the twentieth century than barrio residents.

For centuries barrio residents have also produced food, as a leisure activity and to supplement household nutrition. Particularly in the past quarter century, a vibrant *jardinero* movement has turned numerous vacant lots to productive use. *Una explosion de verde, yerbas, floras, verduras y fruta* has resulted from intensive labor that beautifies the city and offers nontoxic food resources for local and regional residents (Pinderhughes 2004).

El barrio thus has important contributions to make to the sustainable urban policy that will be needed in the future: not only in relation to efficient energy use, maximization of existing resources, support for collective public amenities, urban density, adaptive reuse, and eclectic uses of space, but in the role of the *ciudadano,* which exemplifies the vibrant social agency within urbanism that planners of virtually all ideologies hope to restore (Katz 1994; Fung 2001; Calthorpe 1993; Bailly et al. 2000). Arguments to reconceptualize urban design, create open space in neighborhoods, revert to mixed uses, and abandon rational functional zoning logic are all predicated on the vision that Alain Touraine has articulated: "Political and social institutions can no longer be the servants of a supposedly rational order or a progress that is supposedly inscribed in the laws of historical evolution; they must be made to serve the Subject ... to defend the radiant future from the past" (2000, 303). Henri Lefebvre's ([1974] 1991) demand that urbanism challenge the gentrification that has displaced the working class from the center of the city must also be met if this vision is to be fulfilled; the defense of barrio space is thus critical to the project of urban restoration.

Yet planners seeking solutions to the urban crisis have been unaware of the barrio's living demonstration of a rational, economically and environmentally sustainable form of urbanism in their midst. One reason for their ignorance may well be the history of pathetic Eurocentric fear of the other (Doob 1999; Bowser and Hunt 1996). *El barrio* has been stereotyped as a mysterious, dangerous, and threatening space. Unwarranted assumptions about barrio life are reinforced by racist ideology and skew perceptions: thus, for example, *el ciudadano caminando por la calle* is viewed as a frightening figure to be surveiled and controlled rather than a citizen interacting socially with his community. Everyday cultural practices are perceived as sinister resistance to mainstream society, and a suburban mindset imagines cities as zones of crime and degeneracy. Cloaked in mystery, barrio culture has been ignored and misunderstood.

Planners have also had little awareness of the rich and eclectic history of Latino urbanism. Along with the initial settlements of First Nations, barrios and *colonias* have been some of the earliest urban forms in the Southwest, dating from the 1600s. In fact, until the era of railroad expansion, barrios were the only urban centers. The influx of Euro-Americans into the Southwest in the latter stages of the nineteenth century ushered in a fundamental ethnic transition (Rosenbaum 1981), that has been reversed only in the last two decades. The evolution of cities is directly correlated with the growth of barrios and *colonias.* The three largest Latina/o urban communities in the United States are in El Paso, San Antonio, and Los Angeles.

In the past twenty-five years, barrio communities of the Southwest have significantly expanded their territory and are on the verge of achieving an ethnic *reconquista* (Diaz 2005; Suro and Singer 2002). The most substantial Latina/o community in the country, East Los Angeles (Valle and Torres 2000; Romo 1983; Acuña 1988), has expanded into what is now considered "the Greater Eastside." This is a zone of approximately 450 square miles, stretching east of the Los Angeles River into the central San Gabriel Valley and south from Highland Park into the small cities that constitute Southeast Los Angeles County. This ethnic and cultural transformation is the most fundamental aspect of urban change associated with virtually every city in the Southwest and, increasingly, cities throughout the nation. Barrios are rapidly making inroads into surrounding urban communities and working-class suburbs and in some areas are taking over entire counties. Los Angeles County is now 50 percent Latina/o and is largely a system of barrios showing the polynucleated pattern of growth that Mark Gottdiener, in an enlightened theoretical analysis, projected for suburbs in this region in 1985.

Latinas/os have had a history throughout the last century of challenging planning and spatial relations. It has spanned land grant battles in New Mexico from the 1880s through the 1960s (Peña 2005; Rosenbaum 1981); rent strikes in Spanish Harlem in the 1940s (Cayo-Sexton 1965); and numerous struggles, over the decades, to save Chicano neighborhoods from urban renewal, whether Chavez Ravine in Los Angeles in the 1940s and 1950s (Lopez 2002; Parson 2005), Varrio Viejo in Tucson in the 1960s (Dimas 1999), or Chicano Park in Logan Heights, San Diego, in the 1960s and 1970s (Cockcroft and Barnet-Sanchez [1990] 1993). The Crusade for Justice in Denver, one of the first organizations of the Chicano Power Movement, evolved from a critique of that city's racist redevelopment and redistributive policies (Vigil 1999). Throughout the Southwest, barrio social movements like La Raza Unida in the 1960s engaged cities over their failure to provide the most basic urban amenities, such as sewer and water systems, storm drains, paved streets, and recreational facilities for youth (Vigil 1999). One of the first Chicano protest movements in California was a result of the dismantling of the entire western sector of Barrio Logan by California's state transportation agency; by claiming land for a community park where Chicano artists painted murals that portrayed Chicano politics and history, the protesters gave cultural workers a unique interventionist role in redefining space in a distinct culture image. Since the 1970s, the Chicano environmental justice movement has attempted to halt the environmental poisoning of working class Latino communities.

Oppositional movements have been barrio leaders' only recourse, due to the fact that Latinos both in and on the periphery of planning have had limited agency in advancing the promise of Model Cities, advocacy planning, and working-class community revitalization. These social actors, marginalized by the profession, have had few avenues available to proactively shape policy. Yet in any project of barrio revitalization, those most at risk should have the most influence over matters that will be affecting their everyday lives. Self-determination, direct control over actions that have potentially have long-term or even permanent impacts on individuals, families, and communities, is a fundamental human right.

The legacy of planning documents the opposite. Barrio residents have sensed that they are under attack by urban policy mandates that they have had no political influence to challenge (Acuña 1988). From the beginning of eminent domain in the post–World War II era of redevelopment and transportation route designations, the state has viewed barrio space as vulnerable and expendable. The destruction of barrios, involving the demolition of massive amounts of affordable housing, the dismantling of zones of minority property ownership, and radical reconfigurations of space, has been carried out with a dismissal of minority concerns that expressed a racist contempt for marginalized communities. In the aftermath of the enlightened federally financed War on Poverty, only minimal influence has been ceded to representatives from disenfranchised zones of the city. Since that era, as documented in this volume, the relationship between a Euro-American planning profession and Latinas/os has been oppositional and conflictive rather than egalitarian and inclusionary. But through a long history of being marginalized economically and politically, Latina/o communities have asserted their right to active participation in land use decisions (Darder and Torres 2004).

Planning Literature and Barrio Reality

Despite the many lessons that planners might draw from the long history of Latino urbanism, mainstream literature has rarely situated Latinas/os in the center of urban crises or in relation to oppositional movements critical of urban revitalization policy (Valle and Torres 2000; Peña 2005; Diaz 2005). Latina/o environmentalists, including Devon Peña, Benjamin Marquez, and Laura Pulido, as well as critical theorists Rodolfo Torres and Nestor Rodriguez, have developed the most important urbanist analyses of barrios and planning. Mike Davis is one of the very few non-Latino urbanists who has written on urban policy and Latinas/os with analytical specificity and incisive social critique. His book *Magical Urbanism* (2000) contains a wealth of information and is a major contribution to understanding the emerging Chicano and Latino urban landscape in the United States.

Why has this failure to incorporate Latinas/os into planning literature persisted into the twenty-first century? Given that they constitute a significant ethnic community and that barrios are a fundamental component of every major city in the Southwest and other powerful cities across the country, why have planners remained so ignorant of them and so narrowly focused on the "lily white" suburbs nurtured by the profession since the post–World War II suburban expansion? To answer this question, a few key aspects of city planning—racism, classism, and endorsement of discriminatory exclusion in public policy—will be briefly explored.

Planners' failure to acknowledge, much less learn from, ethnic others in the domains of theory, policy formulation, and practice is reflective of an earlier era of segregation, a construct designed to nurture, celebrate, and defend white privilege (Almaguer 1994; Doob 1999; Bowser and Hunt 1996; Young 1990). A predominantly Euro-American discipline, in its staunch resistance to incorporating other, existing visions of urban spatical relations, continues to practice, on an intellectual level, the kind of segregation more broadly and thoroughly enforced in an earlier period of U.S. history.

Planning has long resisted acknowledging its history of racism in education, practice, and policy (Darder 1995; Hoch 1994). From its earliest inception in the modern era (since 1950), planning has actively resisted minority voices concerning urban policy. The result was a series of historical contradictions to any claims of a pluralist democracy in urban policy through the late 1980s. Planning remained one of the most segregated professions well into the 1980s. Planning schools practiced a de facto "color line" in annual admissions. University of California Berkeley (where one of the authors attended) was, and is, notorious for the paltry numbers of Latina/o graduate students admitted through the 1990s, though California has by far the highest percentage of Latinas/os in the nation. In addition, the scarcity of Latina/o doctoral students in planning is nothing less than a social crime, given the importance of urban policy and planning to the future of barrio revitalization.

Structural racism resulted in a distinctly racist social and professional environment for Latina/o planners through the 1980s (one that many would argue still exists today). Yet the 1980s was the critical period of federally supported revitalization programs. In the era when redistributive benefits should have substantially enhanced barrios, minorities were forced into marginalized roles with virtually no power. Those that resisted were professionally repressed or blacklisted from the city planning profession.

Obviously, this had severe, detrimental impacts on barrio redevelopment and reconstruction. In fact, few attempt to claim that any meaningful level of tangible benefit actually accrued to barrios during this era. Racism and resistance to ethnic difference were key factors necessitating the evolution, in numerous cities, of barrio social movements engaging in desperate *luchas* for the very survival of barrios. Barrio leaders, instead of participating in principled inclusionary, egalitarian planning, were forced into confrontational roles in defense of barrio spatial relations and Latinas/os in cities.

Classism and sexism were also prominent forces in city planning practice through the early 1980s. City bureaucracies, like colleges, were reluctant to admit women and minorities into their ranks (Hoch 1994). For minorities in general and Latinas in particular, seeking a professional degree and a career in planning was a highly risky venture. Situated in an economy that supported systemic exclusion (Doob 1999), city planners often acted in defense of class privilege. Consequently barrio constituencies came into conflict with planners and criticized a range of failures in urban policy (Feagin 1989; Rodriguez 1993; Davis 2000; Diaz 2005). The key goal of the profession was legitimation of elite interests rather than actual revitalization of deteriorating neighborhoods. A sequestered profession made up of Euro-American men developed a siege mentality in relation to the universe outside the "gates of city hall." They normatively rejected oppositional voices, less on the basis of the merits of proposals than on the basis of maintaining their own total control over planning knowledge and urban policy (Taylor 1998). Thus they kept barrio residents from establishing proactive, community-based alternatives to rational-functional planning practice.

The political exclusion maintained during the critical early stages of Model Cities was and remains a central cause of the current crisis in planning. As we enter the fifth decade of predominantly Eurocentric control over the policy apparatus of the state, the only historical lesson is that of stark failure to assist, much less actually revitalize, barrios, almost anywhere. The demise of advocacy planning, the only true reform movement within planning, doomed the profession to a series of conflicts with barrios in which aggressive protests were the sole avenue for Latinos' political expression and critique of planners' constant policy ineptitude.

Thus, it is no surprise that by the late twentieth century the topic of Latinas/os' relationship to space had yet to assume a central place in planning discourse. The sole arena was environmental justice. In a famous 1989 *Amicus* journal article (Russell 1989), planners "proudly" pronounced the "discovery" of environmental racism. But while addressing racism in any of its forms is important, claiming a "new" racism in the late twentieth century shows either lamentable ignorance or a hypocritical cover-up of the long-standing history of environmental insults to Latino communities and the vibrant social justice movements that arose as early as the 1940s and 1950s to address these problems.

Racism in planning practice has correlated directly with an exclusion from planning literature of studies focused on urban policy's effects on barrios. For decades, the existence of any semblance of such a literature was due mainly to Chicana/o sociologists and historians who ethically could not escape documenting the urban planning injustices perpetrated on barrios as a subset of other narratives. A few ethnic historians, Rodolfo Acuña being the most prominent, have analyzed the Latina/o urban experience far more significantly than planners have (though Acuña's most significant contribution, *A Community under Siege: A Chronicle of Chicanos East of the Los Angeles River* [1984], has been largely ignored by both Chicano and non-Chicano urbanists). Eminent domain, freeway destruction, land banking, targeted disinvestment, racism in public policy, and the devastation of Latina/o spaces were readily apparent to this field of academia. Further, literature from the fields of public health, education, social welfare, and law has at least occasionally touched on planning in descriptions of such issues as poverty, inadequate housing, and lack of infrastructure in Latino communities. Yet in planning, similar documentation was virtually absent well into the 1990s.

Finally, one of the most fundamental failures in the literature has been the inability to recognize how barrios are in the vanguard of sustainable urbanism. It is the height of Eurocentric arrogance to declare a New Urbanism when every feature of that framework has long been and continues to be exhibited as a vibrant and enduring reality in barrios through the country. Devon Peña and Raquel Rivera-Pinderhughes are among the leading voices addressing barrios' traditions of sustainable urbanism and local economic relations. And in the past decade, as mentioned earlier, Latina/o urbanists and a few others have directed attention toward the urban crisis and the inherent value of barrio urbanism in the United States. Increased attention to the Southwest, in relation to civic plazas

Failures in urban planning

(Arreola 2002), the use of open space as community space (Rojas 1999; Gámez 2002), integrated business districts (Dávila 2001), and environmental justice (Peña 2005, 1998, 1997; Marquez 1998; Pulido 1996), has initiated a spatial discourse of the barrio. But ironically, adherents to the L.A. perspective, which has famously claimed to "make the invisible visible," have apparently failed to incorporate Latinas/os.

Organization of This Book

This book, then, is part of a broader recent effort to address numerous issues related to barrio urbanism that have long been neglected in the planning literature. In the next chapter, "Barrios and Planning Ideology," David Diaz, coeditor of this volume, challenges current planning ideology by claiming that what is being called "New Urbanism" is in reality "barrio urbanism" or "Latina/o urbanism." The social function of the city that New Urbanists are trying to restore still exists in barrios and has not fundamentally changed over the past century. The barrio's cultural logic of a communally oriented spatial arena that reflects rich interrelationships and social networks has intrinsic value for planning and urban sociology. Yet New Urbanism, in what is only the latest form of racialized and exclusionary urban visions, has not even so much undervalued barrio urbanism as totally ignored it. Why? What purpose is served when yet another "new theory" is propounded that fails to acknowledge enlightened urbanist practice that already exists?

The answer is that New Urbanists, especially architects and planners, want to evade accountability for the failure of suburbia. The fundamental crisis has finally reached the consciousness of suburbanites who are trapped on gridlocked freeways, stressed out, frightened by the economy, and freaking out over housing costs. New Urbanism advocates a reformulation of zoning and design principles that will compel a return to civic society and restore a social realm. It is a perspective grounded on the acknowledgment that because of suburban sprawl the concept of urban citizenship has virtually disappeared.

Diaz's chapter shows how the everyday life of *el barrio* exemplifies a workable, enduring alternative to the suburban model that has persisted throughout the decades of failed suburban policy. Compact development, easy access to shops, live-work spaces, actively used open space, the cultivation of gardens and farms, and an emphasis on walking and public transportation all produce a vital public realm with flourishing social interaction. This historic urbanism is not "new."

Chapter 3, by Johana Londoño, entitled "Aesthetic Belonging: The Latinization and Renewal of Union City, New Jersey," is an analysis of the politics of aestheticizing urban places that focuses on a working-class suburban barrio outside New York City. During the past two decades Union City has been gradually revitalized through New Jersey's Urban Enterprise Zone (UEZ) program. Though Bergenline Avenue, the city's main commercial boulevard, features a colorful, multitextured built environment that exemplifies the "Latinization" of urban space, upwardly mobile aspirations among the city's Latina/o population and gentrification pressures generated by Union City's geographic proximity to New York City have resulted in the UEZ's promotion and financing of its replacement by a modern "Main Street American" look similar to that of many New Urbanist developments, characterized by muted "classic" colors and clean-cut sign typography. Thus, the aesthetic Latinization of commercial space in Union City has come into conflict with the UEZ's definition of what constitutes a "proper urban aesthetic" for economic development, one that will encourage investment by projecting an image of regulation and uniformity. According to Londoño, the saying *Entre gustos no hay disgustos,* which translates to "In matters of taste there is no debate," actually dismisses the power relations involved in the implementation of aesthetics: *el gusto*'s visual manifestation in cities is laden with discourses of power constituted by class and racial hierarchies, and the visual aestheticization of cities is a process by which opinions and perceptions focused on urban spaces are defined by specific groups with multiple interests. Londoño argues that economic redevelopment projects in barrios outlying large global cities engage with culture and ethnicity in different ways from those in historic central cities, a key factor when analyzing federally urban redevelopment programs: location plays an important role in whether a Latina/o-identified place will be appreciated and sustained for its economic, social, and cultural value.

Chapter 4, "Placing Barrios in Housing Policy," by Kee Warner, examines the magnitude of the housing crisis in Latina/o communities and traces the history of the policies that have created it. Before the civil rights era, federal housing policies and programs blatantly excluded racial and ethnic minorities, but even passage of civil rights laws in the 1960s did not eliminate discrimination in public housing. Challenges to redlining of neighborhoods and to racist exclusion from public housing projects and programs sought to redress these inequalities, but beginning in the 1970s a devolution of housing policy from federal to state and local levels and from public to private initiatives generally weakened programs. Their emphasis shifted from directly assisting low-income consumers of housing, such as renters, to increasing the number of home owners—a project that in combination with unregulated subprime lending has for many Latina/os, changed their housing problem from gaining housing in the first place to keeping it. Programs also have tended to shift funds from affordable housing to community development that favors elites and the middle class over those most in need. Latinos certainly have not significantly benefited from HUD-funded programs and reallocation policies initially adopted to address deteriorating residential neighborhoods. The legacy of national legislation established to assist lower-income areas to improve the housing stock, revitalize the local economy, and improve social conditions has not reversed a history of underdevelopment, continuing neighborhood decline, and harmful land speculation. Instead, the funding from federal affordable housing programs has been confiscated by local elites for civic center-, sports- or office-oriented development, so that little has been directed toward increasing home ownership in barrios. A number of historical factors have blocked a proactive reallocation strategy, including overt racism, exclusion of Latinos from the political arena, elite control over land policy, manipulation of federal programs by local elites, rational-functional planning practice, and the inability of federal agencies to ensure the transfer of knowledge to the community level.

In chapter 5, "Urban Redevelopment and Mexican American Barrios in the Socio-Spatial Order," Nestor Rodriguez addresses the effects of urban redevelopment on Mexican American barrios. As he shows, redevelopment policy has conferred little benefit, social or economic, on barrio communities in decline since the 1960s; indeed, more housing for the poor has been destroyed than created. Antipoverty programs originally designed to provide affordable housing for poor and working-class communities have been abandoned or manipulated by real estate and investment banking interests through legislative modifications that have allowed funding to be diverted to nonresidential development and the building of commercial districts.

During the most influential period of redevelopment, from the era after World War II until the early 1970s, barrios absorbed the worst abuses associated with urban reconstruction. Despite campaigns of resistance by barrio residents, numerous communities were destroyed, partially dismantled, and/or excluded from the benefits of redevelopment programs. In fact, the logic of redevelopment destabilized rather than reinvigorated the economy of the barrio. Redevelopment policy as practiced in this society viewed barrios as expendable in relation to regional economic development strategy. Barrios, being generally located near downtown business districts, were prime targets for redevelopment, and residents generally lacked the political power to prevent their being exploited by outside economic interests.

Redevelopment has never achieved its legislative mandate. It has failed to increase affordable housing supply, reverse structural decline in minority business districts, empower communities through direct control over land policy, end employment discrimination, or significantly increase in employment opportunities—all major urban demands of Latina/o communities to this day.

In chapter 6, "A Pair of Queens: La Reina de Los Angeles, the Queen City of Charlotte, and the New (Latin) American South," José Luis Gámez explores the "invisible terrain" occupied by new Latina/o migrants in East Los Angeles and Charlotte, North Carolina. In East L.A., established Latina/o residents and new migrants inhabit separate worlds that rarely intersect: the latter rarely frequent the public and commercial spaces of Latina/o East L.A. because they lack the money and social connections to do so. Often their main social connections are to their homelands. New migrants are less likely to be home owners, more likely to seek privacy from a variety of prying eyes, more likely to share housing with other families who are not related by kinship so that even within one house barriers of privacy are maintained, and less likely to project their identity into their surroundings in obvious ways. Public socializing does occur but often in makeshift and temporary spaces out of the view of greater Los Angeles. In Charlotte, most of the Latina/o population consists of such new migrants, who have moved into aging auto-oriented suburban landscapes no longer attractive to middle-class residents, and who maintain a very similar way of life to that of the migrants in L.A. Even here, however, migrant communities have initiated spatial transformations: vendors' trucks, for example, are revitalizing nondescript, marginal suburban spaces, though such transformations are often resisted by civic officials as evidence of urban decline or nonconformity to local regulations.

In chapter 7, "Fostering Diversity: Lessons from Integration in Public Housing," Silvia Domínguez reports the author's fieldwork concerning two sets of Latina/o residents in public housing in Boston in 2000: residents of Maverick Gardens in East Boston, near a busy Latina/o enclave, and

CHAPTER 7

residents of Mary Ellen McCormack in South Boston, in an Irish American neighborhood. These public housing developments, like others in Boston, had been court-ordered to integrate in 1988. The author expected a particularly hostile reception to Latina/o immigrants in South Boston, given that white neighborhood's long history of antagonism toward integration. But she found that although South Boston was historically prepared to engage in a black-white struggle, there were no cognitive frames for a struggle against Latina/os. Further, the Latina/os, who also had no such cognitive frames, tended to defuse antagonism directed toward them by white community members and to point out problems and issues that the two groups shared. Racism was openly voiced in public forums, but the threat of gentrification, affecting all residents, made racial struggles increasingly irrelevant.

In East Boston racial tensions had decreased as the onetime majority Italian Americans diffused into surrounding neighborhoods and as wave after wave of Latina/o immigrants entered. But systematic, unvoiced racism continued to operate in the Maverick Gardens Tenant Task Force, where the Italian American minority maintained undemocratic control and cultivated patronage ties with the Boston Housing Authority. And for Maverick Gardens residents, the presence of co-ethnics in the neighborhood did not prove to be an advantage, since members of the Latina/o community outside the project often resented the "free ride" that project residents were getting. The economic fortunes of residents in the two projects turned out to depend primarily on the professionalism of the two tenant task forces: Maverick's did not show leadership in disseminating information, democratizing the board of directors, or forging ties with local service organizations, whereas McCormack's task force provided culturally responsive services that enabled many project residents to achieve economic and residential mobility.

In chapter 8, "Mexican Americans and Environmental Justice: Change and Continuity in Mexican American Politics," Benjamin Marquez traces the history of the Latina/o environmental justice movement and assesses its future prospects. This movement arose from a break with the mainstream, Anglo-dominated environmental movement; Latina/o activists criticized it as being more concerned with the preservation of pristine recreational areas than with the issues most likely to affect poor and nonwhite communities, primarily exposure to toxins from illegal dumping, lead paint in aging homes, commercial pesticide use, dangerous working conditions, and the location of polluting industries in regions whose residents have the least power to exclude them. Marquez recounts some of the many victories achieved by Latina/o environmental activists during the 1990s. Recently, however, such victories have been harder to obtain. Polluting corporations that once arrogantly assumed minority communities could not organize significant resistance are now far more legally circumspect and place more effort into public relations. Further, the Supreme Court decision that plaintiffs must prove intent to discriminate in environmental cases has greatly reduced the number of legal challenges to corporations. Thus the movement faces an uncertain future, but its activists are committed to the long-term struggle that will be necessary.

In the final chapter, Victor Valle and Rodolfo D. Torres make the general case for grounding a twenty-first-century critical Latina/o urbanism in something they provisionally call "cultural political economy" in an attempt to resolve lingering theoretical tensions between socioeconomic (structural) and culture-based (semiotic) approaches to our neoliberal present. Using this approach, the authors suggest new lines in Latino urban theory that can revitalize Chicana/o studies and progressive politics and confront capital in the neoliberal present.

Together, these chapters posit new directions for urban planning in both theory and practice. The demographic and political transitions in the current era, especially with regard to ethnic integration and the rapid expansion of barrio spaces, offer some level of optimism. Planning *for* the multicultural city must be planning *with* the multicultural city, encompassing inclusion in key decision-making arenas, ownership patterns in private sector consulting, administrative leadership in planning, housing and redevelopment departments, and largely segregated planning schools. Only then can the social, economic, and environmental crises of the city be truly resolved.

REFERENCES

Acuña, Rodolfo F. 1984. *A Community under Siege: A Chronicle of Chicanos East of the Los Angeles River, 1945–1975.* Los Angeles: UCLA Chicano Studies Research Center.
———. 1988. *Occupied America.* 3rd ed. New York: HarperCollins.
Almaguer, Tomas. 1994. *Racial Faultlines: The Historical Origins of White Supremacy in California.* Berkeley: University of California Press.
Arreola, Daniel D. 2002. *Tejano South Texas.* Austin: University of Texas Press.
Bailly, Antoine, Philippe Brun, Roderick J. Lawrence, and Marie-Clare Rey, eds. 2000. *Socially Sustainable Cities.* London: Economica.
Barry, John. 2005. *The State and the Global Ecological Crisis.* Cambridge, MA: MIT Press.

17

Introduction

Beatley, Timothy. 2000. *Green Urbanism: Learning from European Cities.* Washington, DC: Island Press.

Booth, Douglas E. 2004. *Hooked on Growth: Economic Addictions and the Environment.* New York: Rowman and Littlefield.

Bowser, Benjamin P., and Raymond G. Hunt, eds. 1996. *Impacts of Racism on White Americans.* 2nd ed. Thousand Oaks, CA: Sage Publication.

Bullard, Robert D., Glenn S. Johnson, and Angel O. Torres. 2000. "Race, Equity and Smart Growth." Policy paper, Environmental Justice Resource Center, Clark Atlanta University, Atlanta, GA.

Calthorpe, Peter. 1993. *The Next American Metropolis: Ecology, Community, and the American Dream.* New York: Princeton Architectural Press.

Cayo-Sexton, Patricia. 1965. *Spanish Harlem: Anatomy of Poverty.* New York: Harper Colophon Books.

Cockcroft, Eva Sperling, and Holly Barnet-Sanchez. [1990] 1993. *Signs from the Heart: California Chicano Murals.* Albuquerque: University of New Mexico Press.

Darder, Antonia. 1995. "Introduction: The Politics of Biculturalism: Culture and Difference in the Formation of *Warriors for Gringostroika* and *The New Mestizas.*" In *Culture and Difference: Critical Perspectives on the Bicultural Experience in the United States,* edited by Antonia Darder, 1–20. Westport, CT: Bergin and Garvey.

Darder, Antonia and Rodolfo D. Torres. 2004. *After Race: Racism after Multiculturalism.* New York: New York University Press.

Dávila, Arlene. 2001. *Latinos Inc.: The Marketing and Making of a People.* Berkeley: University of California Press.

Davis, Mike. 2000. *Magical Urbanism: Latinos Reinvent the US Big City.* London: Verso.

Deleage, Jean-Paul. 1994. "Eco-Marxist Critique of Political Economy." In *Is Capitalism Sustainable?,* edited by Martin O'Connor, 37–52. New York: Guilford Press.

Diaz, David. 2005. *Barrio Urbanism: Chicanos, Planning and American Cities.* New York: Routledge.

Dimas, Pete R. 1999. *Progress and a Mexican American Community's Struggle for Existence.* New York: Peter Lang.

Doob, Christopher Bates. 1999. *Racism.* 3rd ed. New York: Longman.

Feagin, Joe R. 1989. *Racial and Ethnic Relations.* 3rd ed. Englewood Cliffs, NJ: Prentice Hall.

Frey William H. 2001. *America's Future Defined by Diversity.* Washington, DC: Brookings Institute.

Fung, Archon. 2001. "Beyond and below the New Urbanism: Citizen Participation and Responsive Spatial Reconstruction." *Boston College Environmental Affairs Law Review* 28:615–35.

Gámez, José Luis. 2002. "Representing the City: The Imagination and Critical Practice in East Los Angeles." *Aztlan* 27 (1): 95–120.

Galarza, Ernesto. 1964. *Merchants of Labor: The Mexican Bracero Story.* Notre Dame: University of Notre Dame Press.

———. 2011. *Barrio Boy: 40th Anniversary Edition.* Notre Dame: University of Notre Dame Press.

Gottdiener, Mark. 1985. *The Social Production of Urban Space*. Austin: University of Texas Press.

Hoch, Charles. 1994. *What Do Planners Do?* Chicago: Planners Press.

Katz, Peter. 1994. *The New Urbanism: Toward an Architectural Community*. New York: McGraw Hill.

Lefebvre, Henri. [1974] 1991. *The Production of Space*. Oxford: Basil Blackwell.

Lopez, Ronald W., II. 2002. "Displacement and Resistance: The Gendered Politics of Community Struggles in Chavez Ravine." Paper presented at the Pacific Coast Council on Latin American Studies, East Los Angeles College, Los Angeles, November 7–9.

Marquez, Benjamin. 1998. "The Mexican-American Environmental Justice Movement." *Capitalism Nature Socialism* 9 (4): 43–60.

Parson, Donald C. 2005. *Making a Better World: Public Housing, the Red Scare, and the Direction of Modern Los Angeles*. Minneapolis: University of Minnesota Press.

Peña, Devon G. 1997. *Terror of the Machine*. Austin: CMAS Books / Center for Mexican American Studies.

———. 1998. "Los Animalitos: Culture, Ecology, and the Politics of Place in the Upper Rio Grande." In *Chicano Culture, Ecology, Politics*, edited by Devon G. Peña, 25–57. New York: Guilford Press.

———. 2005. *The Mexican American Environmental Movement*. Tucson: University of Arizona Press.

Pinderhughes, Raquel. 2004. *Alternative Urban Futures: Planning for Sustainable Development in Cities throughout the World*. Lanham, MD: Rowman and Littlefield.

Pulido, Laura. 1996. *Environmentalism and Economic Justice*. Tucson: University of Arizona Press.

Rodriguez, Nestor. 1993. "Economic Restructuring and Latino Growth in Houston." In *In the Barrios: Latinos and the Underclass Debate*, edited by Joan W. Moore and Raquel Pinderhughes, 101–27. New York: Russell Sage Foundation.

Rojas, James. 1999. "The Latino Use of Urban Space in East Los Angeles." In *La Vida Latina in L.A.: Urban Latino Cultures*, edited by Gustavo Leclerc, Raul Villa, and Michael Dear, 131–38. Thousand Oaks, CA: Sage Publications.

Romo, Ricardo. 1983. *East Los Angeles: History of a Barrio*. Austin: University of Texas Press.

Rosenbaum, Robert J. 1981. *Mexicano Resistance in the Southwest: "The Sacred Right of Self Preservation."* Austin: University of Texas Press.

Russell, Dick. 1989. "Environmental Racism: Minority Communities and Their Battle against Toxics." *Amicus Journal* 11 (Spring).

Suro, R., and A. Singer. 2002. "Latino Growth in Metropolitan America: Changing Patterns and New Locations." Center on Urban and Metropolitan Policy and Pew Hispanic Center, Washington, DC, July.

Taylor, Nigel. 1998. *Urban Planning Theory since 1945*. Thousand Oaks, CA: Sage Publications.

Touraine, Alain. 1988. *Return of the Actor*. Minneapolis: University of Minnesota Press.

———. 2000. *Can We Live Together? Equality and Difference*. Stanford: Stanford University Press.

Valle, Victor M., and Rodolfo D. Torres. 2000. *Latino Metropolis*. Minneapolis: University of Minnesota Press.

Vigil, Ernesto. 1999. *The Crusade for Justice: Chicano Militancy and the Government's War on Dissent*. Madison: University of Wisconsin Press.

Young, Iris Marion. 1990. *Justice and the Politics of Difference*. Princeton: Princeton University Press.

Barrios and Planning Ideology

The Failure of Suburbia and the Dialectics of New Urbanism

David R. Diaz

There is no "New" in "New" Urbanism. Given the everyday life of the culture of *el barrio* and the legacy of compact, mixed uses that is characteristic of barrio urbanism, any claim to these design features as new in planning discourse is unjustified. A Eurocentric and market-driven profession has appropriated them as its own in a blatant attempt to evade accountability for the systemic failures arising from its long-term adherence to the suburban model of planning. Though that model has proved to be a burden on cities, causing environmental pollution, traffic congestion, and social alienation, planners are still refusing to admit or analyze their role in producing critical irrationalities in land use policy and practice.

Barrio urbanism predates the entire construct of what planners are claiming to be new. But in defense of a racist ideology of Euro-American control over both the apparatus of planning and land use policies, the profession continues to reify the belief that Latina/os have no important contributions to make to planning thought (Hoch 1994; Diaz 2005). At the same time, the profession's adoption, starting in the 1980s, of a "new" approach to planning is implicitly a recognition that quite possibly the entire guiding rationale of the planning function in relation to post-World War II suburban expansion may have been a colossal blunder with drastic social and environmental consequences (Bullard, Johnson, and Torres 2000a; Booth 2004; Deleage 1994; Paehlke 1989). Blind allegiance to the demands of capital (Checkoway 1984; Cox 1978) has led to sprawl and thus to wasteful use of land, excessive use of nonrenewable resources, pollution, overconsumption, lengthy commutes, a weakening of bonds of citizenship, and psychological stress (Aronowitz et al. 1998; Jackson 1985). Sprawl has been further encouraged by the zone separation that has functioned as one of the guiding principles of the planning profession since the initial phase of the suburban evolution in spatial policy (Lewis 1997). Hence the recent trendy discourse of "Smart Growth" is really an acknowledgment that this history has led to what Bullard, Johnson, and Torres (2000b) have called "Dumb Growth." Suburbia today constitutes a failure of planning and of the modern U.S. environmental movement (Diaz n.d.).

Planning's Eurocentrism has led to another fundamental failure, the inability to recognize and adapt to existing forms of urban social and spatial relations. Barrio urbanism has been practiced since the late 1800s (Peña 2005; Diaz 2005). Because barrios have been segregated, by Euro-American discriminatory practices, from ethnically cleansed zones of the city (Massey and Denton 1993), space there has been culturally conceptualized in eclectic patterns rarely emulated elsewhere (Rojas 1999; Gámez 2002). These patterns have supported extensive social interaction among neighbors and have given residents a role to play in their communities as *ciudadanos*, urban citizens.

A central premise of planning approaches that seek to reshape suburbia is that suburbanites need to be retrained as *ciudadanos*. There is a recognition that at the apex of modernism in planning, the role of the urban citizen almost completely disappeared in the suburban ideology that placed a high value on distance from both the city and one's neighbors (Boyer 1983). When people are isolated in dormitory zones, lack communal spaces, are dependent on cars for all mobility, are satiated with consumption emporiums, are locked into a highway logic, and rely on electronic imagery as a substitute for real-world experience, the 'social realm becomes less and less real' (Touraine 1995). But the suburban project has proven so unworkable that planners are desperately chasing a different course of action and attempting to replace an entrenched belief system that has persisted for almost fifty years. Such an ideological shift requires fundamental reconceptualization.

Barrio urbanism, in its modern formulation, is the vanguard for reforming planning practice, if this change in paradigm has a valid premise. But those who proclaim their own visions of the city and its future, whether theorists of a new school of planning identified with a particular city such as the "L.A. school," architects and designers enamored with their own writing, the heads of graduate planning programs, or the last adherents to the old model of planning still employed in city government, have largely failed to recognize the workable model of urbanism that is right in front of them, in cities across the United States. This failure is especially egregious among planning experts in California, where the largest Latina/o community in the history of the United States, East Los Angeles, has been constantly expanding for over seventy years, and where the country's most significant system of urban barrios has, in the past three decades, created a virtual spatial *reconquista*. Perhaps because the profession is too threatened by ethnic others to truly engage with the differences that ethnic communities exemplify (Young 2000; Darder 1995), let alone learn directly from *ciudadanos* the richness of urban culture within a barrio spatial logic, the connection between barrio urbanism and the project of constructing and assessing alternatives to the suburban model is not being made.

With respect to the goal of retraining people in urban citizenship, *el barrio* offers innumerable lessons for the reform of planning practice, internal and external, to guide urban reconstruction and transformation, not only in housing, commercial, and transit policies, but in broader realms spatially, culturally, and artistically. The real challenge to planning is, Will there be a new beginning, or will an ideology of hierarchy, exclusion, and Eurocentric intellectual isolation persist in the modern period of multiethnicity?

Everyday Life and Barrio Culture

El barrio is the foundational logic of Chicana/o urbanism in the Southwest: its space is central to cultural expression, as well as to conflict with and resistance to the dominant culture. Historically the barrio is the result of uneven development, segregation, repression, and discriminatory urban policies. It is characterized by the exorbitant extraction of ground rents, a population that is an urban repository for low-wage labor, and intense demands on a socially constricted housing supply. Yet with regard to everyday life it is a reaffirmation of culture, an ethnically bounded sanctuary, and the spiritual zone of Chicana/o Mexicana/o identity (Ponce [1993] 1995; Acosta and Winegarten 2003). It is also an intense space defining the independence and resistance of a culture that predates Euro-American influences on city life and urban form (Peña 2005, 1998). It is a location bound up with an economic rationale and racial injustice in civil society and the state, but also with cultural solidarity, political mobilization, and empowerment.

A central social practice in the barrio is walking, which involves communal learning and engaging with others in a communally oriented cultural arena. This learning and relearning occurs in countless, often benign, interactions, face to face and personal, that energize and celebrate cultural solidarity. Given the concern, in the larger Eurocentric culture, to reconstruct the social realm and bring about what Alain Touraine has called "the return of the social actor" (1988), barrio culture presents a salutary challenge to modernist trends in urban planning that have alienated people from their own humanity.

Further, barrio urbanism is far more environmentally sustainable than other patterns of urbanism in the United States (Peña 2005; Davis 2000; Díaz 2005). Barrio communities historically utilize public transit, feature mixed-density zoning, and consume fewer resources, all of which, as Robert Paehlke has noted, can serve, in the larger society, as pragmatic responses to limit the environmentally damaging impacts of industrialization and overconsumption (1989, 247-51). Thus while the planning profession attempts to respond to the environmental crisis, *el gente del barrio*, outside the planning hierarchy and its "privileged, technical knowledge," have practiced environmental sustainability for decades. A walk through any barrio will amply demonstrate "chaotic urban environmentalism" in its most organic presentation (Peña 2005).

The mixed density that is characteristic of barrio spatial relations has established vibrant, functioning neighborhoods that are the "life blood of cities" (Jacobs 1961). In contrast to traditional planning's rigid separation of commercial establishments from residences, and of single-family from multifamily dwellings, barrio spatial relations are characterized by a mix of single-family homes, bungalow flats, single-story apartments, multistory apartments, an occasional condominium, and *tiendas* in the internal streets of the city. Whereas mixed use has been militantly rejected throughout the modern history of planning, the strictures against it have been quaintly ignored in barrios.

The logic of mixed density is intertwined with the history of how space is produced and reproduced (Gottdiener 1985). A history of vicious racism, segregation, and exclusion initially produced barrios' tight integration of commercial and residential development. When racism precluded trips to Eurocentrically cleansed zones of the city, when businesses refused bilingual service, when ethnic products were limited in their location, and when the combination of low wages and high commodity pricing severely limited what minorities could buy, barrio commercial establishments were relied upon for their provision of daily household goods, and residents' commercial transactions inside the barrio were closely intertwined with their social life. But even after access to the totality of the city increased for Latina/os, mixed use persisted because of its vitality and importance to internal barrio social relations.

For most barrio residents, direct access to commercial establishments is one of their neighborhood's most important spatial amenities. Whereas in many places across the United States poor urban planning makes a car trip necessary to supply every household need, in the barrio *la gente* ordinarily walk or send their children for quick purchases. Such trips, whether spanning one or two blocks or over a mile, are means of socializing and socialization: residents come to know the community, build relations of loyalty and reliance with business owners, and establish a humane way of conducting the tasks of everyday life that builds on the legacy of culture. They establish patterns of consumption, purchase small carts to facilitate purchasing, link trips to social interaction with neighbors, and establish long-term social relations with individuals who own or work in commercial spaces. Mixed use thus makes possible a way of life that limits car use (along with its related problems of pollution, congestion, and reliance on nonrenewable resources) and promotes improved health.

Barrio residents have historically constituted an important segment of public transit users in metropolitan areas. Public transit has been an essential resource for Latino Americans since the earliest urban omnibuses and streetcars were introduced in the early 1900s in the Southwest. Several factors, mainly income status and structural underemployment, have resulted in a high demand for public transit service. Users include young adults entering the labor market and/or students, who often lack the resources to purchase and maintain a car. Seniors on fixed incomes also depend on bus systems for a range of daily trips. Renters, an important component of the local housing market, may be unable to afford more than one car per family, if that, and may be limited as to the parking space allotted per unit. Because so many jobs pay less than a living wage, significant sectors of the labor market—particularly janitors, hotel staff, service workers in others' homes, fast-food workers, and clerical workers—rely solely on public transit for daily work-related commutes. Some workers buy a used car, carpool, or rely on family members, but when these informal systems break down they must often turn to public transit as well.

In response to this level of demand, virtually all urban transit systems have structured route corridors to address the shifting needs of barrio users. Working-class users make up a major proportion of farebox revenue for public transit (Cervero 1998). This has resulted in an interdependence between barrio users and transit agencies in cities throughout the country. In fact, most public transit agencies would experience severe financial crisis if minority users fundamentally shifted their mobility option to cars. A phalanx of buses traversing the barrio is a common sight in cities across the nation.

Another underappreciated aspect of barrio culture is the tradition of recycling. The concept of adaptive reuse was essentially pioneered in barrios in relation to the composting of *jardines*, water resource management, and a thriving trade in *segundas*, including building materials and all kinds of household items. Such practices continue to this day. In Mexico, home construction firms along the *frontera* are active in the home demolition sector of the building industry, but instead of merely bulldozing structures and dumping the debris, as is the norm for U.S. firms, they "manage" the dismantling of homes by preserving, inventorying, and reselling or reusing lumber, especially large beams; windows and doors; wrought iron; cabinets; mirrors; pipes; electric lights and switches; and copper. These practices reduce consumption, encourage reuse of materials, maximize existing resources, provide entry-level local employment, and reduce demands on forests. Imagine the benefits, ecological and economic, if barrio urban practices were emulated throughout this society, just within the housing market.

Historically, barrio residents have been at the vanguard of urban recycling, though more spontaneously, for economic reasons, than for reasons of compliance with a socially produced environmental mandate. A wide range of used products have been consistently recycled. The most readily accessible materials have been glass, paper, cans, and pipes. These types of materials have had a local resale or reuse value from which their gatherers have supplemented their incomes. Recycling practice consists of collecting resources from streets, alleys, parks, parking lots, and highway verges, and at the sites of trash bins, lumber yards, industrial zones, department stores, and other spaces of opportunity where this "throwaway society" blithely litters the planet with resources that are still functional.

Barrio recycling includes autos, plumbing and electrical supplies, light fixtures, household amenities, clothing, tires, metals, plastics, and reusable furniture. While relatively unorganized and unregulated, this sustainable practice is an important aspect of these communities. In fact, the United States could quite possibly resolve its trash generation crisis by allowing either domestic or Third World trash *collectivas* to bid on managing our landfills. They would probably view the inventory, the gross overabundance of reusable items, as a guaranteed avenue to personal wealth. Paying a fee for the franchise seems minimal in relation to the tremendous level of value to be re-extracted and resold on international markets. Just a thought.

Still another historic environmental practice among barrio residents has been the maintenance of urban gardens, both for decorative purposes and to supplement food resources. The resulting green and colorful landscape—a kaleidoscope of flowerbeds, trees, vines, cactuses, roses, and fruit trees—is characteristic of an interactive land use ethic (Pinderhughes 2004; Peña 1998). Although garden spaces may be small and the plants mainly non-native, they show families' connection to and appreciation for nature, and the actively cultivated flowerbeds and trees are celebrations of local space.

These *jardines de la familia* create a sense of accomplishment and entitlement to the earth. They offer a respite from the hurried pace of urban life, a connection to the eternal cycles of nature as opposed to the forward-driving changes of modernity. And they contribute to the barrio's social life, in that passersby and visitors linger to appreciate their beauty and to talk with the gardeners.

The important urban farm movement, which has adapted the principles of *collectiva* relations to U.S. cities, has transformed many desolate, underutilized tracts of land and has evolved into a sophisticated approach to urban food production that has introduced unique herbs, vegetables, fruits, and medicinal plants into urban zones (Pinderhughes 2004). Some gardens are relatively large plots on the periphery of barrios or in abandoned industrial areas. These *jardines* are established by Latina/os interested in gardening or newer immigrants attempting to replicate the cultural practices of their homelands. They have normally functioned on the basis of a *collectiva* structure. Collective decision making establishes guidelines, defines growing spaces, ensures egalitarian sharing of costs, addresses conflicts, and generates trust. This system fosters stability and equity within the *jardines*, thus minimizing friction and dominance by one sector of a particular *collectiva*. This approach to governance is the oldest type of administrative relationship in North America (Peña 2005).

Initially, the vast majority of *jardines* operate without interference of either city officials or property owners. The plots are small and the use is benign and unobtrusive. Innumerable collective gardens have functioned undisturbed for over a decade in cities around the country. However, once they become seemingly permanent features of the barrio urban landscape, these *collectivas* have been forced to engage in defensive political tactics to fight for their preservation.

While cities countenance the open spaces and plazas designated by redevelopment plans, open space in barrios that is actively used by residents is viewed as having limited value for urban life. The irony is that *jardines* provide significant social and cultural benefits to lower-income areas. They are an arena for socializing, generational bonding, and learning;

they represent an advanced ecological practice aspect in mass consumer culture; their small-scale food production is an important economic supplement to the income of working-class households; their green spaces reduce the harmful impacts of air pollution; and they introduce area consumers to new food products that enhance diets. The fact that urban officials and planners demean these benefits and uses is a prime example of the lingering racism in public policy. *Jardines* counteract some of the negative features of impoverished urban zones: youth alienation, underemployment, racism, lack of appreciation of the local environment, and high levels of conflict. The serenity alone constitutes a legitimate defense of barrio *jardines.*

Thus all these features of barrio spatial relations—mixed use, multidensity housing, public transit, *familia, collectivas, jardines,* adaptive reuse of materials, and, above all, the centrality of walking—are components of the reformulation of urban ideology in the current period. Planning discourse need only visit what exists, *el barrio,* to learn the future.

The Failure of Suburbia and the New Urbanist Response

In this era the social, environmental, and economic repercussions of the planning of suburbia are reaching such a point of crisis that planners will soon be forced to openly admit their historic failure (Bullard, Johnson, and Torres 2000a; Barry 2005; Booth 2004). But already, approaches by such names as Smart Growth, New Urbanism, mixed use, and/or a return to the city are implicitly recognizing some part of that failure in that they are predicated on fundamentally challenging conventional planning and suburban sprawl. The most influential component of this ideology is mixed density (Fung 2001; Calthorpe 1993; Katz 1994; Bailly et al. 2000). This is a retrograde strategy attempting to rectify the consequences of sprawl. The main themes are high-density housing developments, with commercial establishments on their ground floors, in close proximity to major transit corridors. The densification of both residential and commercial uses constitutes a reintroduction of the historic city into current planning discourse. The major objectives are to maximize land use, substantially influence the mode of mobility, re-create the synergy of neighborhoods, and reduce excessive use of nonrenewable resources.

Crucially, this ideology attempts to reduce the absolute dependency on cars for virtually every activity. It optimistically predicts that the linkage of mixed-density developments with transit corridors will significantly increase public transit utilization for work commutes and other mobility necessities (Cervero 1998; Walter, Arkin, and Crenshaw 1992). The effects of such usership—substantial reductions in congestion, air pollution, fossil fuel demands, the costs of transportation infrastructure, and the psychological stress and lost work and leisure time associated with long commutes—could in turn lead to a transformation in federal and state transportation policy that would support public transit more and car use less (Cervero 1998).

Advocates of a transition to mixed density postulate that the close proximity of commercial and residential spaces will encourage walking. Densification is automatically assumed to foster intense, street-level socializing and a communal sense of place. Architectural design will re-create a community atmosphere in which civic society will directly engage itself on the street, enriching and enhancing everyday life in the city (Katz 1994). "In . . . cities, spaces and places are designed and built: walking, witnessing, being in public, are as much a part of the design and purpose as is being inside to eat, sleep, make shoes or love or music. The word *citizen* has to do with cities, and the ideal city is organized around citizenship—around participation in public life" (Solnit 2000, 176). The assumption is that, at the most basic human scale, suburbanites can be retrained in the responsibilities of the *ciudadano*.

In an effort to enhance this opportunity, planners are now advocating zero-lot-line plottage, establishing miniparks in new subdivisions, and changing the relationship between cars, streets, and parking in an effort to facilitate pedestrian activity (Calthorpe 1993). Further, architects have reconceptualized past practice by "introducing" a front porch into housing design (Katz 1994), with the goal of increasing social interaction between residents and pedestrian passersby.

Though the incorporation of these features into new approaches to planning shows a recognition of some of the problems generated by planning over the past several decades, other problems remain unacknowledged or addressed, such as planners' involvement in exclusionary practices based on race and class hierarchies. For example, most New Urbanist developments are devoid of working-class housing. City officials and real estate developers have adopted a range of strategies to ensure the exclusion of lower-class residents from their projects. Many cities now require developers of elite projects to pay into a housing fund for construction of more affordable housing elsewhere, but such agreements continue class and ethnic segregation and often only minimally address the critical shortage of lower-income housing. For although developers are the ben-

CONTEMPORARY PLANNING EFFORTS

eficiaries of significant state concessions, zoning bonuses, infrastructure improvements, urban rail systems, local transit improvements, and redevelopment funding, they remain adamant that neither New Urbanism nor Smart Growth mandates the inclusion in their projects of working families seeking affordable home ownership opportunities. Redevelopment subsidies have been funneled to favored economic zones (Feagin 1984; Weiss 1985; Beauregard 1993), while the impoverished communities for which the policy was created have been ignored. The abandonment of any meaningful policies to house truly needy families, as opposed to middle-class professionals with direct access to credit and capital (Squires 1994), is a major failure of this "new" ideology in planning. What have been developed are expensive, elite zones of the city characterized by blatant class and ethnic exclusion (Massey and Denton 1993). Thus New Urbanism and Smart Growth are emerging as contributors to a new system of residential apartheid in the city.

Planning and SUV Culture

One problem confronting New Urbanism is whether the paradigm shift it envisions can have any salience with a mass consumer society wedded to the suburban model and "SUVism," a fast-paced way of life that is predicated on a great deal of driving, with its attendant lifestyle of social isolation and overconsumption (Goldman 1992; Booth 2004; Levenstein 2003; Fine and Leopold 1993). The dominant reliance on one form of mobility, automobiles, has significant residual environmental impacts such as air pollution, stress, and a permanently unbalanced demand for oil and gas reserves.

SUVism has produced and reproduced social alienation (Fishman 1987; Boyer 1983), structuring social relations on an atomized, alienating logic in which daily activity is reduced to working for and then purchasing consumption amenities. A daily routine centered on overconsumption of almost every product available—clothing, gas, food, illegal substances, household accessories, and electronic equipment—has been reinforced by media and advertising (Levenstein 2003; Booth 2004). A sedentary lifestyle and the abuse of the capacity of the human body to absorb consumption items have led to a public health crisis, particularly among children (CSPI 2003). The explosion of diabetes is correlated with overeating and leisure activity based on a screen and a couch (McCann and Ewing 2003). Other health problems result as well: heart disease, high blood pressure, diabetes, psychological stress, joint stress. Vast sectors of society refuse to meet one of our most basic evolutionary needs, one that in prior generations was a fundamental aspect of life, the need to *walk*. The longest trip of the day is often from the living room to the refrigerator and back.

The crisis of urban mobility, worsening seemingly by the moment, is a result of an irrational and insensitive assault on the land (Beatley 2000; Bullard, Johnson, and Torres 2000b; Barry 2005). Since the post–World War II era the planning profession has facilitated capital's voracious requirement to expand development through constant sprawl envisioned as a panacea to the evils of the city. The proliferation of modern subdivisions mimicking the estates of the initial elite suburbs has created a crisis in that these far-flung neighborhoods are predicated on highways for access (Walter, Arkin, and Crenshaw 1992). Inherent in this everyday reality is the utter failure to implement any semblance of an environmentally rational land use strategy in the past five-plus decades (Beatley 2000; Barry 2005; Peña 1998). In particular, the disconnect between transportation planning and land use policy during this period has been a glaring omission in the profession.

In the late 1980s planners belatedly and perplexedly recognized this disconnect. Their response was to produce a "new" paradigm in response to it, transit-oriented planning (Cervero 1998) and then traffic calming (Hoyle 1995; Burden 2000). Planners raced to incorporate transportation engineers into planning and land use policy and to reestablish planning policies that would substantially improve mobility in cities and regions. Portland, Oregon, became the poster city for these developments. For the next decade, the literature was flooded with books and articles on the topic. But then as now, the "new" served to cover over past failure. How could planners have completely ignored the transportation function of the city when developing public policy since the 1950s? Quite an embarrassing "mistake," one that has had profound, negative consequences to the social production of urban form. Meanwhile, minority planners have remained puzzled as to why planning took so long to recognize the centrality of public transit to rational planning practice. Barrio residents would be amused to learn that highly educated planners considered as "new" one of the most essential aspects of their everyday lives.

This leads us back to this chapter's initial contention: there is no "New in New Urbanism." The recent paradigm shift is a response to the irrationalities, failures, crises, and costs related to the failure of suburbia (Bullard, Johnson, and Torres 2000a, 2000b; Barry 2005; Beatley 2000). Planning, in distancing itself from its past, inherently signals the structural failure of planning for almost fifty years.

The ideological transition within the planning profession has resulted in new models, typically featuring a combination of mixed-use development, increased residential density, community building to address the social alienation of civic society, sustainable urban planning practices, substantial expansion of public transit systems and usership, and environmentally oriented land use relationships. Yet these models only weakly mimic what has existed in barrios for over a century. Meanwhile, a Eurocentric approach to planning, which persists even at this critical juncture, neglects Latina/o urbanism as if it had no value to the discourse in the field.

Such professional arrogance is typical of American racism. A future of mistaken policy seems to be better than listening to ethnic others and possibly comprehending that different visions have more inherent value than those embedded in a rational-functional ideology.

The Planning Literature's Neglect of Chicana/o Urbanism

One of the planning literature's most egregious failures is its silence with regard to the Chicana/o urban experience. This ignorance is especially reprehensible in New Urbanists from either California or the Southwest. This region has experienced a historic spatial *reconquista*. The largest Latina/o community, East Los Angeles, is a powerful cultural and social space influencing public policy in Southern California. Major barrios in San Antonio, El Paso, Denver, San Francisco, San Jose, San Diego, Phoenix, and el Valle del Rio Bravo are among the most significant features of the regional built environment (Arreola 2002; Diaz 2005; Peña 2005; Rodriguez 1993; Mendez 2003). Latina/os have had a major impact in this region spatially, politically, and economically for over a century. Since the mid-1900s, barrios have emerged in New York's Spanish Harlem, Chicago's Pilsen, Miami's Calle Ocho, Kansas City, and the Pacific Northwest. In the current era, Latina/o urbanism is one of the most controversial issues in the United States.

The defense of spatial relations *en el barrio* has been central to conflict and controversy between Latina/os and planning (Marquez 1998; Peña 1998; Pulido 1996; Diaz 1989). However, a review of conventional planning literature would lead to the assumption that the second-largest ethnic group in the United States was virtually nonexistent. Part of the failure of the literature has stemmed from a decidedly eastern bias with regard to the minority populations that have received the most attention. But another factor is racism in planning (Hoch 1994). The profession, having encountered conflict with African Americans over planning issues, has been extremely reluctant to address difference, racism, and class bias with another major minority community as well. The extremely limited attention in the city planning literature to barrio urbanism, especially in relation to California and the Southwest, is an embarrassment to the entire planning field.

Yet the history of the conflictive relationship between Latina/os and planners mirrors the entire modern history of planning. From the struggles over illegal and racist theft of land grants in New Mexico and Colorado to Puerto Rican-led rent strikes in Spanish Harlem, spirited opposition against eminent domain in Segundo Barrio in El Paso and Viejo Varrio in Tucson, massive protests against displacement in Chavez Ravine in Los Angeles, fights in East L.A. over racism in public housing and unprecedented destruction of communities from freeways in the 1950 and 1960s, and the establishment of the Crusade for Justice in Denver at the beginning of the Chicano Power era, Latina/os, contrary to exclusionary planning literature, have been engaged in land use, planning, redevelopment, affordable housing, social justice and environmental *luchas* for over a century.

Chicana/o social movements and critiques of planning have been a permanent feature of urban policy controversy since the era of Model Cities and the creation of the Office of Economic Opportunity in the 1960s. Confronting racism, classism, and an elitist hierarchy, barrio leaders, intrinsically comprehending inequity in redistribution policy, the manipulation of eminent domain, and the legacy of underdevelopment, have confronted planning in the cities of virtually every state in the Southwest and Midwest as well as those of other regions throughout the country. Similar confrontations have occurred in rural zones as well (Peña 2005, 1998; Marquez 1998).

One of the most fundamental realities in urban policy is planning's failure to address the crises in barrios. From the first Chicana/o political majority in the small South Valle jurisdiction of Crystal City (Garcia 1989), the failure of urban policy has been a central issue of political opposition. The legacy of acute neglect of infrastructure throughout the Southwest is legendary. Through the 1980s, innumerable barrios lacked a range of basic urban amenities such as storm drain systems, sewer mains, water systems, paved streets, and gas lines.

Affordable housing, parks and youth recreational facilities, revitalization, economic development, historic preservation, environmental protection, and community empowerment have all been issues around which barrio social movements have continually mobilized against a racist planning cartel. The rampant use of eminent domain to confiscate barrio space and/or destroy entire *colonias* is a component of this legacy. Reaction to proposed or actual destruction of barrios during the modern, post-World War II history of planning has led to a vibrant social justice movement throughout the Southwest. Whether planning will ever acknowledge this history remains an open question.

The memory of these contested spaces is a permanent legacy of barrio cultural history. In fact, the attacks against the integrity of barrio spatial relations, a continuation of a history of conflict from the 1940s and 1950s, fueled the youth revolt in barrios during the 1960s and 1970s Chicana/o Power era. Challenges to racism in political institutions were soon followed by *luchas* against reactionary city planning practice and urban policy. Yet planning literature remains devoid of specific analysis of the destructive impact of redevelopment, freeway construction, and eminent domain on barrios, and only limited attention has been given to the structural underdevelopment of the barrio economy. The profession also appears reluctant to document and assess the influence of barrio social movements against the urban cartel, with which planning has been directly aligned.

When will planning place the *barrio* and Chicana/o urbanism in the center of urban policy? Latina/os' transformation into the second-largest ethnic population indicates the importance of addressing their influence within urban spatial relations. The social construction of the rich cultural zone of the barrio offers significant lessons to the future of planning. The spatial *reconquista* occurring in the Southwest will only accelerate in the next quarter century and is already socially and culturally transforming the urban environment.

The L.A. Perspective and Chicana/o Urbanism

Up through the early 1990s, the topic of urbanization and its coinciding socio-demographic influences in the Los Angeles region was, at best, incidentally treated in the planning literature. The key texts addressed two major factors leading to irrational land use patterns: fragmented governmental jurisdictions (Fogelson's *Fragmented Metropolis,* 1967) and polynucleated development (Gottdiener's *The Social Production of Urban Space,* 1985). One book, *Thinking Big* (Gottlieb and Wolt 1977), documented the evolution of the *L.A. Times* and the Chandler family's deployment of print media, land use investments, a staunch right-wing political philosophy, and membership in the Group of 25 into a direct role in land development policy for over eighty years. These three books, along with a few tomes on architecture and car culture, served to document the evolution of urbanization and sprawl endemic to Southern California. But in the early 1990s an event and a book combined to ignite renewed interest in L.A. urban issues: the Rodney King insurrection and Mike Davis's *City of Quartz*.

Discourse on L.A. is important in relation to the magnitude of the sprawl in the region. While sprawl is not at all unique to L.A. or even historically new (it occurred in Rome and other historic city-states in other eras), it was substantially more significant in L.A. than in any other comparable region through the 1980s. The so-called "L.A. school" has attempted to ascribe to L.A. a uniqueness with regard to planning issues that the urban history of this region fails to justify. The forces that the school addresses—globalization, immigration linked to demands for low-wage labor, economic restructuring, the establishment of ethnic marketplaces, information technology manufacturing centers, and other economic factors (Dear 2001)—are part of the evolution of cities and have already occurred in other regions of the country. Discussions related to the influence of these urban, economic, demographic, and social impacts are valuable, but claims to a "new" discourse in relation to planning stretch the legitimacy of this perspective.

The main urban patterns described by the L.A. school, fragmented jurisdictions and autonomous, decentralized citylike agglomerations, were first theorized in Fogelson's *Fragmented Metropolis* and Gottdiener's *The Social Production of Urban Space*. Ironically, few advocates of the L.A. perspective properly situate in its time this initial literature and its precise analysis of urbanization patterns and impacts. New York, Chicago, San Francisco, and for that matter the global cities of Europe all have similar urban dynamics. Thus the patterns of urbanization that are termed new actually replicate the transitions and transformations of other cities in U.S. urban history. L.A. is not unique with regard to global capital's influence on spatial relations, a structural reliance on immigrant labor in a wide range of economic sectors, the series of economic transformations beginning in the 1970s, the reproduction of new ethnic-based regional markets (which started a century ago), or a vibrant informal economy. Los Angeles mimics other major cities; it has not led urban policy in relation to these or other urban policy transformations.

Two important aspects of the urban history of this region potentially are significant to future planning discourses: the magnitude of the pending social, tax, environmental, and economic costs of unfettered sprawl, and the spread of barrio urbanism, to an extent that is unprecedented in this society. However, both themes have been virtually ignored by advocates of the LA perspective.

Limitless sprawl, manipulation of land use policy, and the impacts of irrational planning are all important topics for planning policy. Los Angeles is significant, if not solely for the substantial environmental destruction that has been wrought throughout the region. Public health costs, lost wages, lowered work productivity, taxation to maintain and expand infrastructure, transportation crises, a weak public transit system that most commuters view as worthless, industrial pollution, economic stagnation, and abandonment of some suburban zones are and will continue to be significant, harmful impacts on government revenues and expenditures. Yet the L.A. school has not seriously critiqued the ravages of constant and total sprawl in this region or the hegemony of the growth machine (Molotch and Logan 1984)—perhaps because real estate and development interests are the main funders of the research institutes that support advocates of the L.A. perspective.

The other issue that these advocates have not sufficiently addressed is barrio urbanism. Though they consider the Latina/o population in relation to a range of issues including economic restructuring, immigrant labor, capital mobility, and ethnic demographic trends, insufficient assessment of their impact on the culture and on urban spatial relations is a major failure. Given the explosion of Chicana/o urbanism in East Los Angeles since the mid-1970s and the unprecedented suburban expansion of minorities (a majority of whom are middle-class Chicana/os), the L.A. perspective has bypassed a major opportunity to inform planning about its own future.

There is no region in the United States where one ethnic group has so reconstituted space in its own cultural vision as Southern California, which Latina/os are spatially and culturally continuing to transform (on such reconstitution of space, see Lefebvre [1974] 1991). Gottdiener's prediction in 1985 that development would produce systemic, decentralized subregional zones remains the most relevant observation to the explosion of new barrios in this region in the past quarter century. His analysis of the "polynucleated pattern of administrative decentralization" (1985, 61) articulated a logic of deconcentration, arguing that "the production of space has occurred in the main not because of economic processes alone but, more specifically, because of a joint state-real estate sector articulation which forms the leading edge of spatial transformations" (241). This assessment of urban restructuring offers a rationale for the underdevelopment and dispersal of barrios.

Southern California's trajectory toward becoming 50 percent Latina/o is having a dramatic impact on the culture of communities, transforming it into barrio-oriented everyday life. The creation of the Chicana/o City (Valle and Torres 2000) and the dynamic expansion of the region related to demographic changes seem to have been a key rationale for analysis of Los Angeles. The evolution of the spatial logic of barrios reflects Gottdiener's concept of polynucleated development: "Consequently, the present form of metropolitan expansion represents less the desires of its . . . residents . . . than the uncoordinated activities of . . . capital disguised by the ideology of growth. The outcomes of this development process are renegotiated by those who bear its costs. Thus the socio-spatial environment represents both the interests involved in the property sector and the materialized scars of the political renegotiation between the initial profit takers and the eventual users of settlement space, as the latter vainly battle to recreate some form of consociation within the hostile environment of unrelenting secondary circuit activity and its constant turnover of land" (Gottdiener 1985, 249-50). Thus the proliferation of barrios is re-creating sociocultural enclaves within a hostile capital-state relationship structured to extract labor and rent.

The L.A. perspective has yet to make a credible contribution to the future of planning. It is anchored in the dated contention that sprawl in L.A. is supposedly "unique" and the weak argument that the influences of globalization in L.A. are somehow different from those of other powerful cities (Chicago, New York, Toronto, Paris, Vancouver, London, Rome, Shanghai, etc.). At the same time, this perspective ignores the barrio urbanism that aspect of the region that are unique and inform planning. Barrio urbanism, in particular, will necessarily emerge from other schools and from other regions.

Racism, Gentrification, and "New" Urbanism
What are actually being developed under the new regime in planning are gentrified spaces that exclude both class and ethnic others. Cities that facilitate densification are establishing zoning and land use concessions allowing capital to dictate policies oriented toward professional middle-

class housing markets. In numerous jurisdictions developers have the option of paying into funds for affordable housing elsewhere, in lieu of being tainted by the inclusion of affordable units for working-class families in their own projects. This capability to transfer the location of affordable ownership opportunities blatantly contradicts any claim of a "smart" or "new" urban logic. It is simply an updated version of residential apartheid (Massey and Denton 1993).

Similar barriers are being imposed in relation to access to capital in the real estate market (Squires 1994; Dymski, Veitch, and White 1991), thus excluding ethnic working-class constituencies from the benefits of virtually all New Urbanist developments in the past decade (Rast 2006). The cost of housing within dense mixed-use developments pragmatically ensures that truly needy working families will never qualify for a home loan in these developments. The mortgage banking industry is also reluctant to break up the class homogeneity of New Urbanist projects, thereby reifying the lingering racist stereotype that minority home ownership automatically translates into reduced valuation of an entire project—a logic that would irrationally imply that minorities want to purchase a home in order to destroy it!

In the abstract, New Urbanism and Smart Growth endorse the goals set forth by the American Planning Association, the American Collegiate Schools of Planning, and other leading organizations: equity, class integration, housing opportunity for all income groups, and the reproduction of a version of the historic city in which all ethnicities will be incorporated into new developments. This creation of myths harks to an earlier era in which rational-functional planners proclaimed themselves to be serving the common good (Taylor 1998).

The reality, however, is that planners and developers continue to control access to the city and to deny housing opportunity to working-class households in desperate need of the structural benefits of ownership. Despite New Urbanist writings that endorse a multiethnic, multiclass restructuring of urban social relations (Rast 2006; Fung 2001), what has occurred to date is business as usual: with the acquiescence of planning, the development industry is utilizing every tactic available to deny affordable ownership within their projects. This reflects what Rast terms 'a profound middle-class bias" in planning (2006, 249; I would argue it is upper-class) that clearly signals a new formulation of class gentrification and exclusion within this ideology.

The failure of planning to ensure equity, which is only the latest iteration of racism within the profession, is occurring despite a range of essential state concessions that capital has stipulated as preconditions for their support of Smart Growth or New Urbanist projects. The state basically finances a host of infrastructure requirements without which capital claims projects are not feasible. Developers demand substantial housing density bonuses to underwrite significant profitability. Local and regional governments finance expensive rail transit centers and enhance local transit systems to improve access for consumption, work, and leisure. They provide innumerable subsidies through redevelopment agencies, divert federal funds earmarked for affordable housing, and offer low-interest development loans. Without these massive state concessions developers often refuse to engage in developments (Checkoway 1984; Cox 1978), mixed-use or otherwise.

Despite their position of authority based on technical knowledge and expertise, planners continue to exhibit political capitulation and weakness. In lieu of demanding fair and equitable conditions, especially mandating a minimum 20 percent of truly affordable units for working-class families, they legitimate class exclusion. New labels cannot mask the continuing racism and classism of urban policy.

As city centers become increasingly gentrified, New Urbanism, without state-mandated policies that regulate real estate capital in relation to government tax costs and support, is contributing to the establishment of elite zones from which minorities and lower-income working people are excluded. The distribution of state resources is skewed in favor of capital, with planners serving as cheerleaders for elites aligned with powerful urban cartels. The new, expensive, subsidized residential projects that adhere to a New Urbanist philosophy are in fact perpetuating an old tradition by deepening the divide between privileged and minority communities.

New Urbanism and Smart Growth are contributing to geographies of exclusion (Peña 2005; Frazier, Margai, and Tettey-Fio 2003) in that developers of New Urbanist projects are manipulating urban form to reassert class and ethnic difference. This is most evident in the types of services and retail amenities that these communities contain. Restaurants, boutiques, recreational opportunities, and personal services are all predicated on a consumer pricing level designed to create distinct economic barricades that implicitly limit access to working-class families, even though the state offers significant subsidies to capital as a precondition to development (Checkoway 1984; Cox 1978). Multicultural, multilingual planning practices could give barrio residents opportunities to provide input regarding development, but in the current era anti-immigrant sentiment tends to be translated into opposition toward urban policies that might benefit barrio residents.

One of the problems with the rush to densification is an acute lack of social space within New Urbanist design. Contrary to what is proclaimed in planning discourse, most developers tend to maximize the "profitability of space" (Harvey 1973). Residential areas thus have very little social space, and apartment balconies are too small. Architects have failed to tier units to offer outdoor spaces, either communal or personal. And the neighborhood community room, if it exists, is generally a sterile, functional space that normally requires reservations for social events. Commingling with residents or, heaven forbid, strangers is frowned upon. A majority of new urban developments function as glorified hotels! Thus the chaos of the city, implicit in mixed use, practiced in barrios, celebrated by the *ciudadano,* is regulated out of existence by both architectural design and formal contractual policy.

What good is New Urbanism or Smart Growth if the eclectic relations of the city are regulated out of existence prior to the sale of units? How does this race to a new planning ideology differ, if at all, from the legacy of exclusion and racism that haunts the profession? These gentrified spaces are rapidly assuming the characteristics of residential apartheid. Should working-class constituencies expect anything less from a profession wedded to advancing the interests of capital at the expense of the poor?

Latina/o Urbanism and the Future of Planning

The urban and cultural environment of barrios and *colonias* has been characterized by the interlacing of mixed-use relationships and vibrant communal activities since the 1800s. These zones, distinctive in their cultural patterning, initially evolved from segregated areas within the framework of racist urban practices dictated by Euro-American elites. The internal cultural resistance to racism in public policy was (and is) reflected in social practice, communal relationships, and ethnic solidarity that link commerce, housing, and labor in a relatively dense physical space. The built environment has reflected a range of land uses, varying structural heights, and maximal utilization of physical space.

The relationships in this dense land use matrix have resulted in culturally oriented social networking based on walking. The proximity of shops and public transit to housing has resulted in the evolution of an active street culture (Rojas 1999; Gámez 2002). Density, which is a fundamental characteristic of barrios, has also influenced active recycling of a wide range of materials, facilitated an underground economy that simultaneously relies on an informal barter system and a cash economy, maximized common social space in residential areas, and fostered a context of social sharing and mutual economic, social, and cultural support. The conceptual framework of the *ciudadano,* encompassing active citizenship in all its manifestations, is a product of barrio everyday life.

Because racism in public policy resulted in inequitable redistribution of public funds to barrio neighborhoods and thus inadequate recreational facilities for youth, barrios responded by maximizing the use of open spaces as recreational zones, whether front and side yards, streets, or vacant lots. Other cultural practices informally created and supported by locals include ballet folklorico, mariachi music, rock, hip-hop, *reggaeton,* and public art such as graffiti art (Viesca 2000). The modern public art movement evolved from the politically inspired Chicana/o mural movement of the 1960s and 1970s (Cockcroft and Barnet-Sanchez [1990] 1993), in which walls, private and public, became important urban canvases that both informed and beautified barrio space.

Thus barrio everyday life offers an array of lessons for current discourse on transforming the future of the city. A trip to the barrio provides direct evidence of how social networks have functioned and thrived for decades, and the close relationship between *viviendas y tiendas* effectively contradicts over half a century of Eurocentric planning ideology. The social, economic, and environmental benefits of this type of land use have only recently been proclaimed as the wave of the future of planning. When will planning admit that that observation is ahistorical and racist, since what is claimed as the future is a feature of long standing within the arena of barrio urban land use?

In relation to public policy, the mixed-use urban form has resulted in a number of important characteristics of Latina/o urban culture and everyday life. One critical aspect of the urban crisis today is congestion and the failure of public transportation systems to address mobility. The exception is in barrios and other historically segregated communities that were denied economic and political rights until the latter stages of last century. Residents there have actively used public transit and sought residential and workplace locations accessible to existing systems. This de facto public policy has resulted in relatively few single-vehicle commutes, relatively low consumption of nonrenewable energy, lowered air pollution, close proximity to barrio commercial zones, walking for both necessity and leisure (and, as importantly, personal health), and the only social sector that has staunchly defended state support for public transit during the entire history of sprawl. Planning should be reminded of its own failure and negligence with regard to public transit up to the point when, in the 1990s, transit-oriented planning reemerged.

Terms such as *sustainable development* and *environmentally oriented planning* are associated with this recent shift in planning discourse. One of the main objectives of the U.S. environmental movement, though wholly undervalued in relation to actual effort, is to dramatically reduce the energy utilization footprint (Gottlieb 1993; Hays 1987; Peña 2005, 1998), which has been much enlarged by the constant sprawl associated with the hegemony of the real estate industry over planning (Checkoway 1984; Feagin 1984). But what is being situated as an essential reformulation of land use and planning logic is nothing new to the barrio experience. Barrio residents have actively recycled; they are an important segment of public transit users; barrio spaces are dense and mixed use; live-work arrangements are common; youth maximize existing open space; cultural workers have recaptured urban walls; vacant lots and other abandoned and marginal spaces are turned into small-scale gardens and farms for personal enjoyment and/or food production.

Barrio urbanism is the future of the city. Fundamentally, any strategy aimed at reacculturating suburbanites to socially function in a dense urban environment implies their learning to be *ciudadanos*. Lessening the use of cars and restoring social life in communities mandates a return to the human scale of the city through walking. Though barrio residents would find it comical that this societal return is the latest fad in planning, walking is central to the reformulation of planning and land use policy in the current era.

Why create gentrified, exclusionary spaces through a "new" planning paradigm? What value is derived from resegregating the city? Why should massive state subsidies demanded by capital to densify the city not be leveraged with mandates for ethnic and class inclusion in any new developments receiving this level of financial benefit?

When will the planning profession finally acknowledge successful sustainable urban practices, especially those in minority zones of the city? Finally, when will they set aside intellectual racism and technical hierarchy to admit failure and begin to relearn the culture of the city from existing examples?

Barrio urbanism is more than willing to assume the task, whatever the time frame, to initiate the transformation of disengaged Euro-American suburbanites into *ciudadanos*. Any rational approach to creating the sustainable city of the future depends on this social logic. Is a Eurocentric planning profession capable of engaging this challenge?

REFERENCES

Acosta, Teresa Palomo, and Ruthe Winegarten. 2003. *Las Tejanas: 300 Years of History.* Austin: University of Texas Press.

Aronowitz, Stanley, Dawn Esposito, William DiFazio, and Margaret Yard. 1998. "The Post-Work Manifesto." In *Post-Work: The Wages of Cybernation*, edited by Stanley Aronowitz and Jonathan Cutler, 31–80. London: Routledge.

Arreola, Daniel D. 2002. *Tejano South Texas.* Austin: University of Texas Press.

Bailly, Antoine, Philippe Brun, Roderick J. Lawrence, and Marie-Clare Rey, eds. 2000. *Socially Sustainable Cities.* London: Economica.

Barry, John. 2005. *The State and the Global Ecological Crisis.* Cambridge: MIT Press.

Beatley, Timothy. 2000. *Green Urbanism: Learning from European Cities.* Washington, DC: Island Press.

Beauregard, Robert A. 1993. *Voices of Decline: The Postwar Fate of US Cities.* Oxford: Blackwell.

Booth, Douglas E. 2004. *Hooked on Growth: Economic Addictions and the Environment.* Lanham, MD: Rowman and Littlefield.

Boyer, M. Christine. 1983. *Dreaming the Rational City: The Myth of American City Planning.* Cambridge, MA: MIT Press.

Bullard, Robert D., Glenn S. Johnson, and Angel O. Torres. 2000a. "Race, Equity and Smart Growth." Policy paper, Environmental Justice Research Center, Clark Atlanta University, Atlanta, GA.

———, eds. 2000b. *Sprawl City: Race, Politics, and Planning in Atlanta.* Washington, DC: Island Press.

Burden, Dan. 2000. *Streets and Sidewalks, People and Cars: The Citizens' Guide to Traffic Calming.* Sacramento, CA: Local Government Commission for Livable Communities.

Calthorpe, Peter. 1993. *The Next American Metropolis.* New York: Princeton Architectural Press.

Center for Science in the Public Interest. 2003. *Pestering Parents: How Food Companies Market Obesity to Children.* Washington, DC: CSPI.

Cervero, Robert. 1998. *The Transit Metropolis: A Global Inquiry.* Washington, DC: Island Press.

Checkoway, Barry. 1984. "Large Builders, Federal Housing Programs, and Postwar Suburbanization." In *Marxism and the Metropolis: New Perspectives in Urban Political Economy*, 2nd ed., edited by William K. Tabb and Larry Sawers, 152-73. New York: Oxford University Press.

Cockcroft, Eva Sperling, and Holly Barnet-Sanchez. [1990] 1993. *Signs from the Heart: California Chicano Murals.* Albuquerque: University of New Mexico Press.

Cox, Kevin R. 1978. *Urbanization and Conflict in Market Societies.* Chicago: Maaroufa Press.

CSPI. See Center for Science in the Public Interest.

Darder, Antonia. 1995. "Introduction: The Politics of Biculturalism: Culture and Difference in the Formation of *Warriors for Gringostroika* and *The New Mestizas*." In *Culture and Difference: Critical Perspectives on the Bicultural Experience in the United States*, edited by Antonia Darder, 1-20. Westport, CT: Bergin and Garvey.

Davis, Mike. 2000. *Magical Urbanism: Latinos Reinvent the US Big City*. London: Verso.

Dear, Michael, ed. 2001. *From Chicago to L.A.: Making Sense of Urban Theory*. Thousand Oaks, CA: Sage Publications.

Deleage, Jean-Paul. 1994. "Eco-Marxist Critique of Political Economy." In *Is Capitalism Sustainable?*, edited by Martin O'Connor, 37-52. New York: Guilford Press.

Diaz, David. n.d. "Population Zero, the Consumption Crisis and SUV Environmentalism." Unpublished manuscript.

———. 1989. "Environmental Regulation: Immigrants in a Changing Economic Structure." *California Sociologist* 12 (Summer): 213–41.

———. 2005. *Barrio Urbanism: Chicanos, Planning and American Cities*. New York: Routledge.

Dymski, Gary, John Veitch, and Michelle White. 1991. "Taking It to the Bank: Poverty, Race, and Credit in Los Angeles." Working Paper in Economics, University of California, Riverside, Department of Economics.

Feagin, Joe R. 1984. "Sunbelt Metropolis and Development Capital: Houston in the Era of Late Capitalism." In *Sunbelt/Snowbelt: Urban Development and Regional Restructuring*, edited by Larry Sawers and William K. Tabb, 99-127. New York: Oxford University Press.

Fine, Ben, and Ellen Leopold. 1993. *The World of Consumption: The Material and Cultural Revisited*. London: Routledge.

Fishman, Robert. 1987. *Bourgeois Utopias: The Rise and Fall of Suburbia*. New York: Basic Books.

Fogelson, Robert M. 1967. *The Fragmented Metropolis: Los Angeles, 1850-1930*. Cambridge, MA: Harvard University Press.

Frazier, John W., Florence M. Margai, and Eugene Tettey-Fio. 2003. *Race and Place: Equity Issues in Urban America*. Boulder, CO: Westview Press.

Fung, Archon. 2001. "Beyond and below the New Urbanism: Citizen Participation and Responsive Spatial Reconstruction." *Boston College Environmental Affairs Law Review* 28: 615-35.

Gámez, José Luis. 2002. "Representing the City: The Imagination and Critical Practice in East Los Angeles." *Aztlan* 27 (1): 95-120.

Garcia, Ignacio M. 1989. *United We Win: The Rise and Fall of La Raza Unida Party*. Tucson: University of Arizona Press.

Goldman, Robert. 1992. *Reading Ads Socially*. London: Routledge.

Gottdiener, Mark. 1985. *The Social Production of Urban Space*. Austin: University of Texas Press.

Gottlieb, Robert. 1993. *Forcing the Spring: The Transformation of the American Environmental Movement*. Washington, DC: Island Press.

Gottlieb, Robert, and Irene Wolt. 1977. *Thinking Big: The Story of the Los Angeles Times*. New York: G. P. Putnam's Sons.

Harvey, David. 1973. *Social Justice and the City*. Baltimore: John Hopkins University Press.

Hays, Samuel P. 1987. *Beauty, Health, and Permanence: Environmental Politics in the United States, 1955-1985*. Cambridge: Cambridge University Press.

Hoch, Charles. 1994. *What Do Planners Do?* Chicago: Planners Press.

Hoyle, Cynthia L. 1995. *Traffic Calming*. Planning Advisory Service Report no. 456. Chicago: American Planning Association.

Planning 167 (Spring): 31-32.

Jackson, Kenneth T. 1985. *Crabgrass Frontier*. New York: Oxford University Press.

Jacobs, Jane. 1961. *The Death and Life of Great American Cities*. New York: Random House.

Katz, Peter. 1994. *The New Urbanism: Toward an Architectural Community*. New York: McGraw Hill.

Lefebvre, Henri. [1974] 1991. *The Production of Space*. Oxford: Basil Blackwell.

Levenstein, Harvey. 2003. *Paradox of Plenty: A Social History of Eating in Modern America*. Berkeley: University of California Press.

Lewis, Tom. 1997. *Divided Highways: Building the Interstate Highways, Transforming American Life*. New York: Viking.

Marquez, Benjamin. 1998. "Mobilizing for Environmental and Economic Justice: The Mexican-American Environmental Justice Movement." *Capitalism Nature Socialism* 9 (4): 43-60.

Massey, Douglas S., and Nancy A. Denton. 1993. *American Apartheid: Segregation and the Making of the Underclass*. Cambridge, MA: Harvard University Press.

McCann, Barbara A., and Ried Ewing. 2003. *Measuring the Health Effects of Sprawl*. Washington, DC: Surface Transportation Project.

Mendez, M. A. 2003. "Latino Lifestyle and the New Urbanism: Synergy against Sprawl." Unpublished M.A. thesis, Massachusetts Institute of Technology.

Molotch, Harvey, and John Logan. 1984. "Tensions in the Growth Machine: Overcoming the Resistance to Value-Free Development." *Social Problems* 31 (5): 483-99.

Paehlke, Robert C. 1989. *Environmentalism and the Future of Progressive Politics*. New Haven: Yale University Press.

Peña, Devon G. 1998. "Los Animalitos: Culture, Ecology, and the Politics of Place in the Upper Rio Grande." In *Chicano Culture, Ecology, Politics*, edited by Devon G. Peña, 25-57. New York: Guilford Press.

———. 2005. *Mexican Americans and the Environment: Tierra y Vida*. Tucson: University of Arizona Press.

Pinderhughes, Raquel. 2004. *Alternative Urban Futures: Planning for Sustainable Development in Cities throughout the World*. Lanham, MD: Rowman and Littlefield.

Ponce, Mary Helen. [1993] 1995. *Calle Hoyt*. New York: Doubleday.

Pulido, Laura. 1996. *Environmentalism and Economic Justice*. Tucson: University of Arizona Press.

Rast, Joel. 2006. "Environmental Justice and the New Regionalism." *Journal of Planning Education* 25 (3): 249-63.

Rodriguez, Nestor. 1993. "Economic Restructuring and Latino Growth in Houston." In *In the Barrios: Latinos and the Underclass Debate*, edited by Joan Moore, and Raquel Pinderhughes, 101-27. New York: Russell Sage Foundation.

Rojas, James. 1999. "The Latino Use of Urban Space in East Los Angeles." In *La Vida Latina in L.A.: Urban Latino Cultures,* edited by Gustavo Leclerc, Raul Villa, and Michael Dear, 131-38. Thousand Oaks, CA: Sage Publications.

Solnit, Rebecca 2000. *Wanderlust.* New York. Penguin Books.

Squires, Gregory D. 1994. *Capital and Communities in Black and White.* Albany: State University of New York Press.

Taylor, Nigel. 1998. *Urban Planning Theory since 1945.* Thousand Oaks, CA: Sage Publications.

Touraine, Alain. 1988. *Return of the Actor.* Minneapolis: University of Minnesota Press.

———. 1995. *Critique of Modernity.* Oxford: Blackwell.

Valle, Victor M., and Rodolfo D. Torres. 2000. *Latino Metropolis.* Minneapolis: University of Minnesota Press.

Viesca, Victor Hugo. 2000. "Straight Out of the Barrio: Ozomatli and the Importance of Place in the Formation of Chicano/a Popular Culture in Los Angeles." *Cultural Values* 4 (4): 445-73.

Walter, Bob, Lois Arkin, and Richard Crenshaw. 1992. *Concepts and Strategies for Eco-City Development.* Los Angeles: Eco-Home Media.

Weiss, Marc. 1985. "The Origins and Legacy of Urban Renewal." In *Federal Housing Policy,* edited by J. Paul Mitchell, 253-76. New Brunswick, NJ: Center for Urban Policy Research.

Young, Iris Marion. 2000. *Inclusion and Democracy.* Oxford: Oxford University Press.

Aesthetic Belonging

The Latinization and Renewal of Union City, New Jersey

Johana Londoño

"Entre gustos no hay disgustos." So goes a common adage in Spanish that roughly translates to "In matters of taste there is no debate." The common-sense logic espoused is alluring and meant to demonstrate acceptance and open-mindedness toward taste. This statement also dismisses power relations involved in the implementation of aesthetics. The ingenuousness of the expression is particularly revealed when this saying is applied to aesthetic negotiations regarding the urban built environment. Contrary to the complacency expressed in this saying, in this chapter I show that *el gusto's* visual manifestation in cities and the particular aesthetic experience it connotes, such as that of community belonging, are important and laden with discourses of power constituted by class and racial hierarchies. The visual aestheticization of cities, a process by which judgments about urban forms and places are established by specific groups with multiple interests in urban place, is especially politically and economically salient today for Latino-majority cities in the United States. Popular form-conscious urban planning models such as New Urbanism's traditional architecture and redevelopment, together with neoliberal models of urban growth, aim to cater to and foster contemporary interest in gentrified urban living and consequently press upon the future sustainability of the Latino landscapes of barrios.

This paper focuses on the politics of aestheticizing urban places as manifested in Union City, New Jersey, a working-class suburban barrio, located at the edge of the Hudson River facing New York City, that has over the past two decades been gradually revitalized with monies from New Jersey's Urban Enterprise Zone (UEZ). Operating with the purpose of economic development and community betterment, the UEZ has reserved multiple loans for the replacement, on Bergenline Avenue, Union City's main commercial boulevard, of a multitextured built environment and commercial awnings—features that exemplify the so-called Latinization of urban space—with a modern "Main Street" American composition of muted "classic" colors and clean-cut typography that recalls New Urbanist forms. In what follows, I will examine the interrelated ways the

Latinized commercial space in Union City is being reshaped by UEZ's definition of what constitutes a proper urban aesthetic for economic development, by the upwardly mobile desires of Union City's Latino population juxtaposed with new Latino immigration waves into the city, and by gentrification generated by Union City's geographic proximity to New York City.

I argue that the UEZ's revitalization of Union City reveals the ways ethnic and racial relations, politics, and economics are organized by aesthetic judgment in the push toward gentrification. Moreover, this case study shows that economic redevelopment projects in barrios outlying large global cities engage with culture and ethnicity in different ways from those in historic central cities, a fact to consider in analyses of the use of federally allotted funds in urban redevelopment projects and the processes of gentrification that cultural renewal sometimes exacerbates at a metropolitan scale. In general, this case study contributes to a literature of Latino urbanisms by highlighting the importance of geographic location and history as factors that determine whether a Latino-identified place will be appreciated and sustained for its economic, social, and cultural value.

Indeed, the UEZ's manipulation of Union City's built environment is different from the approach taken in other Latino-majority cities by enterprise zones—which were started in the 1980s across the United States to foster economic growth in impoverished communities. Several publications note the ways some enterprise zones celebrate and affirm Latino culture. Places such as El Barrio in New York and Barrio Logan in San Diego, California, are able to market Latino culture, even if under the regulatory framework of enterprise zone management, because of their location in large cities with a history of Latino activism (Dávila 2004; City of San Diego 2006). But Union City, though also a Latino-majority city, is located at the outskirts of a metropolitan area, and its Latino population is diverse, making it less suitable for ethnic branding projects in the service of gentrification. The case of Union City suggests that working-class suburbs must compete even more intensely and deemphasize their Latino urban culture strategically because of their marginal location within the metropolitan gentrification system.

Union City's *Latinidad* is celebrated only by a top-down approach whereby the mayor infrequently announces the naming of a park or a street, or unveils a statue to honor a famous Cuban or Dominican artist or political figure. The bias against the bottom-up Latinization of urban space in Union City is interesting considering that since the 2000 census first documented the Latino demographic explosion numerous media figures, writers, and academics have claimed that the Latino visual reconfiguration of urban space in large cities such as Los Angeles and New York is revolutionary and highly marketable. The impact of Latinos on the visual landscape is variously considered to be a possible vehicle for cultural justice and a commercial boon, with the latter construal being partially responsible for the celebration of Latino culture by enterprise zones. Counter to the discourse that extols the everyday Latinization of cities, other discourses explicitly or implicitly devalue the Latinization of cityscapes and perceive it as a visual manifestation of blight, poverty, and chaos. This latter position promises to have an impact on both the material realities of Latinos and their visual landscape. In this vein Union City shows how enterprise zones, and the aesthetic they privilege in relation to the Latinized environment, negotiate a thin line between celebrating and devaluing urban Latino culture in a neoliberal era of marketable cities.

In what follows I draw from visual analysis, participant observation, press accounts, and informal interviews to examine the contrasting aesthetic constructions of Union City in relation to three issues: immigration, upward mobility, and gentrification. First, I offer a brief history of the social Latinization of Union City from the Cuban immigration of the 1960s to the present-day immigration from Central America, the Caribbean, and South America. Second, I show that despite the celebration of the aesthetic Latinization of American cities, Union City's particular location near New York City's most hotly contested real estate, demographic changes, and some residents' desires for the American dream of upward mobility influence the popularity of the UEZ's strategy for economic and community development and mainstream urban design. Finally, I analyze the ways in which the newly designed awnings and dreams for community improvement dismiss the city's Latino production of space to create a friendlier place for gentrification. Indeed, the case of Union City demonstrates that aesthetics are at the center of a neoliberalization of urban space in which a city's proximity to a global urban center influences its cultural development. I suggest that the dynamic between the contrasting aesthetic constructions of Union City threatens the ability of Latinos to claim space and cultural and social justice via processes of Latinization, and hence the overall capacity of the urban environment to facilitate community belonging.

Social Latinization of Union City

The first wave of Latin American and Caribbean migrants to Union City was initiated by a small number of poor Cuban farm and factory workers who arrived in New York City during Cuba's early twentieth-century Batista regime and quickly relocated to Union City and nearby West New York in search of open space and quiet neighborhoods. By 1959 there were two thousand Cuban exiles, mostly from the rural town of Fomentero in central Cuba (Nieves 1992). This community maintained social networks with Cubans on the island, particularly those living in Havana, Las Villas, and Fomento, and were a major influence in the arrival of the first cohort of postrevolutionary Cuban refugees in Union City and the larger North Jersey area (Boswell and Curtis 1983). In addition to the family and friendly ties attracting Cubans to Hudson County, many of the Cuban migrants that arrived in the first decade following Castro's ascension to power were relocated from Miami to Hudson County under the directorship of the Cuban Refugee Program in the United States. Begun in 1960 by the Department of Health, Education, and Welfare, the Cuban Refugee Program sought to prevent a possible financial burden caused by a mass influx of Cubans in Miami.[1] From 1961 to 1966, of all the states receiving resettled Cuban refugees, New Jersey received the most, an estimated population of twenty thousand. This early Cuban migration to Union City largely replaced an immigrant population of working-class Germans, Irish, and Italians who were simultaneously moving to nearby middle-class suburbs with less industry.

The expansion of the Cuban community was also promoted by the strategic exclusion of other Latino groups. Ramon Grosfoguel (2003) documents, the Cuban Refugee Program invested millions of dollars in the receiving cities where Cubans relocated. The money was primarily allocated for education, welfare, hospitals, and other public services. A portion of the funds was allotted to the Small Business Administration (SBA), which in turn distributed the resources among several business loan and mortgage programs. Puerto Ricans, as well as African Americans, were systematically excluded from attaining start-up capital through the SBA. Whereas almost 80 percent of the first Cuban-owned firms in Union City had relied on SBA bank loans, 75 percent of Puerto Ricans in New Jersey who requested information on loan attainment were given misleading information and blocked from access (Grosfoguel 2003, 169). Similiar to the other cases in a wide range of policies, the administrative work of the SBA at this time favored early Cuban migrants over Puerto Ricans because the former were largely perceived to be white and to have high social and cultural capital, and because the successful integration of Cubans into the American mainstream served a symbolic function during the cold war in which the United States posited itself as the noble guarantor of freedom and upward mobility vis-à-vis communist Cuba. This partially explains the large population of Puerto Ricans and African Americans in nearby Jersey City compared to the still small numbers of Puerto Ricans in Union City.

However, it is misguided to allow stories of political favoritism to make the account of Union City's history of Cuban migration replicate the dominant narrative of early Cuban migration to the United States as an elite, highly educated, privileged cohort. Although a number of early Cuban refugees were upper and middle class, with money capital deposited in U.S. banks before their migration, North Hudson's Cubans included far fewer high school graduates and more female workers (Rogg and Cooney 1980, 15). The Cuban migrants in Union City, and larger Hudson County, came to work in the sweatshops and factories that peppered the North Jersey landscape. Thus, as much as the Cuban influx to northern New Jersey was the result of cold war politics, it was also a necessary industrial workforce. For some Cuban women, working in Union City's garment industry meant downward occupational mobility and a change to their traditional family role. Subsequent migrations of Cubans, particularly the mass exodus of the 1980s "Mariel Boatlift," contributed heavily to Union City's Cuban working class. The "Marielitos," as these refugees came to be known, were mostly Afro-Cuban and peasants from the countryside. Even though these later Cuban migrants had the same socioeconomic standing as earlier Cuban cohorts in Union City, they were greeted coldly by older Cuban residents, who thought this new group brought drug problems and gave "law abiding Union City a bad name" (Cheslow 1988). A combination of racial policies and racist attitudes by older waves of Cuban migrants toward this later cohort, as well as the end of the Cuban Refugee Program, contributed to the inhospitable environment.

Structural forces, kinship ties, and sheer demographic strength led to Union City's development as "the Havana on the Hudson," a Cuban political and commercial stronghold. The city's voters, who were overwhelmingly Democrats, elected their native Cuban American politician Robert Menendez to various offices, first as mayor, then as New Jersey's first Latino congressman and one of the highest-ranking Hispanics in congressional history, and finally as senator. Menendez's prominent status encourages the ethnic solidarity and patronage that has ensured a strong Cuban representation in municipal politics (Gettlemen 2006). Cubans in Union City have also been successful developers and entrepreneurs, starting up thriving restaurants, social clubs, pastry shops, and other retail stores (Prieto 2009).

Despite the Cuban population's successes, Union City remains in the shadow of its sister city "Little Havana" in Miami (Nieves 1992). Union City did not become a Miami ethnic powerhouse for several reasons. First, in the 1980s Union City's Latino population began to grow more diverse. Further, at that time Union City underwent its initial stages of deindustrialization in which jobs became increasingly scarce, forcing competition between old and new immigrants. Cubans who experienced upward mobility deemed the city's changes in population and political economy in the eighties and nineties a threat to their hopes for social and economic mobility, and many first exiles and their U.S.-born children moved away to outer New Jersey suburbs or Miami (Nieves 1992).[2]

Since the 1980s the Latino demographic in Union City has rapidly increased, with mass immigration from Central America, the Caribbean, and South America. Significant numbers of this latter group of immigrants come from the Dominican Republic, El Salvador, Mexico, Peru, Ecuador, Colombia, and Puerto Rico. Union City is now over 90 percent Latino/a. The increase in immigration has made Union City one of the most densely populated cities in the United States. In 2000, the city's average population per square mile was 52,825; New York City's was 26,402.[3] Union City's Latin American diversity and lack of earlier industrial forms of economic incorporation have also placed it among the most impoverished in the United States, a situation heightened by its location in New Jersey, one of the wealthiest states in the country, bordering the "world city" of New York. The mass influx of an increasingly diverse Latin American immigrant population has in its totality surpassed the more established Cuban population, even though the latter continues to be the largest Latino national group in the city. This demographic change is not lost on the Cuban population that remains. It is common to hear stories of Cuban landlords who, in an attempt to keep the old guard in town, selectively accept white and single tenants over recently migrated Latino families. On Bergenline Avenue it is also common to hear from a diverse group of Latinos, not just Cubans, grudgingly remarking that "things are changing" and that Union City is increasingly looking like *"un barrio en* [enter Latin American country of choice]."

Undoubtedly, things have changed, mostly because of a shift toward a service economy. The large and diverse Latin American migration to the city occurred just as the United States began to experience extreme bouts of unemployment and deindustrialization. Saskia Sassen (1998) explains, this is not all that surprising. The increasing internationalization of the economy in the last three decades expedited mass immigration to the United States at the same time that it led to deindustrialization and economic restructuring in the shape of an expanding service sector in urban areas. Union City, like other small industrial cities at the periphery of New York City, experienced a rise in immigration because the shift to a service economy was gradual. Factories located on the industrial periphery of New York City evolved into an urban crust of downgraded manufacturing dependent on low-wage, semiskilled jobs.[4] A few of these factories managed to survive into the late nineties, albeit with difficulty (Strunsky 1997). Residents I spoke to who had experienced the gradual deindustrialization of the city noted that toward the end of their factory employment precarious part-time and temporary employment was available but that workers were frequently sent home without paychecks and that factories temporarily closed without notice. Certainly, Union City has had varying degrees of engagement with New York City throughout its history, but as the New York metropolitan system has been increasingly affected by deindustrialization, gentrification, and "return to the city" movements among professionals, the city has become more dependent on New York City for its future growth.

Consequently, throughout the past decade Union City, once known as "Northern New Jersey, Embroidery Capital of the World since 1872"—as an imposing sign on a New Jersey turnpike overpass proudly declares—has had to turn to other forms of economic growth and sustainability. The city is now lightly marketed in low-quality TV commercials and ads for its diverse cuisine and a low 3.5 percent sales tax, managed by the UEZ. But more salient are the ways municipal government has employed the UEZ to visually renew, market, and gentrify Union City. The following section examines the aesthetic Latinization of Bergenline Avenue, Union City's main commercial area, and the ways the UEZ has altered this landscape.

Aesthetic Latinization and the Urban Enterprise Zone

Union City residents readily point out, the changes in the Latinization of Union City brought by immigration are observable not only in the city's demographics but also in the contrasting aesthetic constructions of Latino and revitalized Bergenline Avenue. By reading the commercial avenue's fast-changing visual landscape one can gauge the diversity in Union City's immigrant population as well as the incoming changes in population and consumption brought about by gentrification.

The visual Latinization of Union City is similar to that observable in other barrios. The city's visual rhetoric is composed of various textures, colors, and scales: hand-painted typography of varied and rich coloring; murals and statues of the Virgin Mary; tiled roofing reminiscent of Latin American roofs; and facades composed of brick, vinyl house siding, and glossy tiles of many materials and patterns. It exemplifies what Mike Davis aptly describes as "tropicalizing cold urban space" (2001, 61) and Agustín Laó-Montes and Arlene Dávila (2001) exuberantly term a "mambo montage." It is a production of sociocultural space gradually accumulated to create a landscape expressive of *Latinidad*. Both excess and economy, aesthetics and politics, expression and need, play a role in the Latino visual reconfiguration of cities. Visual dynamism is certainly present as you walk down Bergenline Avenue. Cuban *pastelerias* and restaurants selling *bandeja paisa* and *ceviche* try to lure you in with their vibrant nationally coded facades. Although some business owners are not Latino, or do not reside in Union City, the audience they market to is the Latino population. When you walk into an Indian- or Korean-owned store you are more likely to be greeted in Spanish than in English. The visual Latinization of space may have different ethnic agents, but their context and self-presentation are products of the Latino community that consumes and provides the overall energy of the street. The visual environment's multiple facets, spatial composition, and ability to signify various social contexts make it vibrant. Michael J. Dear, Raul Homero Villa, and Gustavo Leclerc (1999, 1) consider this type of reconfiguration of cities part of a larger Latino cultural revolution.

However, Union City's Latino landscape is also understood in relation to New York City. A viewer on Bergenline Avenue, on the top of the Palisades Cliffs rising above Manhattan, can observe a divided landscape, with a visual montage of *Latinidad* on the one side and with wealth, as represented by New York City's shiny and tall skyscrapers, on the other. This visual contrast influences the conceptual prism through which Union City, New York, and other North Jersey middle- and upper-middle class suburbs are viewed and represented. The resulting regional perceptions shape the ways in which political and economic forces play out in these places. As Union City shows, perceptions about the city and its geographic location intertwine with changes to its population and political economy.

Indeed, for some Union City residents, politicians, and business owners, the nonlinear configuration of the city sparks anxiety. These people are concerned with fulfilling normative expectations of what upward mobility looks like and fear that the Latinized landscape symbolizes negative cultural capital, especially now that it reflects the increasing numbers of poor working-class and racialized Latinos coming from Mexico and Central America. To counter this symbolism, this group advocates for a neutral and undifferentiated urban aesthetic that may connote belonging to an American national imaginary of upward mobility. Moreover, they believe that changing the visual landscape of Union City into something akin to the cleanliness and homogeneity exuded by already "Manhattanized" North Jersey cities such as Hoboken and Jersey City may foster economic growth. These agents of visual change, primarily public officials and business owners, insist that the expansion of regional shopping malls and discount retailers such as Walmart and Target, and the recently built light rail connecting Union City to these shopping destinations, are putting economic pressure on Union City's commercial district (Miller 2005). But an even more salient, though less noted, explanation for urban renewal is the city's proximity to New York City's exclusive real estate market, which has made Union City prime territory for young professionals looking for less expensive housing (Martin 2005). For all these reasons—to provide social distinction, foster a business climate, and attract New York City professionals—a neotraditional aesthetic has gained favor in Union City. The UEZ's aesthetic redevelopment is at the forefront of this revitalization.

Union City's UEZ is one of many public and private enterprise zones that sprang up across the United States in the 1990s to foster growth in economically distressed areas and to visually project economic vitality (Mossberger 2000, 2).[5] The UEZ's advisory board consists of seven local merchants and two residents, who meet to devise ways and raise funds to clean up Union City's business districts and attract new businesses and developers (Nardone 2001). A result of this active promotion, the UEZ's membership has rapidly increased since its inception to two hundred enrolled businesses. Over the past twelve years UEZ-member businesses have accrued an estimated $6 million in tax revenue generated by a special reduced 3.5 percent sales tax—about half of the average New Jersey sales tax—that retail businesses in Union City may charge their customers. The money is grouped into a special fund for economic development projects and services. Included in the revitalization project is a "facade improvement program" that allocates monies for the redesign of the commercial district's awnings and is the most visible sign of redevelopment. For the fiscal year 2007, $235,000 was approved for storefront facade improvements for businesses that were a part of Union City's UEZ (Rosero 2007b).

Needless to say, the municipal government's support for the UEZ is indicative of the heightened mutual dependence between government and real estate capital. In a neoliberal economy politicians comply with market demands by providing a business-friendly environment they in turn sell to residents as economic progress. What is interesting about this all-too-well-known partnership in Union City is the special consideration for aesthetics. The UEZ's facade improvement program demonstrates how significant the manipulation of urban form is in maintaining a positive government-business relationship. A "good" standard design in Union City promises to provide a pleasant environment that attracts investment, turning the city into what Mayor Brian Stack (n.d.) categorizes as a "business destination about to make its mark."

One indicator of how successful Union City has been in attracting investment since its association with the UEZ is the "investment grade" that the bond rating agency Moody's has given Union City in the past 10 years.[6] Union City's constant rating as investment ready with minimal credit risk explains why old apartments are being renovated and numerous condos are under construction. It also largely explains why city officials pursue facade renovation as a way to prove their credit worth and provide an amenable context for the construction of condominiums.

Just how much does the UEZ aid progentrification business in the city? In the spring of 2010, a manager I spoke with at the new luxury condominium in Union City named the Thread—a reference to the clothing factory that once stood at the site—detailed the tax abatement made possible by the UEZ among the many benefits of buying a condo there. The manager's enthusiasm for the UEZ tax benefit betrayed her mild disapproval and contempt for Union City's poverty and ethnic concentration. But the manager did not seem to recognize that the UEZ benefits were there because of the concentration of poor residents in the city, thus showing how new property developers, and the managers and residents they bring along, benefit from the very people and environment they disparage. Given the progentrification environment, visual change seems more necessary now than ever. The following section examines the ways the aesthetic dimensions of an American dream of economic progress coincide with the neoliberalization of space.

A Visual Consensus: An Aesthetic American Dream and the Neoliberalization of Space

Several authors have linked the gentrification of cities to the neoliberalization of the economy and its preference for private and public partnerships (Brenner and Theodore 2003; Dávila 2004; Hackworth 2007; Smith 1996). Some of these authors relate the culture of place to structural mappings (Dávila 2004; Smith 1996). Similarly, the UEZ facade program shows how the visual rhetoric of an urban development project intersects with economic restructuring. Clearly, aesthetics—whether Latino inspired or neutral, as advocated by UEZ—is at the center of a neoliberalization of urban space. The design of place has become an important factor that determines the ability of a public-private partnership to successfully market a city.

The turn to visual renewal raises the question: Why now? And why, given the consequences of economic growth strategies employed by Union City officials, such as escalating housing prices and a higher cost of living, is there support among the population? I suggest that, as Union City shows, visual renewal is most successful as a gentrification strategy when it gains purchase on the desires of various urban stakeholders. All Union City business owners, mostly Latinos but also South Asians and Koreans, on the main commercial avenues can choose to be part of the revitalization program. The two-hundred-plus members now involved in the UEZ have access to the facade program. While participation is voluntary, the UEZ encourages it by arguing that the program will attract more consumers, create a cohesive look for the commercial avenue, and persuade new businesses to enter the city. Thus the program is in fact operating in an insidious way to benefit capital accumulation. For example, Larry Wainstein, chairman of the UEZ, has stated, "We are working with the Zoning Office and the Building Department to update our sign ordinance, which was last revised in 1996. . . . We want to work in conjunction with the store tenants to help them understand the simple signage effort." Moreover, "Businesses on three major streets will be told to avoid cluttering up their windows with excess signs, and to taken [sic] advantage of grant money to improve their facades" (Rosero 2007a). Both quotes devalue the avenue's previous signage and imply that with the use of a firm hand the delivery of a superior aesthetic knowledge will perform its ideological work and convince business owners of the merits of renewal.

Since the implementation of the facade program many business owners have agreed to change their facades to a neotraditional aesthetic composed mostly of burgundy and hunter green awnings with white sans serif type. The signs of a Cuban bakery, a Mexican restaurant, furniture shops, and ninety-nine-cent stores have now become an indistinguishable linear plane of burgundy. Several UEZ stores have chosen different colors and relief lettering, but even the colors and layout are tamed to fit some sense of what commercial design *should* be. Added to this traditional beautification scheme of the city are the Victorian street lamps, newly paved sidewalks with an interlocking pattern, and omnipresent American flags dotting Bergenline Avenue. It seems that the New Urbanist paradigm for community design is being implemented in Union City and quickly replacing the city's fragmented and chaotic visual Latinization.

Though this universal design has amounted to a visual mechanism with social implications, UEZ participants are unlikely to realize that the economic and aesthetic imperatives they espouse make them active players in the city's creative destruction process and progentrification scheme. Because the UEZ posits itself as offering Union City businesses a competitive edge, it gains a purchase on business owners' desires for the American dream of upward mobility. By using rhetoric that conflates business interests with the needs of the community, and relying on locals' acceptance of the program, the UEZ's recommended changes for redevelopment and visual renewal are naturalized and deemed necessary for progress. In this way the UEZ has managed to build consent among business owners by playing up the economic growth and the community revitalization that residents and business owners desire as they project their insecurities about demographic change and class mobility onto the visual landscape. In making Union City's residents complicit with an economic development scheme that pushes standardization, the UEZ creates the conditions by which taste is conflated with a normative aesthetic. The result of the dynamic process between municipal government, investment capital, residents, and business owners is visual *re-form*.

The renewal of the built environment has not led to the total vitiation of Latino culture, though it certainly limits its visuality. Union City officials have made an effort to represent the Latino community in the urban environment by naming a street and plaza after Cuban singer Celia Cruz, a school after Cuban national hero José Martí, and a children's park after

Juan Pablo Duarte, the founding father of the Dominican Republic (Cave 2005). Arlene Dávila's work on El Barrio shows, it is necessary to critically analyze how Latino culture is conceptualized in projects of urban development to avoid the negation of the material conditions of *Latinidad* (Dávila 2004). In a similarly critical vein, the memorials being built in Union City are sculptures and placards that memorialize future displacement and alienate residents from their history. The new visual rhetoric clears away a Latino reconfiguration of space that signifies immigration, change, and socioeconomic status from the landscape. City officials have opted for discrete forms of cultural representation to cater to city voters, while at the very same time working against everyday cultural expressions to accumulate more capital. Union City's policies and the landscape it polices point to the ways ethnic communities will continue to be managed to simultaneously keep a working-class labor supply, please voters, and attract an inflow of new investment and wealthier residents.

This instrumentalization of *gusto* in Union City masks socioeconomic relations and contributes to a neoliberal reconfiguration of space. My argument parallels the critique made by some urbanists that New Urbanism's neotraditional design masks neoliberal processes of inequality by evoking community and diversity through its design.[7] It also parallels larger debates on the cultural regulation of neoliberal economics. As various scholars have noted, neoliberal processes of public and private cooperation transform urban cultures into a resource for profit that requires heightened measures of cultural management, including the manipulation of aesthetics (Dávila 2004; Street 2000; Yudice 2004). In Union City the UEZ and the entrepreneurial and government visual brokers of the city value a standard homogeneous urban environment over the heightened visibility of Latino commerce. The manipulation of form mediates the wants of a neoliberal economy and the aesthetic responses of the population, dictating the shape that a district should take to bring in desired commercial investment. As Sharon Zukin (1991) has noted, landscapes can control social relations. Toward that end, Union City officials offer, in lieu of a guarantee, a depiction of a population's desire for mainstream lifestyles. This visual renewal limits the political possibilities of Latinization, celebrated by scholars and designers, and creates a welcoming space for gentrification.

The neoliberalization of Union City also occurs through a strategy of spatial regulation that conspicuously demarcates public and private space. Once businesses in Union City extended out into public streets.

Now merchants are beginning to use glass facades to enclose the spectacle of commercialization. On occasion, specially designated "sidewalk sale" days allow merchants to sell their goods along commercial corridors (Low and Smith 2006). This regulation of the public display of clearance goods helps create a progentrification environment.

The visual process of neoliberalizing urban culture brings up the question: Should one react to the subsumption of *Latinidad* by arguing for the importance of eclectic, organic urban *Latinidad*? I suggest that to do so would mean risking physical determinism by creating a simplistic narrative whereby a Latinized landscape would be radical and UEZ's re-form would be fascist. After all, it is difficult to argue without falling into essentialisms that the Latinization of cities is representative of a Latino identity. But it is also important to remember that these landscapes reflect economic and political processes of Latinization. The point, then, is not to declare the Latino visual reconfiguration of commercial space as more authentic or conducive to economic growth than the revitalization program of the UEZ. Rather, I suggest that the visual agents of the city should strive to construct an aesthetic debate to better understand the destruction of visual Latinization by a dominant process of urbanism that is purportedly more American, and the mode of community belonging that is at stake in this process.

My concern in this chapter has been to show the ways in which upwardly mobile desires among the Latino population in a poor working-class community conflict with public and private interests and how these manifest in the aesthetics of the built environment. The urban changes I detail here are primarily a result of the UEZ, a program that is part of a larger set of urban policies initiated during the Reagan administration in what would later become known as the formative years of neoliberal urbanism. Union City shows how the UEZ has rethought the city at a metropolitan scale and, in neoliberal fashion, has aided business and outside investment at the expense of empowering the gradual development of the community's urban landscape.

Certainly in this last year of economic recession, a critique of the cultural changes to the urban environment must consider the material conditions facing American cities. On the one hand, the Obama administration's new White House Office of Urban Affairs has fueled high expectations for the future of urban centers and has led some media and political figures to express hopes for the restoration of American cities from the general malaise and marginalization they suffered during Republican administrations. Certainly this is the first time in decades that a president has put a spotlight on urban issues and promised to understand and promote the ways in which cities and their regions interrelate. Conversely, the recession of 2010 has partially tarnished these hopes, bringing with it disinvestment that has directly affected enterprise zones in New Jersey cities. Yet urban redevelopment projects such as the UEZ continue to play a major role in economic growth strategies (Cowen and Flaccomio 2010). Both government officials and business owners lament cuts in the UEZ and the opportunities it has provided local businesses in the form of reduced sales taxes for customers and business improvement grants. In light of this pressing economic situation, a debate on the aesthetic judgment employed by the UEZ may seem superficial and unimportant and the funding of UEZs the most crucial imperative. I maintain, however, that urban policies implemented in a future, more robust, economy will be most successful and equitable if they also engage with the cultural dimensions of cities.

Union City demonstrates that what is at stake in urban development is more than economics and politics; the visual culture of the built environment and its ability to connote community belonging are also important. Middle-class fears and desires along with developers' ideas of a proper visual environment are played out in aesthetic negotiations over the look of the built environment. Moreover, Union City's geographic location near New York City and its history of Latinization have opened the way to a visual renewal that threatens the social and cultural representation of Union City's Latino population and thus thwarts the ability of the urban environment to foster community belonging. Despite a postmodern, multicultural celebration of difference, Union City proves that value does not accrue to all urban forms, especially those that are marginalized by their metropolitan region and political economic context. The politics of aesthetics in urban places should therefore be further considered.

This is particularly so in a national context in which other cities are also becoming simultaneously entrepreneurial and designed, and consequently giving political economic processes an affective and visual order. In addition, as the Latino population continues to grow outside inner cities the Latinization process observed in Union City, and its disparagement and erasure by various governmental entities and the established population, might very well become ubiquitous across the United States. To this end, Union City presents an opportunity to examine a very diverse Latino working-class suburb with a dissimilar fate to that of inner-city barrios facing urban development. Moreover, a study of Union City shows how essential it is to understand the political significance of *el gusto*—the role that a dominant aesthetic form and aesthetic experience play—in the decline of a sense of community cohesion and the neoliberalization of space at a metropolitan level.

NOTES

1 The Cuban Refugee Program was aided by religious organizations around the country that organized the Cuban migrants' arrival in particular cities. In Hudson County the Catholic Church was an important agent in Cuban relocation (Rogg and Cooney 1980, 16; Thomas 1967, 51-52).

2 In addition to Evelyn Nieves (1992), see McHugh, Miyares, and Skop (1997), who note that Miami grew as a magnet for Cubans in the Northeast during the decade spanning 1985-95. By far, northern New Jersey experienced the most out-migration to Miami. Reasons provided include closeness to Cuba, warm weather, and a thriving ethnic economic niche.

3 These data were taken from the 2000 U.S. Census.

4 For a description of the dynamic interactions of immigration with political and economic forces, see Sassen's (1998) chapter entitled "America's Immigration 'Problem.'"

5 Information on the Urban Enterprise Zone of Union City can be found at Union City's website under "Our UEZ": www.firstlooksagency.com/unioncity/uez.html.

6 From 1992 to 2007, Union City consistently received an "AAA" investment grade, the highest rating possible (from Moody's Investor Service; see www.moodys.com/cust/default.asp). Such assessment sets the stage for increasing outside investment, a process that has become evident in the landscape of the city. Jason Hackworth's *The Neoliberal City* (2007) is particularly helpful in showing the ways in which bond rating agencies and the grades they assign to cities contribute to the neoliberalization of urban space.

7 Neil Smith (1999) offers a compelling argument against New Urbanism, contending that the New Urbanist paradigm legitimizes the revanchist city that promotes gentrification by masking it as "good design." For more on the design principles of New Urbanism, see Duany, Plater-Zyberk, and Speck (2001).

REFERENCES

Brenner, Neil, and Nik Theodore. 2003. *Spaces of Neoliberalism: Urban Restructuring in North America and West Europe.* New York: Wiley-Blackwell.

Boswell, Thomas D., and James R. Curtis. 1983. *The Cuban American Experience: Culture, Images, and Perspectives.* Totowa, NJ: Rowman and Allanheld.

Cave, Damien. 2005. "Union City Journal: A Park's Dominican Name, Reflecting Quirky Diversity." *New York Times,* August 15. http://query.nytimes.com/gst/ fullpage.html?res=9F02E5DA123FF936A2575BC0A9629C8B63.

Cheslow, Jerry. 1988. "Union City Angered by Cuba Pact." *New York Times,* January 3. http://query.nytimes.com/gst/fullpage.html?res=940DE3D9123EF930A35 752C0A96E948260.

City of San Diego. City Planning and Community Investment Department Communications Program. 2006. "Barrio Logan Redevelopment Project Area, Fact Sheet." www.sandiego.gov/redevelopment-agency/pdf/barriologanfact.pdf.

Cowen, Richard, and Keri Ann Flaccomio. 2010. "New Jersey Budget Woes Threaten Urban Enterprise Program." *NorthJersey.com,* June 18. www.northjersey.com/ news/96632419_FISCAL_CRISIS_THREATENS_URBAN_ENTERPRISE_ZONES. html.

Dávila, Arlene. 2004. *Barrio Dreams: Puerto Ricans, Latinos, and the Neoliberal City.* Berkeley: University of California Press.

Davis, Mike. 2001. *Magical Urbanism: Latinos Reinvent the US Big City.* New York: Verso.

Dear, Michael J., Raul Homero Villa, and Gustavo Leclerc. 1999. *Urban Latino Cultures: La Vida Latina en L.A.* Thousand Oaks, CA: Sage Publications.

Duany, Andres, Elizabeth Plater-Zyberk, and Jeff Speck. 2001. *Suburban Nation: The Rise of Sprawl and the Decline of the American Dream.* North Point Press, 2001.

Gettlemen, Jeffrey. 2006. "On Politics; A Cuban Revolution, Only It's in New Jersey." *New York Times,* February 5, http://query.nytimes.com/gst/fullpage.html?res=9C05 E2D61F3FF936A35751C0A9609C8B63.

Grosfoguel, Ramón. 2003. *Colonial Subjects: Puerto Ricans in Global Perspective.* Berkeley: University of California Press.

Hackworth, Jason. 2007. *The Neoliberal City: Governance, Ideology, and Development in American Urbanism.* Ithaca: Cornell University Press.

Laó-Montes, Agustín, and Arlene Dávila. 2001. *Mambo Montage: The Latinization of New York.* New York: Columbia University Press.

Low, Setha, and Neil Smith, eds. 2006. *The Politics of Public Space.* New York: Routledge.

Martin, Antoinette. 2005. "Residential Up-and-Comer: Union City." *New York Times,* October 2. www.nytimes.com/2005/10/02/realestate/02njzo.html.

McHugh, Kevin E., Ines M. Miyares, and Emily H. Skop. 1997. "The Magnetism of Miami: Segmented Paths in Cuban Migration." *Geographical Review* 87 (4): 504–19.

Miller, Jonathan. 2005. "An Orgy of the Senses, a Checkered History." *New York Times,* December 18.

Mossberger, Karen. 2000. *The Politics of Ideas and the Spread of Enterprise Zones.* Washington, DC: Georgetown University Press.

Nardone, Christine. 2001. "The Ins and Outs of Business: Most Hudson Companies Not Yet Affected by Recession This Year." *Hudson County Reporter,* December 30. www.hudsonreporter.com/site/index.cfm?BRD=1291&PAG=461&dept_ id=523584&newsid=2861542&rfi=8.

Nieves, Evelyn. 1992. "Union City and Miami: A Sisterhood Born of Cuban Roots." *New York Times,* November 30. http://query.nytimes.com/gst/fullpage.html? res=9E0CE4DE 1E39F933A05752C1A964958260&sec=&spon=&pagewanted=print.

Prieto, Yolanda. 2009. *The Cubans of Union City: Immigrants and Exiles in a New Jersey Community.* Philadelphia: Temple University Press.

Rogg, Eleanor Meyer, and Rosemary Santana Cooney. 1980. *Adaptation and Adjustment of Cubans: West New York, New Jersey.* Monograph 5. New York: Hispanic Research Center, Fordham University.

Rosero, Jessica. 2007a. "Shopping District Gets Makeover, UEZ Hosts Dinner Meeting, Introduces Facade Improvement Program." *Hudson County Reporter,* March 17. http://hudsonreporter.com/view/full_stories_home/2411391/article-Shopping-business-district-gets-makeover-UEZ-hosts-dinner-meeting—introduces-fa-231-ade-improvement-program.

———. 2007b. "What's Happening at Your Meeting? Various Resolutions Passed at Union City Board of Commissioners Meeting." *Hudson County Reporter,* August 26. www.hudsonreporter.com/site/news.cfm?newsid=18746021&BRD= 1291&PAG=461&dept_id=523590&rfi=6.

Sassen, Saskia. 1998. *Globalization and Its Discontents: Essays on the New Mobility of People and Money.* New York: New Press.

Smith, Neil. 1996. *The New Urban Frontier: Gentrification and the Revanchist City.* New York: Routledge.

———. 1999. "Which New Urbanism? The Revanchist 90's." *Perspecta* 30:98–105.

Stack, Brian P. n.d. "Welcome to Union City, New Jersey: A Message from the Mayor." www.firstlooksagency.com/unioncity/home.html.

Street, John. 2000. "Aesthetics, Policy, and the Politics of Popular Culture." *European Journal of Cultural Studies* 3 (1): 27–43.

Strunsky, Steve. 1997. "For 125 Years, a Big Industry That Produces Delicate Lace." *New York Times,* August 31. http://query.nytimes.com/gst/fullpage.html?res=980DE6D6 1331F932A0575BC0A961958260.

Thomas, John F. 1967. "Cuban Refugees in the United States." *International Migration Review* 1 (2): 46–57.

Yudice, George. 2004. *The Expediency of Culture: Uses of Culture in the Global Era.* Durham: Duke University Press.

Zukin, Sharon. 1991. *Landscapes of Power: From Detroit to Disney World.* Berkeley: University of California Press.

Placing Barrios in Housing Policy

Kee Warner

Even as Latinos have surpassed African Americans as the largest minority group in the United States, we are also the population with the most severe housing needs. Housing programs from the federal level on down have scarcely addressed the backlog of needs, much less anticipated the future. Long-term problems with barrio housing have been compounded by a deepening affordability crisis and by the diversion of public resources to profit-driven urban redevelopment. Official data clearly underestimate the severity of housing needs by not including the growing numbers of the undocumented. But those who blame the housing crisis on the latest wave of immigrants are misguided. This chapter will first describe the character and the magnitude of Latino housing needs and then describe how this results from patterns of urban place-building practices in the United States and the failure to address barrio housing at all levels of public policy.

Magnitude of Latino Housing Needs

For Latinos, securing decent, affordable housing continues to be a challenge. Some achieve the middle-class dream of home ownership, but many remain inadequately housed, including some home owners, particularly in comparison with white Americans. According to a 1999 report, "Hispanics are about twice as likely as Whites with similar resources to be inadequately housed and more than three times as likely to live in overcrowded conditions" (Yzaguirre, Arce, and Kamasaki 1999, 161). Housing costs continue to climb in a boom mode, but incomes do not keep pace and housing programs are grossly inadequate. These broader realities have particular force for Latino populations, who tend to live in high-cost housing markets, are overrepresented in the low-wage service sector, and have benefited less from public housing policy.

It is no surprise that Latinos live in the hot housing markets. Latinos, including undocumented workers, are a critical component of the construction industry (Frey et al. 2009). In 2006 undocumented immigrants (mostly Latinos) were estimated to constitute 29 percent of the roofers and drywall installers in the country and 14 percent of all construction workers (Passel 2006). In the year 2000, of the twenty cities with the highest Latino populations, 80 percent were above the national average in housing costs and 20 percent were among the "top-ten least affordable cities in the country" (Bowdler 2004, 4). Latinos are drawn to booming cities for employment, and many sprawling cities of the Sunbelt, such as San Diego, Phoenix, and Dallas, both are closer to the border, putting them in the middle of migrant streams and have historically large Latino populations.

In the 2000 census, median family income for Latinos ($34,397) was almost one-third lower than the median for all families ($50,046) (Ramirez 2004, 14). Latino men were concentrated in the lower-wage occupations in service, construction, production, and transportation, whereas women were in sales and service. A substantially lower proportion of Latinos worked in higher-paid occupations as managers and professionals (Ramirez 2004, 13). And these data include only households that are counted in the formal labor force! The combination of high costs and inadequate incomes forces Latinos to pay too much for housing. By traditional measures, 41.8 percent of Latino families paid too much for housing in 2001, compared to 29.6 percent of all families, and almost one out of five households (18.6 percent) spent more than half of their income on housing (Bowdler 2004, 4).

The accepted standard for housing affordability in the United States is that families should not pay more than 30 percent of their income for housing. This somewhat arbitrary guideline has been used for the analysis of housing needs and to design criteria for housing programs. Unfortunately, it may not capture the real impact of housing costs on a family's livelihood. For one thing, it is not sensitive to family size and it does not reflect the cost of other basic household necessities. The concept of *shelter poverty* is designed to address these deficiencies (Stone 2006a, 54). Stone compares what is left in the family budget after paying the actual cost of housing with what the family needs to pay for "a basic market basket of non-shelter necessities" (45). Following this methodology, a married couple with two children earning $30,000 a year in 2001 would be able to afford to spend only 21 percent of their income on housing (46). Their real need would not be captured if they were expected to pay 30 percent of their earnings on housing. Shelter poverty tells us most about the distribution of housing needs within the United States. Shelter poverty is worse for larger households, renters, people of color, and female-headed households. Understandably, the combined effects for Latino populations are severe. "In 1997, 50 percent of Latino-headed, 45 percent of Black-headed (non-Latino) and 35 percent of Asian-headed households were shelter-poor, compared with 27 percent of white-headed households" (54).

Latinos are paying more than they can afford for housing and are getting less than they need. In 2001, "The share of Latino households reporting poor building conditions ha[d] declined slightly since 1991, but [it was] still more than twice that of Whites" (Bowdler 2004, 6). And in that same year the proportion of Latino households living in overcrowded conditions was more than five times the national average (6). These conditions were even worse for Latino immigrants, 40 percent of whom were living in crowded housing conditions (7).

Access to decent housing and to home ownership has immediate impacts on living conditions but also shapes opportunities for the future. Home equity is the most valuable wealth asset that most American families own and can be leveraged to improve the prospects of coming generations. The median net worth of Latino households in 2002 was only $7,932, less than one-tenth of the median net worth for non-Hispanic white households (Kochhar 2004, 2). Less than half of the Latino population owned homes at all, and those that did owned much less home equity than white households. The median value of home equity for Latino home owners was $49,840 in 2002, 60 percent of the median home equity for white home owners (17).

Quality housing generally coincides with "good" neighborhoods. Neighborhood location determines proximity to amenities and hazards, the condition of infrastructure, and, perhaps most importantly, the quality of services such as public education. Latinos are not as segregated from whites as African Americans, but they became more segregated from 1980 to 2000 due to population growth, and foreign-born Latinos were even more segregated than native-born (Denton 2006, 64). Latinos are spreading out from the metropolitan areas where they were concentrated in past (particularly Los Angeles and New York) into other areas of the country, including rapid-growth cities and suburban areas (Frey 2006). However, moving into the suburbs does not always equal improving opportunities, as the gap between wealthy and poor suburbs is also widening (Swanstrom et al. 2004) and older ring suburbs are disadvantaged in regional hierarchies. Because Latino families are younger, the concentration of Latino youth in certain school districts is even more pronounced (Frey 2006). These many inequalities reflect public policies that have failed to improve housing for Latinos or support the vitality of barrios as places to live and work. We will now examine the context of housing policy in the United States to understand why.

Impact of Housing Policies and Inattention to the Barrios

Before housing became an explicit public policy concern in the United States in the early twentieth century, life in the barrios was shaped by a history of conquest in which land grabs, racial violence, and blatant discrimination relegated many poor Latinos to the worst conditions imaginable, including shacks that were made of scrap materials and had no bathrooms (Acuña 2000, 198). Early housing policy promised decent housing for all, but some of the same prejudices against Mexicans were embedded in institutional practices. In other respects, housing policy has failed to serve barrios because it was designed from the beginning to serve real estate and finance interests more than poor and working-class people. A pervasive *privatism*, in which urban policy serves private business interests (Orum and Chen 2003, 65), explains much of what was included and what was not included in housing policy. We will review the origins of housing policy and how this privatist bent has been reinforced ever since.

The Privatism of Urban Public Policy

The push to create public housing programs in the United States came from social reformers known as the "housers" in the early twentieth century (Diaz 2005, 97). Their vision was eventually captured in the 1949 Housing Act commitment to "provide a decent home and a suitable living environment for every American family" (Bratt, Stone, and Hartmann 2006, 1). But the policies and structures created to accomplish this vision were consistently designed to work mostly through the private sector by providing state supports, incentives, and guarantees for the private complex of building, real estate, and finance industries. The universalistic mission of housing policies did not recognize the particular needs or assets that might be found in specific communities such as the barrios.

Federal housing policy beginning in the 1930s effectively gave birth to the modern real estate/finance complex. Federal mortgage insurance, introduced in 1934 with the creation of the Federal Housing Administration (FHA), provided public backing for private mortgage lending and began to open up housing markets to middle-class markets (Schwartz 2006, 49). In 1938, the Roosevelt administration created the Federal National Mortgage Association (FNMA—now known as Fannie Mae) as a mechanism to channel investment capital into home finance by providing a secondary market for FHA loans. The secondary mortgage market assumed even greater importance over the years (Schwartz 2006, 52).

Even as the FHA facilitated the flow of capital into housing production, it institutionalized guidelines that provided minimal construction standards and created the type of home mortgage that became typical in the United States for many years: 5 percent down-payment, thirty-year, fixed interest rates. Unfortunately, the FHA guidelines for appraising the real estate values guidelines were biased against areas that contained "inharmonious racial or nationality groups" (Schwartz 2006, 51). FHA loans were more readily available in growing suburban areas than they were in the central cities. From 1934 to 1962, less than 2 percent of the $120 billion in housing financing underwritten by the government went to minorities (Mead 2003). Homer Hoyt, noted economist and sometimes consultant to the FHA, went as far as ranking racial and ethnic groups in terms of their impact on land values. "From most favorable to least favorable, the list was: 1) English, Germans, Scotch, Irish, Scandinavians; 2) North Italians; 3) Bohemians or Czechs; 4) Poles; 5) Lithuanians; 6) Greeks; 7) Russian Jews ("lower class"); 8) South Italians; 9) Negroes; and, lowest on the list, 10) Mexicans" (Abrams 1955, 161).

The impact of federally insured mortgages was expanded after World War II with creation of similar loans for returning GIs through the Veterans Administration. The growth of the suburbs was also spurred by other government initiatives, including the creation of a national highway system and support for large-scale builders such as Levitt & Sons who were developing mass-production techniques (Kleniewski 2002, 103). Regressively, Levittown would not sell to African American families, and more than fifty years later the development remained almost all white (Mead 2003).

New Deal legislation opened the way for the federal government (through local housing authorities) to play some direct role as a provider of public housing (comparable with *social housing* in other countries), but this was a minor component of housing policy. The creation of this program "owed nearly as much to public housing's potential for employment generation and slum clearance as to its ability to meet the nation's need for low-cost housing" (Schwartz 2006, 101). "Slum clearance" was also promoted by urban renewal projects intended to clear the way for private development. The total stock of public housing in the United States has declined since 1993 and constitutes a tiny proportion of housing in the U.S. market—1,234,555 units in 2004 (102). Public housing has been supplemented by programs that support the construction of affordable housing by private interests and nonprofits and by rent subsidies that constitute the largest public housing program.

The housing subsidy with the greatest impact in the United States mostly benefits people in the middle class and above—it is the tax deduction home owners are allowed for the payment of mortgage interest. "Whereas fewer than 7 million low-income renters benefited from federal housing subsidies in 2003, nearly 150 million homeowners took mortgage interest deductions on their federal income taxes. Federal expenditures for direct housing assistance totaled less than $32.9 billion in 2004; however, mortgage interest deductions and other homeowner tax benefits exceeded $100 billion. . . . The lion's share of these tax benefits . . . go to households with incomes above $100,000" (Schwartz 2006, 5). The incentives built into the tax code are hardly considered a publicly funded housing program but have instead taken of the character of an entitlement. Thousands of Latinos have benefited from the opportunity to become home owners, even more so in the past twenty years with the boom in housing construction and rising levels of home ownership. Even more, have been left behind in overcrowded conditions and in diminishing rental markets.

To this point, we have described the basic institutional structure of housing policy in the United States as it emerged through the twentieth century. It is an institutional realm dominated by privatism: that is, it operates through the private market institutions undergirded by government support systems. This orientation has spanned partisan divisions, with liberal and conservative policy makers differing over levels of funding and modes of delivery but sharing this basic paradigm (Marcuse and Keating 2006). Housing policy, as it exists today, has been shaped by two significant and often contradictory political forces: the civil rights movement and the devolution of urban policy.

Civil Rights and Housing

The civil rights movement, which peaked nationally in the 1960s and early 1970s, exposed the failure of housing policy to serve the needs of minority populations, including Latinos. The Fair Housing Act of 1968 made the discriminatory practices that had preserved white privilege in housing illegal and provided the legal groundwork for minorities to assert their rights to equal opportunity. Race-restrictive covenants had already been outlawed by a Supreme Court ruling in 1948 (Schwartz 2006, 239), but real estate agents and others had found many other ways to limit the housing options of minorities. With the new civil rights legislation it was no longer legal "to deny a dwelling; to declare that a dwelling is not available when, in fact, it is; to offer different terms, conditions, or privileges of sale or rental" on the basis of race, color, religion, or national origin (Yinger 1999, 94). The act also prohibited discrimination in marketing, real estate services, and mortgage lending. Unfortunately, passage of the law has not eliminated housing discrimination. The federal government conducted national housing discrimination studies in 1977 and 1989 and "found widespread discrimination against both Blacks and Hispanics" (Yinger 1999, 95). A third study in 2002 (Turner et al. 2002) found that discrimination had decreased since 1989 except in the case of Hispanic renters, who were subject to even more discrimination than African American renters. Local fair housing groups have been active in opposing housing discrimination, filing 1,160 fair housing lawsuits between 1990 and 1997 (Yinger 1999, 96).

The civil rights movement and so-called "urban unrest" in American cities also spurred a more activist federal government role in urban issues, including housing. In 1965, President Johnson created the Department of Housing and Urban Development (HUD) at the cabinet level to consolidate urban programs and coordinate new initiatives. One of these was the rather short-lived Model Cities program, which provided funding for designated neighborhoods to devise innovative responses at the local level to address education, health, recreation, and employment issues (Kleniewski 2002, 320).

The civil rights movement challenged, not only long-standing discrimination against individual minorities, but also discrimination against entire neighborhoods by lending institutions. Some lenders drew a red line around those areas of the city that they considered too risky, usually inner-city areas with high proportions of minorities. Residents of these neighborhoods were effectively barred from borrowing money even from the institutions in which they had deposited their own funds, no matter how impeccable their credit was. The Home Mortgage Disclosure Act (HMDA) of 1975 required banks and lending institutions to disclose where they were making loans by census tract. Over the years this was expanded to include a range of other types of financial institutions. The Community Reinvestment Act (CRA) of 1977 went even further by requiring lenders to serve the "credit needs of all the communities from which they draw deposits" (Schwartz 2006, 242). The CRA made it possible for community groups to challenge mergers and acquisitions that required regulatory approval for lenders that had not met their community obligations. This became a leverage point for communities to engage lenders in community reinvestment activities and to get them involved in community development corporations and organizations such as the neighborhood housing services. Over time, the impact of CRA has declined as more and more mortgage lending falls outside the scope of traditional lending institutions.

The Devolution of Urban Policy

Even as civil rights and community activists demanded that policy makers respond directly to the conditions of minority communities, countervailing movements emerged to reduce the role of the federal government and of the public sector altogether in housing. The "devolution" of urban policy from the federal level to state and local levels and from public programs to private and nonprofit initiatives has been called by different names as political winds have shifted—new federalism, retrenchment, retreat, and even "reinvention" of urban policy—but with similar outcomes of reducing support for housing in Latino communities.

President Richard Nixon's "new federalism" replaced seven federal programs that had provided funds to cities for specific uses (categorical programs) with Community Development Block Grants (CDBGs) that shifted funds and decision making to the local level—this was enacted through the Housing and Community Development Act of 1974 (Kleniewski 2002, 321). Entitlement grants were provided to major cities throughout the country according to a standard formula based on population characteristics and community need. Programs and priorities could be set locally on the condition that they gave priority to serving low- and moderate-income families, eliminating slum and blight, and addressing urgent health and welfare needs (HUD 2005). In practice, the transfer of responsibilities seems to have weakened programs. "Given the flexibility to design their own programs, cities and states have tended to spread housing and community development monies more widely, instead of concentrating CDBG funds in areas most in need; they have tended to shift funds from affordable housing to economic development and public facilities; and they have favored homebuyer assistance over tenant assistance" (Davis 2006, 387).

The Section 8 rent subsidy program was introduced as an alternative to public housing. It was designed to provide affordable housing through the private housing market by making up the difference between what low-income households could afford (at a rate of 25 percent to 30 percent of household income) and the "fair market rent" (Harloe 1995, 439). In the typical privatist approach, these subsidies were paid by HUD directly to the property owner under long-term contracts rather than to the tenants. Landlords were given the option of buying out these contracts after twenty years to go "market rate," creating an additional drain on the stock of affordable housing (Achtenberg 2006, 163).

Into the 1980s, lawmakers cut urban programs, including housing, even further. The administration of the first President Bush featured "the elimination of the major urban development grant program, federal assistance for local public works, and general revenue sharing payments; a 54 percent decrease in the community development block grant funding, a 69 percent decrease in job training, a 78 percent decrease in economic development assistance, and a 25 percent decrease in mass transit funding" (Kleniewski 2002, 323). The emphasis of federal policy shifted to providing direct assistance to low-income consumers of housing, always with an eye toward creating home owners (rather than increasing the amount of public housing) and to promoting the general economic health of cities under the belief that benefits would accrue to all. Typical of this approach were the "urban enterprise zones" that were intended to jump-start economic activity and neighborhood revitalization by supporting business development in special districts with such incentives as tax reductions, subsidized land, and relaxed regulation. In most enterprise zones, there was no guarantee that low- and moderate-income people would even be recruited for the jobs created through tax reductions (276). Resolving housing needs by building urban economies remained a distant possibility at best.

Political leaders such as Jack Kemp, HUD secretary and subsequent vice presidential nominee, embraced privatization as an explicit value, looking for ways to get government out of the business of public housing by turning tenants into home owners. The number of public housing units peaked in 1994 at 1.4 million and by 2004 had been reduced by 12 percent despite continuing population growth and housing need (Schwartz 2006, 102). This eliminated possibilities for Latinos, even though as a population they had received a very low proportion of federal housing aid. According to a HUD study in 1993, Latinos constituted 23 percent of poor families but only 13 percent of those renting public housing or receiving tenant-based rent subsidies through the Section 8 program (Yzaguirre, Arce, and Kamasaki 1999, 164).

While the Clinton administration revived the language of "empowering" urban communities with comprehensive solutions in the 1990s, the level of tangible support remained very limited. The HOPE VI program

"URBAN ENTERPRISE ZONES"

was established in 1993 to address problems with "distressed public housing" (Schwartz 2006, 117). The models of public housing developed by this program were certainly more humane and holistically designed to meet community needs. But while solving the problem of decrepit public housing, the program did not substantially address housing needs for the population eligible for public housing. "The 217 HOPE VI redevelopment grants awarded from 1993 through 2003 involved the demolition of 94,500 public housing units. These will be replaced by 95,100 units. However, only 48,800 of these new units can be considered equivalent to public housing in that they receive permanent operating subsidies of the magnitude necessary to support households with very low incomes" (119).

Supporting Private Housing Solutions

By far, the emphasis in housing policy since 2000 has been on promoting home ownership. This is in accord with the ideology of individual accountability, it echoes the *privatist* approach that characterizes U.S. urban policy, and it rides the wave of a boom in home ownership that arguably has more to do with the deregulation of financial institutions than it does with housing programs. New programs have been created to support lower-income home buyers, dating back to the 1990 HOME Investment Partnership program's provision of additional block grants for state and local governments to support housing, and including no-down-payment mortgages from the FHA's American Dream program and state housing finance authorities' innovations. The surge in home ownership, however, has been privately financed and fed by the secondary mortgage markets. The growth in mortgage lending after the recession of the early 1980s was unprecedented. From 1981 to 2003 the number of loans reported under the Home Mortgage Disclosure Act increased from 1.28 million to 41.56 million—more than 3,000 percent (FFIEC 2004).

Since the recession of the 1980s, Latino home ownership has grown, though not reaching the level for white Americans. This is true even though Latinos, particularly those that are Spanish-language dominant, are less confident that they will be able to obtain home financing (Fannie Mae 2003). Ironically, this has created a different set of risks because "the increase in homeownership among people of color since the 1990s is disproportionately attributable to the specially targeted mortgage programs and subprime lending of the recent decade" (Stone 2006b, 96). Subprime loans usually charge the customer more in the way of interest rates and fees to compensate for histories of bad credit or no credit. Some fear that subprime lenders are more likely to engage in such predatory practices as reverse redlining (where loan terms for minorities are not based on their individual credit risks), negative amortization, prepayment penalties, and excessive fees (Williams, Nesiba, and McConnell 2005, 188).

The higher rates of delinquency and foreclosure that accompany subprime lending may shift the problem from that of becoming an home owner in the first place to that of affording home ownership over the long term. The higher debt burden carried by lower-income people also makes them most vulnerable to economic recession. Stone summarizes this problem succinctly: "The new era of housing finance has ensured a high volume of mortgage money by creating new vehicles and opportunities for profitable investment in housing. But with this abundant supply of capital has come extensive promotion and acceptance of dangerously high levels of debt for buying homes, refinancing existing mortgages and tapping home equity" (2006b, 98). In the same vein, Williams and his colleagues conclude, "The old inequality, which denied many access to homeownership, has slowly diminished. The result has been record growth in the rates of homeownership for minorities and other members of underserved markets. But for many of these homeowners, a new inequality has replaced the old. This new inequality is characterized by less desirable loan terms, exposure to predatory practices, and a lack of consumer protection" (Williams, Nesiba, and McConnell 2005, 201).

The costs of growing home ownership through high-risk lending became glaringly apparent with the national mortgage meltdown and housing crisis of 2008: the human impacts were felt particularly in communities of color. "In 2007, 27.6% of home purchase loans to Hispanics and 33.5% to blacks were higher-priced loans, compared with just 10.5% of home purchase loans to whites that year" (Kochar, Gonzalez-Barrera, and Dockterman 2009, i). We also know that counties with higher shares of immigrants had higher foreclosure rates (though this does not directly prove that the immigrant home owners are the ones suffering foreclosure in these counties [vi]). According to a *Wall Street Journal* report, the Congressional Hispanic Caucus, in partnership with subprime lenders, played a key role in promoting this approach for housing Latinos (Schmidt and Tamman 2009). As a result of the crisis, the incoming Obama administration was compelled to devote significant resources to stabilizing housing finance and ameliorating the impacts of foreclosure and economic contraction (HUD 2010).

To this point, we have focused on how programs and policies relate to the housing needs of Latinos, rather than considering how public policies affect barrios as places. This reflects the people-based rather than place-based orientation of most federal poverty programs (Gyourko 1998). However, there is a different set of governmental activities that are directed to the places where people live, including barrios. These include explicit and implicit housing elements within such frames as redevelopment, urban renewal, community revitalization, and neighborhood improvement, to name a few. In the past twenty years, a number of cities have seen the remarkable transformation of urban zones that include onetime barrios, places such as the Mission District in San Francisco, the San Antonio Riverwalk, Lower Downtown Denver, and downtown Santa Fe. These success stories were the product of intense collaboration between city officials, landed interests, developers, builders, architects, and other elements of the local growth machine.

Tools such as land underwriting, eminent domain, public infrastructure, and discounted financing were all put in play in the name of public-private partnerships for economic growth. "Local officials placed community issues in a position secondary to the interests of civic centers and zones favored by land speculators. Cities generally complied with federal mandates by developing affordable housing components within their annual CDBG applications. However they were selective as to the specific housing projects that actually were developed" (Diaz 2005, 112). In 2004, only 27 percent of CDBG funds went to housing. Of this amount, almost three-quarters went for housing rehabilitation, most of which served home owners, though we know most Latinos are renters. Also the income eligibility guidelines (set at 80 percent of the median income) were out of reach of the 40 percent poorest households, and 30 percent of the CDBG allocations had no income limits (Schwartz 2006, 182).

The flexibility built into the program continually tempts localities to use CDBG funds to pay for standard infrastructure costs (streets, gutters, bridges, etc.) that would usually come from general revenue, and beyond this to subsidize marquee development projects such as arenas, ball fields, and convention centers. The booster role of city leaders has been taken to another level, as entrepreneurial mayors try to make their hometown the most attractive entertainment venue and convention destination. Cities outdo each other in the construction of festival centers and luxury sky-boxes—this in spite of evidence that "the economic effects of stadium investments, casino projects, convention centers, and other entertainment amenities generally show up on the negative side of the balance sheet" (Eisinger 2000, 318). There is even less reason to believe that benefits spill over into the surrounding urban neighborhood. For example, "Baltimore's investment in the Inner Harbor festival marketplace in the 1970s certainly did not spontaneously stimulate development in adjacent poor residential areas, nor did it generate surplus revenues that the city could use for neighborhood development projects" (330).

Even beyond the fiction of spillover benefits, barrios have been actively disrupted for grand development schemes and highways. In the long tradition of "urban renewal," these development zones often went through earlier phases of population displacement and land clearance before the formally "blighted" areas were packaged for private development. It would be a challenge to find a city that has *not* disrupted at least one barrio. A few examples include clearing the barrio from Chavez Ravine to build Dodger Stadium, cutting the Coronado Bridge through Barrio Logan in San Diego, displacing the downtown barrio to build the Tucson Convention Center (now envisioned as Rio Nuevo), and displacing the Auraria neighborhood of Denver for a combination of university and professional sports facilities.

The grand plans that put cities "on the map" and bind together urban regimes have little to do with meeting the housing needs of Latinos or enhancing life in America's barrios, even when Latino mayors are at the helm. Indeed, the core issues of how urban place building is publicly guided and supported—based often on the implicit dominance of private development interests—are usually considered a matter entirely apart from such "social welfare" considerations as barrio preservation. With few exceptions, the approval and support of new high-rises, subdivisions, and gated communities proceed with little regard for the fate of less advantaged urban zones. If anything, mainstream development agendas are designed to exclude lower-income people and minorities by limiting zoning for multifamily housing and minimizing low-income housing programs and social service support (James 1994, 105).

People in Place—Barrios as a Resource

Rather than people-based or place-based urban policy, a third option considers the needs and possibilities of particular populations in particular places: that is, "people in place." One of the most established examples is the Neighborhood Housing Service (NHS) approach, which has been widely applied across the United States. With national funding from government and foundation sources, the Neighborhood Reinvestment Corporation, established by Congress in 1978, promoted a model for NHSs as locally controlled nonprofit organizations serving and representing delineated neighborhoods (Neighborhood Reinvestment Corporation 2006). NHSs were conceived as partnerships between community residents, city government, and the private sector, controlled by a board of directors with a majority of residents but relying on critical resources from the other partners. More than 240 organizations in fifty states are linked together in a network supported by the Neighborhood Reinvestment Corporation under the name NeighborWorks America.

The selection process for NHSs favored neighborhoods with demonstrated housing needs, but with a base of home owners and infrastructure rather than the poorest urban neighborhoods. Over the history of NeighborWorks these have included a number of barrios. Such organizations provide an opportunity not only to deliver housing services but more holistically to strengthen neighborhoods for the current residents. One of the benefits has been to provide an organizational base for planning and leadership development. There are also limitations to the program. One is the number of neighborhoods that can be served. For example, currently eighteen organizations are listed as part of the network in California of the thousands of neighborhoods in that state. Second, NHS programs, like U.S. housing policy in general, mostly rely on home ownership as the solution for housing needs, though they have developed some supports for multifamily housing and mutual housing. Finally, NHSs and other community development corporations tend to operate as alternative institutions within the housing markets rather than challenging the *privatist* policy framework for housing or the development agendas of local government. While the organizations provide a framework for democratic involvement, this is often overshadowed by the exigencies of sustaining themselves as nonprofit developers and as sources of capital for home ownership and home rehabilitation. Such neighborhood-based organizations could play a greater role within barrios if public support were solidified and expanded and the community-building emphasis were reinforced.

Connecting Housing with Development

I conclude by considering some ways to fundamentally address the housing needs of Latino communities by building public considerations into the privatized systems of producing housing and urban places. I emphasize local and regional approaches because of the retrenchment of federal housing programs and with the hope that policy makers will be made aware of the needs and assets of particular communities—people in place. Rather than tapping federal revenues to support the buying power of poor people within private housing markets, these strategies generate resources through local development processes.

Inclusionary housing requires private developers to address community housing needs, particularly for affordable housing as a condition of project approval, rather than letting developers sell or rent housing for whatever the market will bear. Inclusionary housing programs have been introduced in a growing number of U.S. cities— particularly in suburbs and in robust housing markets—through inclusionary zoning or through the terms of specific development project approvals (Porter 2004). Some cities give developers the option of paying in-lieu fees to a housing fund rather than including affordable housing on site. This creates new resources for funding housing programs, but barrios may benefit from more strongly advocating mixed-income developments within their boundaries. Such income mixing creates a form of new development (or redevelopment) that addresses community needs rather than simply gentrifying the neighborhood.

Linkages expand the concept of inclusionary housing to look at the demand for affordable housing created by commercial development approved by a city. These programs are less prevalent in the United States, and localities must be prepared to justify in court the direct connection between a project's impact and the fees that are charged (Warner and Molotch 2000, 114). One mechanism is to incorporate such "linkage" fees into development agreements between the city and private developers. While some housing resources may be generated from commercial developments within barrios, the greater potential is to introduce this agenda into some of the city's grand redevelopment schemes. The remaking of downtowns and civic centers, which is supported by public entrepreneurialism and resources, creates impacts on surrounding barrios and on the construction and service labor forces. Community housing needs should be integrated as a condition for public backing of redevelopment so that there is a direct flow of resources rather than an imaginary trickle-down. This should occur within planning frameworks that address the full range of development impacts, so that linkages do not simply trade development approvals for housing funds.

Real estate transfer taxes are another local mechanism for tapping resources for housing. Property owners derive direct benefits from local government efforts to stabilize and enhance real estate values. People who own more valuable properties and real estate speculators gain more from this system than renters or people with lower-priced real estate. Transfer taxes have been used to capitalize housing trust funds and provide another support for housing programs in a number of states and municipalities (Schwartz 2006, 192). While these programs have had limited application, they have the advantage of more equitably distributing the windfalls that accrue from rising housing markets.

Housing proposals based on inclusionary housing, linkages, and transfer taxes are likely to evoke a clamor that such innovations will send developers running to more lenient jurisdictions. This is premised on the traditionally fierce competition between cities to attract revenue sources (particularly commercial development) and to externalize such costs of growth as affordable housing and public schools because of the fragmented structure of local governance in the United States (Orfield 1997). *Regional equity* provides an overarching framework for broadening the scope of housing policy in ways that make affordable housing integral to the development of urban regions. With the backing of careful research documenting how current practices produce severe regional inequities, community organizations, housing advocates, and funders are pushing for ways to share resources throughout regions and to hold localities accountable for doing their *fair share* in addressing regional needs in transportation, housing, economic opportunity, land use and infrastructure, education, environmental justice, and health (PolicyLink 2002). Some envision regional equity as the rallying cry for a significant new civil rights movement in the United States (Glover Blackwell and Fox 2004). Coalitions of inner cities and older suburbs have successfully established a regional framework for planning and revenue sharing in a few major cities. The case for regional equity is similar to that for environmental sustainability: it is not only the "right" way but also the "smart" way. There is evidence that regions that are more equitable are also more economically competitive (Pastor et al. 2000). The regional equity agenda has the potential of opening up housing opportunities for Latinos in new areas of urban regions as well as generating resources to invest in the infrastructure, services, and capital needs of existing and emerging barrios from jurisdictions that are not doing their fair share.

Bringing It Back to the Barrio

I have emphasized policy directions that focus on people in place, but this may not be enough to bring the barrio into thinking about housing policy.

And we should not assume that all Latinos' needs are contained within barrios. The final ingredient, or perhaps it should be the first, is to think explicitly about barrios and Latinos in designing and implementing housing policy. This shift in thinking would be of equal benefit for other disadvantaged ethnic communities and cultural groups. Housing policy in the United States has been designed to meet the needs of a generic consumer within an abstracted private housing market. In this sense, housing programs have mostly been "culture-blind"—obscuring particular needs and possibilities associated with ethnicity, race, gender, and immigration status, to name the most obvious. Efforts to be culturally responsive are focused at individual consumers—such as providing services and materials in Spanish and other languages. Other than the efforts of some neighborhood nonprofits, policies are not designed to address the needs of Latino *communities* or to build upon the things that work about barrios. Cities have typically treated barrios as holding zones for future redevelopment and sometimes as an opportunity for theming revamped "spaces for consumption" in the style of Santa Fe and other southwestern communities. Meanwhile, the New Urbanists aspire to solve what is wrong with American communities by rediscovering design elements to revive urban life—front porches, walkability, mixed uses— that have been working in barrios all along, without even a nod to what Diaz (2005) calls "barrio urbanism."

Developing housing policy for people in place means going beyond the one-size-fits-all approach that has failed so often. This is all the more critical for housing Latinos and for strengthening barrios because of the wide diversity in both of these categories—from Chicanos to Puerto Riqueños to Salvadoreños; from Spanish land-grant families to those who have just crossed the border; from rural to urban to suburban; from East Harlem to East Los Angeles to the Rio Grande Valley. Barrio housing policy should respond to the distinct human needs and community characteristics shaped by local and regional contexts. The people-in-place approach has found new resonance at the federal level with the election of President Obama. New programs such as HUD's Choice Neighborhoods Initiative (HUD 2010, 20) and the Promise Neighborhoods program of the U.S. Department of Education (www2.ed.gov/programs/promiseneighborhoods) build on a more holistic approach linking investment with internal assets and bridging such areas as infrastructure investment, housing, and early childhood education. This is an important shift in paradigm (see, for example, McKoy, Bierbaum, and Vincent 2009) but remains a minor component of housing policy. Compared with the $250 million slated for the Choice Neighborhoods Initiative, HUD secretary Donovan committed $75 billion to help home owners facing foreclosure to modify their loans (Donovan 2009). For every dollar committed to people in place in "choice" neighborhoods, three thousand dollars will be spent on foreclosure assistance, shoring up a market-based housing system that is "too big to allow to fail."

Bringing "the barrio" in requires a shift in thinking by policy makers and also by barrio advocates, who need to be at the table in discussions of regional and downtown development. It is not enough to advocate for more of the same housing funding, and the task of succeeding as a nonprofit housing developer often exhausts the energies of our strongest advocates without producing systemic change. The regional equity movement is a promising development, and Latino communities—urban, suburban, and rural—should make themselves a distinctive part of the mix of stakeholders that reform place-building practices in the United States.

Housing programs and institutional support are still needed from the state and federal levels. We cannot simply expect local communities to take care of housing needs on their own any more than we can expect the market to provide decent housing for all. Leading housing advocates make a convincing case that housing should be considered a fundamental right and a precondition of economic security (Bratt 2006). This does not sound all that different from the initial goals of the Housing Act of 1949, but the *right* to housing has been lost in the complexities of a *privatist* system of building, financing, and owning housing. Public housing policy and programs should provide substantial support to community-based and regional solutions, but without abdicating the responsibility of ensuring that everyone living in our nation has a right to decent housing.

REFERENCES

Abrams, Charles. 1955. *Forbidden Neighbors: A Study of Prejudice in Housing.* Port Washington, NY: Kennikat Press.

Achtenberg, Emily Paradise. 2006. "Federally-Assisted Housing in Conflict: Privatization or Preservation." In *A Right to Housing: Foundation for a New Social Agenda,* edited by Rachel G. Bratt, Michael E. Stone, and Chester Hartman, 163-70. Philadelphia: Temple University Press.

Acuña, Rodolfo. 2000. *Occupied America: A History of Chicanos.* 4th ed. New York: Longman.

Bowdler, Janis. 2004. "Hispanic Housing and Homeownership." *National Council of La Raza Statistical Brief,* no. 5, June.

Bratt, Rachel G. 2006. "Housing and Economic Security." In *A Right to Housing: Foundation for a New Social Agenda*, edited by Rachel G. Bratt, Michael E. Stone, and Chester Hartman, 399-426. Philadelphia: Temple University Press.

Bratt, Rachel G., Michael E. Stone, and Chester Hartman. 2006. "Why a Right to Housing Is Needed and Makes Sense: Editors' Introduction." In *A Right to Housing: Foundation for a New Social Agenda*, edited by Rachel G. Bratt, Michael E. Stone, and Chester Hartman, 1-19. Philadelphia: Temple University Press.

Davis, John Emmeus. 2006. "Between Devolution and the Deep Blue Sea: What's a City of State to Do?" In *A Right to Housing: Foundation for a New Social Agenda*, edited by Rachel G. Bratt, Michael E. Stone, and Chester Hartman, 364-98. Philadelphia: Temple University Press.

Denton, Nancy. 2006. "Segregation and Discrimination in Housing." In *A Right to Housing: Foundation for a New Social Agenda*, edited by Rachel G. Bratt, Michael E. Stone, and Chester Hartman, 61-81. Philadelphia: Temple University Press.

Diaz, David. 2005. *Barrio Urbanism: Chicanos, Planning, and American Cities*. New York: Routledge.

Donovan, Shaun. 2009. "Prepared Remarks for Secretary of Housing and Urban Development Shaun Donovan at the Esperanza State of Hispanic Housing Dinner." June 17. U.S. Department of Housing and Urban Development. http://nhl.gov/news/speeches/2009-06-17.cfm.

Eisinger, Peter. 2000. "The Politics of Bread and Circuses: Building the City for the Visitor Class." *Urban Affairs Review* 35 (3): 316-33.

Fannie Mae. 2003. *Understanding America's Homeownership Gaps: 2003 Fannie Mae National Housing Survey*. Washington, DC: Fannie Mae. www.fanniemae.com/global/pdf/media/survey/survey2003.pdf.

Federal Financial Institutions Examination Council. 2004. "FFIEC Reports—Nationwide Summary Statistics for 2003 HMDA Data." www.ffiec.gov/hmcrpr/hmda03.pdf.

FFIEC. See Federal Financial Institutions Examination Council.

Frey, William H. 2006. *Diversity Spreads Out: Metropolitan Shifts in Hispanic, Asian and Black Populations since 2000*. Living Cities Census Series. Washington, DC: Brookings Institution. www.brookings.edu/reports/2006/03demographics_frey.aspx.

Frey, William H. J., Alan Berube, Audrey Singer, and Jill H. Wilson. 2009. *Getting Current: Recent Demographic Trends in Metropolitan America*. Washington, DC: Brookings Institution, Metropolitan Policy Program. www.brookings.edu/~/media/Files/rc/reports/2009/03_metro_demographic_trends/03_metro_demographic_trends.pdf.

Glover Blackwell, Angela, and Radhika K. Fox. 2004. *Regional Equity and Smart Growth: Opportunities for Advancing Social and Economic Justice in America*. Coral Gables, FL: Funders Network for Smart Growth and Liveable Communities. www.fundersnetwork.org.

Gyourko, Joseph. 1998. "Place-Based Aid versus People-Based Aid and the Role of an Urban Audit in New Urban Strategy." *Cityscape* 3 (3): 205-29.

Harloe, Michael. 1995. *The People's Home? Social Rented Housing in Europe and America*. Cambridge, MA: Blackwell.

HUD. See U.S. Department of Housing and Urban Development.

James, Franklin J. 1994. "Minority Suburbanization in Denver." In *Residential Apartheid: The American Legacy,* edited by Robert D. Bullard, Eugene Grigsby III, and Charles Lee, 95-121. Los Angeles: Center for Afro-American Studies.

Kleniewski, Nancy. 2002. *Cities, Change, and Conflict: A Political Economy of Urban Life.* 2nd ed. Belmont, CA: Wadsworth.

Kochhar, Rakesh. 2004. "The Wealth of Hispanic Households: 1996 to 2002." Pew Hispanic Center Report, October 18. http://pewhispanic.org/files/reports/34.pdf.

Kochhar, Rakesh, Ana Gonzalez-Barrera, and Daniel Dockterman. 2009. *Through Boom and Bust: Minorities, Immigrants and Homeownership.* Washington, DC: Pew Research Center.

Marcuse, Peter, and W. Dennis Keating. 2006. "The Permanent Housing Crisis: The Failures of Conservatism and Limitations of Liberalism." In *A Right to Housing: Foundation for a New Social Agenda,* edited by Rachel G. Bratt, Michael E. Stone, and Chester Hartman, 139-62. Philadelphia: Temple University Press.

McKoy, Deborah, Ariel Bierbaum, and Jeffrey Vincent. 2009. *The Mechanics of City-School Initiatives: Transforming Neighborhoods of Distress and Decay into Neighborhoods of Choice and Promise.* Berkeley: Center for Cities and Schools. http://citiesandschools.berkeley.edu.

Mead, Julia C. 2003. "Memories of Segregation in Levittown." *New York Times,* May 11.

Neighborhood Reinvestment Corporation. 2006. "The History of NeighborWorks® America and the NeighborWorks Network." www.nw.org/network/aboutUs/history/default.asp.

Orfield, Myron. 1997. *Metropolitics: A Regional Agenda for Community and Stability.* Washington, DC: Brookings Institution.

Orum, Anthony, and Xiangming Chen. 2003. *The World of Cities: Places in Comparative and Historical Perspective.* Malden, MA: Blackwell.

Passel, Jeffrey S. 2006. "The Size and Characteristics of the Unauthorized Migrant Population in the U.S.: Estimates Based on the March 2005 Current Population Survey." Pew Hispanic Center Research Report, March 7.

Pastor, Manuel, Jr., Peter Dreier, J. Eugene Grigsby III, and Marta Lopez-Garza. 2000. *Regions That Work: How Cities and Suburbs Can Grow Together.* Minneapolis: University of Minnesota Press.

PolicyLink. 2002. *Promoting Regional Equity: A Framing Paper.* Oakland: PolicyLink. www.policylink.org/publications.html.

Porter, D. R. 2004. "The Promise and Practice of Inclusionary Zoning." In *Growth Management and Affordable Housing: Do They Conflict?,* edited by Anthony Downs, 212-48. Washington, DC: Brookings Institution.

Ramirez, Roberto R. 2004. *We the People: Hispanics in the United States.* Census 2000 Special Reports, CENSR-18. Washington, DC: U.S. Bureau of the Census.

Schmidt, Susan, and Maurice Tamman. 2009. "Housing Push for Hispanics Spawns Wave of Foreclosures." *Wall Street Journal,* January 5, A1.

Schwartz, Alex F. 2006. *Housing Policy in the United States: An Introduction.* New York: Routledge.

Stone, Michael E. 2006a. "Housing Affordability: One-Third of a Nation Shelter-Poor."
    In *A Right to Housing: Foundation for a New Social Agenda*, edited by Rachel G.
    Bratt, Michael E. Stone, and Chester Hartman, 38-60. Philadelphia: Temple Univer-
    sity Press.

———. 2006b. "Pernicious Problems of Housing Finance." In *A Right to Housing: Foun-
    dation for a New Social Agenda*, edited by Rachel G. Bratt, Michael E. Stone, and
    Chester Hartman. Philadelphia, 82-104. Philadelphia: Temple University Press.

Swanstrom, Todd, Colleen Casey, Robert Flack, and Peter Dreier. 2004. "Pulling Apart:
    Economic Segregation among Suburbs and Central Cities in Major Metropolitan
    Areas." Brookings Institution, Living Cities Census Series, October.

Turner, Margery Austin, Stephen L. Ross, George C. Galster, and John Yinger. 2002.
    *Discrimination in Metropolitan Housing Markets: National Results from Phase I HDS
    2000*. Washington DC: Urban Institute. www.urban.org:80/publications/410821.
    html.

U.S. Department of Housing and Urban Development. 2005. "Community Develop-
    ment Block Grant Entitlement Communities Grants." Updated December 15. www.
    hud.gov/offices/cpd/communitydevelopment/programs/entitlement/index.cfm.

———. 2010. *FY2010 Budget: Road Map for Transformation*. Washington, DC: U.S. De-
    partment of Housing and Urban Development.

Warner, Kee, and Harvey Molotch. 2000. *Building Rules: How Growth Controls Shape
    Community Environments and Economies*. Boulder, CO: Westview Press.

Williams, Richard, Reynold Nesiba, and Eileen Diaz McConnell. 2005. "The Changing
    Face of Inequality in Home Mortgage Lending." *Social Problems* 52 (2): 181–208.

Yinger, John. 1999. "Sustaining the Fair Housing Act." *Cityscape: A Journal of Policy
    Development and Research* 4 (3): 93–106.

Yzaguirre, Raul, Laura Arce, and Charles Kamasaki. 1999. "The Fair Housing Act: A
    Latino Perspective." *Cityscape: A Journal of Policy Development and Research* 4 (3):
    161–70.

Urban Redevelopment and Mexican American Barrios in the Socio-Spatial Order

Nestor Rodriguez

Latina/o Urban Transformation

What has been the significance of urban redevelopment for Mexican American barrios? Rather than addressing this question narrowly from the perspective of public program impacts on the barrio built environment, this chapter situates the question within broader aspects of the development of Mexican American communities. These aspects include the transition from *colonias* to inner-city barrios, the significance of federal redevelopment policies for Mexican American communities, the effects of an underlying capitalistic spatial system, and internal strategies of community development, including the relocation to communities previously occupied by whites.[1]

It is proper to begin the discussion of urban redevelopment in Mexican American communities with a description of the incorporation of *colonias* into barrios in the larger U.S. urban system, albeit at the margins. This transformation, after all, was an initial process of social redevelopment for the Mexican-origin population, as it redeveloped settlements of *mexicanas/os* into the subculture of Mexican Americans dating from the early 1900s.

By the mid-1900s, many *colonias* experienced a large-scale urban incorporation into inner-city barrios (e.g., see De León 1989; Camarillo 1979). The time line varies by specific setting, and in some cases, such as in the *colonias* of the Texas borderlands, the process remains incomplete. It is likely that the *colonias* adjacent to large urban areas experienced the incorporation first. Before this transformation began, Mexican settlements in U.S. urban areas resembled bantustans, that is, ethnic homelands that were relatively autonomous to pursue their social and cultural life but were restricted from political participation in mainstream society.[2] Some *colonias* experienced significant immigration from Mexico; thus social life in these settings was partly focused on what happened in Mexican society. Spanish-language newspapers, music, radio stations, and cinema theaters enjoyed growth in the *colonias*, creating almost complete communities, which attracted Mexican refugees in times of political crises in Mexico (De León 1989; Romo 1983). Functioning as cultural homelands, *colonias* maintained and reproduced many aspects of the original Mexican culture.[3] This was the general character of *colonias* that existed in urban, as well as in rural, environments (e.g., see De León 1982; Griswold del Castillo 1979; Madsen 1973).

The social separation of the *colonias* from white communities reinforced political exclusion. Racist practices kept *colonia* residents outside the political mainstream (Feagin and Feagin 2010; Acuña 1972). In turn, as ethnics and as members of the working class, some *colonia* residents shied away from the formal political sector, viewing it with distrust as an alien and uninviting sphere controlled by a ruling class to derive social privileges (Grebler, Moore, and Guzmán 1970).[4] Inside the *colonia*, Mexican cultural norms and customs became the primary means of social regulation. A few exceptions to these conditions of political exclusion existed, such as when white politicians used Mexican Americans to build political machines in rural Texas counties (Clark 1999), but, in general, conditions of political disenfranchisement characterized these social sectors (e.g., see Camarillo 1979). Not surprisingly, therefore, many residents went to Mexican consulates, not U.S. governmental offices, to report unfair labor practices or racist abuses by U.S. government agencies (Balderrama 1982).

Colonias represented a social contradiction. On the one hand, they were homelands of rich Mexican culture, but conversely they were social spaces of exclusion. In relation to the urban social order, *colonias* ranked at the bottom, sometimes at the same level as African American communities or just above them. A variety of physical conditions manifested this social stratification. Unpaved streets, lack of street lighting, inadequate sanitation facilities, poor schools, the absence of public parks—all manifested the lower rank of the *colonia* in many cases (e.g., see Governor C. C. Young's Fact Finding Committee [1930] 1974). The spatial dimension of this manifestation should not be undervalued, for the physical characteristics were manipulated as a symbol ("Little Mexico," "Mexican town," "Spanish camp," etc.) to construct social boundaries and create multiple social worlds. One could describe this social-spatial dichotomy as follows: Mexicans were Mexicans because they lived in *colonias*, and the others were others because they lived outside *colonias* (e.g., see Rubel 1973). This, of course, is an oversimplification, but it serves an instructive purpose— the *colonia* was the most significant symbol of Mexicanness in U.S. urban areas. Thus it structured social identity for Mexican-origin people (De León and Cuéllar 1996; De León 1989), and, simultaneously, it was a socio-spatial demarcation utilized by white elites to distribute social resources unequally.

Sometimes the boundaries between the *colonias* and white settlements were as rigidly policed as the boundaries between two countries.[5] Normatively, the political and economic leadership demonstrated only a minimal sense of social responsibility toward the *colonias*, which were seem primarily as worker camps or bantustans whose value consisted in the production of cheap labor power (Taylor [1934] 1971).

The transition into inner-city barrios became increasingly evident after World War II. Several developments inside and outside the *colonias* drove this transition. One internal development, for example, was the emergence of a stronger U.S. focus among *colonia* residents. According to sociologist Rodolfo Alvarez (1973), while a previous migrant generation had kept the Mexican-origin population oriented toward Mexico, an emergent Mexican American generation in the mid-1900s viewed its future as cast in U.S. terms. Some social analysts (e.g., see Saenz and Cready 1997) considered the drafting of many Mexican American men into the U.S. military during World War II to be a key factor that increased the social orientation of Mexican Americans toward the larger society. A second external factor was that cities extended their boundaries into *colonias*. In some cases this occurred because they had became an accepted reality of the larger urban social setting, and in other cases because the *colonias* were intertwined with white neighborhoods that were annexed into the city (De León 1989). No doubt, in other cases this was the result of growth rates in the Mexican American population, which raised concerns about the need to extend municipal regulations (public health, housing, etc.) to adjacent Mexican American settlements.[6]

Where *colonias* already existed in cities, the transition involved a greater interaction, and identification, with the larger urban social structure. No longer "Mexicans," the "Mexican Americans" explored social and economic opportunities in the larger urban scene. Among Mexican American youth, social identities became associated with high schools and neighborhoods in different areas of the city. The city, not just the barrio, became the socio-spatial base of social life for the Mexican American generation (De León and Cuéllar 1996; De León 1989).

In reality, significant advantages were lost in the transition from *colonias* to inner-city barrios. *Colonias* offered residents social and cultural protection from the surrounding white, dominant world. The construction of Mexican American social institutions and self-identity depended largely on the Mexican culture of the *colonia*, no doubt limiting the occurrences of social-psychological problems such as self-hatred and feelings of cultural inferiority. After the social incorporation of the *colonias* into larger urban systems, however, Mexican Americans became "minorities." Among many Mexican Americans the scale of social reference became the larger and more affluent white-dominated society, but without the means of equal competition for social mobility (Dworkin 1970; Simmons 1970). In many dimensions (educational, occupational, etc.) on which Mexican Americans compared themselves to the dominant group, they were structurally marginalized. For Mexican Americans who lacked a political consciousness of their minority group status, and who accepted the explanations of dominant institutions, the group differences produced a sense of inferiority, a belief that the Mexican American subculture lacked a modern value system of individualism, deferred gratification, and drive toward self-actualization through achievement and success (Heller 1966).

During the War on Poverty (1964-68) of the Lyndon B. Johnson administration, it seemed that mainstream resources would be allocated to redevelop Mexican American barrios, where poverty rates exceeded the national average. Administered mainly through the Office of Economic Opportunity (OEO), the War on Poverty social programs were considered a mechanism to enlist local involvement in projects to reduce poverty through long-range planning at the local level. Since the OEO mandated local control, these programs generated a new political vitality and enthusiasm in many barrios, assisting, as a by-product, to promote a new generation of Mexican American activists. However, since these programs rarely received sufficient funding, and were never intended to deal with the core sources of structural inequality, they eventually lost momentum. Most OEO programs did not survive the Nixon administration, and those that did became mostly social service agencies for the poor and underprivileged.

The New Federalism of the Nixon administration in the 1970s ended the infusion of direct federal support into community action programs in the barrio. New Federalism had the goal of reducing federal involvement in local affairs (Logan and Molotch 1987). Through the new program of revenue sharing, the federal government transferred monies for social welfare programs and community projects to the states and local governments. In a period in which minorities still lacked a significant voice in state and local government, the redevelopment needs of the barrios did not receive adequate priority in the new revenue-sharing era, beyond income assistance for families in poverty.

The Carter administration attempted to leverage urban redevelopment with urban development action grants to spur entrepreneurial interest, but with few significant results for declining communities. Although mayors gained support for urban development action grants in the first Reagan presidency, the Reagan years produced a market-oriented philosophy of urban development through private enterprise. In support of this philosophy, the Reagan administration assisted poor renters with housing vouchers, which were supposed to stimulate housing construction by increasing the demand for housing. The vision of federal leadership in the redevelopment of U.S. cities never advanced significantly beyond the Johnson administration.

To comprehend the larger scope of barrio development, it is necessary to situate the process in the larger socioeconomic context of U.S. development. This is the context of capitalist development.

Urban Redevelopment: Reshaping the Spatial Constraints of Capital

The laws of capitalist development project an endless cycle of capital accumulation. As long as resources and markets expand, capital has room for growth. Apart from the cyclical problems of competition, changes in consumer activity, shifting of investor support, and other factors, the only real constraint on capitalist growth seems to be the resistance of the working class to economic exploitation. This is what Karl Marx emphasized in his analysis of capitalist development in volume 1 of *Capital*, where he referred to industrial workers as the "grave-diggers" of the capitalist class (Marx 1967). Historically, the spatial expansion of capitalism has appeared endless as capitalist-driven trade and colonialism have stretched from western Europe to the vast regions of Asia, Latin America, and Africa (Braudel 1984; Wallerstein 1974). As recently as the late twentieth century, new capitalist expansion reached the Chinese mainland, especially the eastern provinces, when foreign capitalists turned to China for manufactured products and new markets among the Chinese population of 1.3 billion people (Bardhan 2010).

In the late twentieth century, a number of Marxist, neo-Marxist, and other social theorists started writing about the political relations of capital to its spatial environments (e.g., see Sassen 1994; M. Smith 1988; Logan and Molotch 1987; Gottdiener 1985; Feagin 1988; Harvey 1982). Their writings focus on how capital reshapes the urban built environment to meet its spatial needs, such as the need to redesign downtown areas to build business command centers. Since frequently this spatial reshaping is accomplished at the expense of other interests, this constant restructuring is the political economy of urban space. This activity is central to the development of the "social factory," that is, the attempts by capital to dominate social and cultural resources in the larger society in order to facilitate the accumulation of capital (Cleaver 1979).[7] The domination of spatial resources is equally important to facilitate the accumulation of capital. In addition to central business districts, the spatial resources include adjacent spaces to develop housing markets and other amenities (theater districts, parks, exercise gyms, jogging and biking trails, etc.) needed to support the lifestyles of corporate executives and employees.

What the Marxist and neo-Marxist analysts demonstrated explicitly or implicitly is that ultimately capital does not develop in a limitless urban arena. To the contrary, the growth of capital is bounded by social spaces regulated by values and norms that give more priority to community culture than to profit. Apart from its dialectical relationship with labor, capital faces spatial contradictions, since the ability to gain control of social space does not always occur without a fight. Examples of this include the struggle from the 1950s to the 1970s of elderly residents and small business owners against the Yerba Buena Center project in San Francisco, the actions from the 1980s to the 1990s of public housing tenants against major corporate and real estate interests attempting to gain control of the Allen Parkway Village and Freedmen's Town neighborhoods of Houston, and the activism in the late 1990s and early 2000s of Union de Vecinos and Comité Pro Uno in Los Angeles (Texas Low-Income Housing Information Center 1998; Hartman 1974).[8]

One could argue that the spatial limitation of capital represents a deeper contradiction than the dialectical relationship with labor. While capital ultimately has the capacity to replace labor with technology, it is confined in the three-dimensional existence of space. Of course, capital has found this confinement highly profitable, as it invariably introduces the commodity form into spatial relations in the form of real estate property (Feagin and Parker 2002).

Capital has played a major role in reconfiguring the urban spatial environment under the guise of urban redevelopment (Logan and Molotch 1987; Feagin 1988). The general assumption is that redevelopment projects produce improvements that benefit all in one way or another. The very term *redevelopment* means making anew, renovation. In reality redevelopment has brought improvements mainly for the benefit of real estate speculators and corporations, often at the expense of neighboring communities. When the affected communities are low-income racial minorities, urban redevelopment is interpreted as a revitalization of the area, with little or no consideration given to the displaced population and their community culture. A recent example of this concerns the redevelopment of New Orleans after the devastation caused by Hurricane Katrina in 2005. For some analysts, the redevelopment of New Orleans has marginalized African American areas, creating a "second disaster" for black neighborhoods in the city (Bullard and Wright 2009).

An often-unacknowledged tendency of capital is to privatize profits but socialize costs. The portrayal of capitalism as the polar opposite of government-supported socialism (e.g., see Friedman 1962) is historically incorrect. Capital has often used government support for its operation. Sociologist Joe R. Feagin (1988), for example, has analyzed the process in which privileged economic actors drew major resources from the federal government to develop the large oil and petrochemical industrial complex of the Houston metropolitan area. In the sphere of urban redevelopment, capital captured significant financial subsidies through the National Housing Act of 1949. The Housing Act supposedly was enacted to reward returning war veterans and to accomplish the goal of providing "a decent home and a suitable living environment for every American" primarily by redeveloping housing in poor areas (U.S. President's Committee on Urban Housing 1969, qtd. in Logan and Molotch 1987, 167). In reality, however, it represented the results of a heated struggle between liberal planners and conservative real estate interests, developers, and bankers on how to redevelop U.S. urban areas (Domhoff 1983). Congress additionally authorized the construction of 135,000 public housing units annually, though only about two hundred thousand units were built during the six years of the legislation (Logan and Molotch 1987).

Major real estate interests and bankers who lobbied for the Housing Act had far more lucrative goals in mind than building public housing for the poor. However, certain requirements of the Housing Act stifled their plans. The requirement that redeveloped residential areas had to be returned to "predominantly" residential use was a particularly onerous criterion for those interests seeking to profit from the Housing Act. Actions by congressional supporters of the real estate sector and the recommendations of a presidential commission appointed by the Eisenhower administration eventually opened avenues for real estate capital and the banking industry to move forward with urban redevelopment projects supported by the Housing Act. The recommendations of the presidential commission, which were adopted by Congress, proposed that 10 percent of urban renewal grant funding could be used for nonresidential development and that urban redevelopment could include slum prevention (for example, by building commercial districts) in addition to slum clearance (Domhoff 1983). By 1967, the percentage of urban renewal grant monies that could be used for nonresidential development was increased to 35 percent.

The Housing Act created a wonderland for real estate capital—at taxpayers' expense—eventually leading to devastating social impacts on low-income neighborhoods. Several case studies demonstrate how local economic and political elites united to manipulate the Housing Act to convert central city areas into higher real estate values and rents (Logan and Molotch 1987). Cities had to provide a third of the renewal costs, but by 1954 changes in the Housing Act allowed private building expenditures by local institutions to count toward this requirement. The scorecard of the Housing Act shows that less than 20 percent of urban renewal land went for housing while over 80 percent went for developing commercial, industrial, and public facilities (Logan and Molotch 1987). Ironically, housing for the poor—a stated major goal of the act—suffered a significant loss, as more housing for the poor was destroyed than was created. Roger Friedland's (1982) analysis of urban renewal projects in 130 cities found that 90 percent of housing for the poor that was destroyed by urban renewal projects was never replaced. Logan and Molotch (1987) report that the development of new industrial and commercial facilities did not alleviate the financial burden of taxpayers in later years.

The history of urban redevelopment exhibits how capital's control results primarily in a process of urban spatial restructuring. The goal is not to redevelop the residential base of neighborhood populations but to reconfigure urban space into a more profitable environment for capital. This may entail replacing neighborhood communities with business districts or replacing low-income housing communities with populations of more affluent home owners and renters. The process of urban spatial restructuring accelerates when urban centers, such as global cities, undergo rapid economic growth and housing markets become highly active (see Davis 1990; Feagin and Parker 2002).

Three conditions place Mexican American neighborhoods in danger of being displaced by urban redevelopment projects. One is simply that the Mexican American residents of these neighborhoods remain disenfranchised from the centers of power in mainstream institutions (Bender 2010). While most Mexican American barrios are confronted by marginalized representation in local governments in the twenty-first century, they are not represented in decision-making arenas, controlled by the power-elite sectors that plan the configuration of U.S. cities. Moreover, the vulnerability of Mexican American barrios may have increased since the 1990s as immigration has swelled the numbers of barrio residents who lack the citizenship status to participate in electoral politics. In Houston, for example, by the end of the 1990s, the majority of voting-age Latinos were foreign born, of whom only a minority had become U.S. citizens eligible to vote (Mindiola, Niemann, and Rodriguez 2002). In Los Angeles, by 2005 Latinos made up almost half of the population but only one-fourth of the electorate (Broder and LeDuff 2005, i).

A second condition is that barrios remain strongly working-class communities. Moreover, many barrios have a substantial percentage of low-wage workers with lengthy spans of unemployment and subemployment (Bender 2010). Often these communities serve as zones of transition for newly arrived low-wage, immigrant workers and thus function with a social infrastructure that reproduces the lower levels of the labor force (needed for the more labor-intensive work of the urban economy). With their small political capital, these barrios simply do not attract the attention of influential political leaders with the power to redirect redevelopment projects and/or funding priorities or to stop the encroachment of outside economic interests (Rodriguez et al. 1994). Poorly protected by zoning ordinances, or, as in the case of Houston, without any zoning protection at all, these barrio communities are easily destroyed and/or destabilized by outside businesses that own storage or manufacturing facilities in the area and decide to expand. Excluded from centers of power within a system of class stratification, barrios remain vulnerable to partial or complete spatial takeovers by business interests.

The third condition that increases barrios' vulnerability to real estate domination by outsiders is that they are often situated adjacent to downtown business districts. In the early twentieth century, or even earlier, when many Mexican-origin settlements originated, the circumferences of urban centers were much smaller than they are today. *Colonias* developed socially distant from urban cores but physically close (De León 1989; Romo 1983). Even if Mexican Americans settlements originated a few miles away from central business districts, today many are considered to be in the heart of the central city and thus have become prime settings for redevelopment into high-price property.

Two patterns of urban real estate development suggest that barrios located near central business districts are at increased risk for partial or complete displacement. One pattern is that, within the limitations of urban space, real estate capital will attempt to exploit the weak links in the spatial order to further its growth. Historically, African American and Mexican American communities have been prime targets in this process. The second pattern is that real estate capital expands according to the value system of the larger social order. For the present, the social order continues to give the greatest economic value to spaces in, and adjacent to, central business districts, with occasional variations. The evidence of this valorization is simple—real estate properties in central business districts are usually the highest priced in cities. From this perspective, barrio spaces adjacent to downtown areas are, or will eventually become, prime targets for real estate restructuring.

The larger implications of the discussion in this section for the development of barrio communities include the following. First, capitalistic business priorities, and not Mexican American ethnic needs, drive the agenda for urban redevelopment in barrios. Second, as a consequence, through the manipulation of War on Poverty projects, urban redevelopment in barrios has translated into destructive urban restructuring. The historical reality of urban redevelopment has been to vitiate the character of the barrio, and not to enhance its spatial or community culture. Third, the lower ranking of many barrios in the stratification systems of urban environments places them at greater risk of spatial exploitation by outside economic interests.

Latina/o Struggles for Community Redevelopment

It would be misleading to discuss the history of barrios in U.S. urban areas solely from the perspective of capitalist priorities. This one-dimensional approach tends to portray Latina/o populations incorrectly as passive bodies doing little or nothing to ameliorate their disadvantaged conditions in the lower strata of the U.S. racial-class system. The opposite is true. Historically, Mexican Americans and other Latina/os in U.S. society have waged various struggles to improve living conditions in their communities (Bender 2010). These have included struggles around housing redevelopment. This section describes some of these struggles with regard to different actors and strategies.

Mexican American and other Latina/os have attempted to improve their residential conditions in a variety of ways (De León 1989; Romo 1983). To some extent, this effort could be considered a geographical continuation of struggles waged in Latin America by poor and working-class populations to seek housing through activism, including micromovements, that confronts, or negotiates with, larger power structures for living space (e.g., see Dosh 2007). Across the Latin American urban landscape, millions of residents have struggled to gain housing in shantytowns on mountainsides at the rims of cities, in new neighborhoods created through land invasions, and in abandoned housing projects liberated by popular occupation (Gilbert 1998; Kowarick 1994; Dosh 2007). In the United States, Mexican American and other Latina/o social struggles for housing and residential improvement have included petitions by individuals and small groups before local governments and commissions, social action organized by community activists, and housing construction with public funding secured by established Latino associations (Bender 2010).

Since the early days of the *colonia*, Mexican Americans have sought to improve living conditions in their communities by presenting community concerns to government officials. These issues include the need for road improvements, quality public education, and an end to police abuse (De León 1989; Romo 1983; Tirado 1974). As mentioned above, in the early era of the *colonia* these concerns sometimes were taken to Mexican consulates, which acted as intermediaries between Mexican-origin communities and U.S. agencies (Balderrama 1982). As *colonias* were transformed into inner-city barrios, Mexican Americans increasingly expressed their community concerns directly to local and federal officials.[9]

In the 1960s, War on Poverty programs introduced new resources for barrio improvement. The community programs introduced by the OEO and the Department of Housing and Urban Development (HUD), such as the Community Action Program, Legal Services, and Model Cities, were designed to generate community participation in the planning and implementing of community improvement projects. This participation merged with increasing social activism in the barrios. The activism led in part to the rise of the Chicano movement, which lasted well into the 1970s (Montejano 2010). In the barrio, the War on Poverty and the Chicano movement connected federal support with a nationalist drive for local community control. Chicana/o activists, working through various organizations (the Mexican American Youth Organization, the Brown Berets, Crusade for Justice, etc.), constructed a cultural and historical interpretation of the

Mexican American experience that contradicted the white, mainstream view (Gómez-Quiñones 1990; Acuña 1981).

In the racist era that led to the emergence of the Chicano movement, many white officials and even scholars viewed Mexican American subculture as a barrier to social mobility (e.g., see Heller 1966). Consequently, Chicana/o activists, scholars, and their supporters adopted a theory of racial oppression (internal colonialism) to explain the socioeconomic conditions of the barrio (e.g., see Barrera 1979; Acuña 1972; Blauner 1972).[10] African American activists had also adopted this theory earlier in the 1960s to explain the subordination of the black population in the United States (Carmichael and Hamilton 1967). From the perspective of racial oppression, Mexican American community redevelopment had to involve political empowerment through social activism (Gonzalez 1973). This activism developed into protests, demonstrations, moratoriums, sit-ins, strikes, school walkouts, and boycotts against the larger social system.

In a parallel process, Chicana/o activists and others in the barrios attempted to draw federal support for community projects, such as Head Start for children, Meals on Wheels for the elderly, public clinics for women and children, and legal aid programs for the poor. Since they viewed the causes of social inequality as originating from outside the barrio, Chicana/o activists mobilized alliances with other interest groups through labor organizing, marches on Washington, demands for bilingual education, and alternative political strategies (e.g., La Raza Unida Party) (Gómez-Quiñonez 1990; Acuña 1981).

The Chicano movement actually globalized the context of the barrio experience by drawing comparisons with national liberation movements in Latin America, Asia, and Africa. As occurred in other influential leftist social movements, the new icons inspiring a sense of Chicana/o liberation and resistance became Emiliano Zapata, Ho Chi Minh, Che Guevara, Nelson Mandela, Gandhi, and Mao. In essence, the Chicano movement's greatest contribution concerning redevelopment in the barrio was to redefine it as a political project and as part of the global struggles of oppressed groups, all as activists struggled to gain support from liberal government programs.[11]

A less politicized movement for urban redevelopment also flowed through the barrios in the 1960s, the 1970s, and later, through the efforts of established Mexican American organizations to gain public support for housing construction and other neighborhood improvement projects.

These organizations worked within the system to achieve their goals. The League of United Latin American Citizens (LULAC), the American G. I. Forum, and local groups like Communities Organized for Public Service (COPS) in San Antonio and the East Los Angeles Community Union in Los Angeles are examples of these organizations (Meléndez 1998; Gómez-Quiñonez 1990). In the Southwest, LULAC obtained government support to provide apartment housing for low-income Mexican Americans as one of its many efforts to promote Latina/o community development. The LU-LAC housing program started in the 1960s for low-income households in El Paso, and by 2000 the organization was developing complexes across various cities.[12] Low-income housing construction by the Association for the Advancement of Mexican Americans (AAMA) is another example of this approach to residential redevelopment in the barrio. Working in Texas, the AAMA created a nonprofit community development corporation in 1988 to construct low-income housing on the Mexican American east side of Houston for the first time in over thirty years.[13]

In San Antonio, COPS developed a reputation for aggressively promoting community development on the predominantly Latina/o west and south sides of the city. Established in 1974 as a unit of the Interfaith Area Foundations network modeled after the community organizing principles of Saul Alinsky, COPS had raised, as of 1990, more than $750 million from public and other sources for various barrio development projects, including new streets, drainage, sidewalks, libraries, parks, and street lighting.[14] It has directed millions of dollars toward the demolition of substandard housing and the construction of new units for low- and moderate-income families. Beyond simply implementing new physical improvements to the barrio, COPS promotes a community, activist philosophy of forming a power base through intercommunity alliances with similarly interested community organizations. COPS also believes that politicians should deliver what they promise and schedules meetings with elected officials to hold them publicly accountable. In its more recent work, COPS has pressured the city government of San Antonio to use tax abatement to attract higher-paying employers, rather than service industries that offer only low-wage, dead-end jobs (McDougall 1998).

Constructing New Communities as a Means of Residential Redevelopment

The actors and organizations described above have played important roles in trying to improve living conditions in barrios, but undoubtedly the largest process of residential mobility among Mexican Americans and other Latinas/os has consisted of families moving from old barrios to other neighborhoods. A host of factors motivates the decision of residents to relocate (see Morris, Crull, and Winter 1976). Among Latinas/os, these have included the desire for better housing after experiencing upward social mobility, housing shortages in old barrio neighborhoods, and neighborhood displacement by encroaching real estate interests. Sometimes households will relocate to low-income neighborhoods near their old barrios, but in many instances, especially in cases of intergenerational mobility, they will resettle in neighborhoods previously occupied by middle-income, white households.[15] In these areas, the newer residents find a host of community resources, such as public libraries, well-maintained city parks, major shopping centers, and so forth, which help improve their quality of life.

To an extent, resettling in a neighborhood area previously occupied by middle-income groups can be considered an alternative strategy of community redevelopment. It is a strategy in which Latina/o families can improve their residential conditions by moving to a neighborhood environment with greater amenities. The consequences may or may not lead to the re-creation of a barrio experience (which depends on the development of a critical mass), but it almost certainly restructures the social life of the resettled community area when the number of Latina/o new residents is substantial.

In the 1980s in Houston, thousands of Latina/os resettled and formed new communities in neighborhood areas that had previously been occupied by middle-income whites in the western half of the city (Rodriguez and Hagan 1992). Real estate capital played a major role in promoting this development when in a moment of crisis it acted to reproduce renter populations out of minorities, especially out of new undocumented Latina/o immigrants. It was a real estate strategy of using immigrants to restructure consumption, similar to manufacturers' strategy of using immigrants to restructure production (e.g., see Morales 1982).

In the 1970s, real estate capital in Houston expanded the housing market dramatically as it constructed thousands of units in single-family homes and large apartment complexes for the growing population of the area. The development of Houston into the technological center of the world oil economy stimulated the population growth and subsequent real estate expansion (Feagin 1988). Real estate capital vaulted over the African American and Mexican American neighborhoods surrounding the downtown area and expanded the housing market for more than twenty miles into the periphery of the city, especially in the western half of the city and outlying suburbs. The construction of apartment mega-complexes with manicured green areas, covered parking, and large swimming pools, designed and priced for middle-income, single office workers (primarily a white population), became a major activity of the real estate expansion (Rodriguez and Hagan 1992).

When overinflated oil prices dropped across the world in the early 1980s, the Houston economy entered a sharp downturn, the first decline in over fifty years of economic growth (Feagin 1988). Production workers in oil fields, petrochemical plants, and factories were the first to lose their jobs, but office workers and others soon followed as corporations and a host of supporting industries closed down. By the mid-1980s, the Houston economy had lost over two hundred thousand jobs (B. Smith 1986). Moreover, the housing market of the area had accumulated a large oversupply of rental units when the crisis hit. This was true especially in the western half of the city, which consisted of a substantial white population residing mainly in apartment complexes. When unemployed workers left the city by the thousands, real estate capital went into a severe crisis, since billions of dollars had been in a market that was evaporating. Without a use value, the thousands of newly constructed apartment units had no exchange value.

A temporary but major form of salvation for Houston real estate capital arrived in the form of minorities from the east side of the city and especially thousands of new undocumented Latina/o migrants fleeing economic decline in Mexico and political violence in Central America. Houston was a logical destination for these new immigrants. The Houston metropolitan area had developed a reputation as a robust center of growth in the 1970s, and it was the top-ten U.S. metropolitan area closest to the core of the Mexican population and the Central American isthmus. Within a brief period, major apartment corporations and mangers changed the cultural environment and marketing of their complexes to attract Latina/o renters. Apartment names were changed to Spanish (e.g., "The Orchards" became "Las Americas"), front-office staff were replaced with bilingual personnel, rental prices were slashed from $500 or more per month to below $200 per month, Latina/o clubs and other amenities were opened on apartment grounds, and rental staff looked the other way when migrants brought their small children or lived two or more families per unit in violation of lease agreements (Rodriguez and Hagan 1992).

It was a temporary strategy to maintain the economic viability of these apartments and thus retain value for the investment market. Some apartment corporations, however, simply used the apartments with Latina/o renters as "cash cows," extracting the maximum rents possible before the units deteriorated to a state of disrepair that rendered them no longer habitable. Other apartment complexes were transferred to the government once they fell into bankruptcy. Numerous repossessed properties were handed over to HUD when lending firms collapsed. Some undocumented immigrants thus ironically found themselves temporarily with the federal government as their landlord until their apartments complexes were recirculated into the private sector.

While many apartment complexes reverted to middle-income tenants after the crisis passed in the early 1990s, many others maintained a Latina/o renter population, especially after the new immigrants gained economic stability in this community (Rodriguez and Hagan 1992). Thus it was through a severe economic crisis that Latinas/os were able to achieve residential mobility in the city into communities originally planned for middle-income whites. Yet the role of the crisis should not be overstated. Eventually, the large oversupply of apartment units would have pressured apartment owners and managers to seek new renter populations to supplement the mainly white renter populations of the large apartment complexes. Much to the dismay of many nearby white home owners, apartment managers rather easily recomposed the ethnic and racial compositions of renter populations, since apartment corporate owners, often residing in other cities or foreign countries, seemed to have little regard for local expectations of racial and ethnic relations. In time, some Latinas/os in these west-side apartments bought homes in adjacent neighborhoods, which simultaneously experienced white out-migration. Other Latinas/os purchased homes in neighborhoods that were developed in a new phase of suburban expansion by real estate capital at the periphery of the city.

It is important not to overemphasize the construction by Mexican Americans and other Latina/os of new communities away from their original barrios. As Telles and Ortiz (2008) have demonstrated in a longitudinal study, large percentages of Mexican Americans remain settled in their original barrios, facing enduring institutional barriers of underfunded schools, discrimination, low-paying jobs, and other conditions of exclusion. The financial gains made from the first to the second generation among the Mexican Americans in the study do not continue for later generations.

Housing Policy into the Twenty-First Century

The end of the first decade of the twenty-first century brought a major economic recession that overshadowed any hope that the federal government would push for a major initiative to help Mexican Americans and other racial minorities gain housing and neighborhood improvements. Reacting to the crisis, the new Obama administration sought to control, not liberalize further, financial lending markets for housing. Hopes of federal financial support for neighborhood improvements also diminished as billions of federal dollars were redirected to the for-profit sector to bail out large private corporations at the brink of a financial collapse that threatened to take down large parts of the national economy with them.

To cope with the economic recession, residents were offered few resources by the federal government beyond limited support for a relatively small percentage of home buyers to avoid foreclosures. The housing policy of the Obama administration changed the goal of previous administrations to promote home ownership to a goal of promoting affordable rental housing (Goldfarb 2010). This strategy enables the federal government to reduce its massive financial support for mortgage lenders but puts low-income earners at a greater disadvantage when seeking loans to buy homes. In other words, the Obama administration has not improved the ability of a large section of the Mexican American population to gain housing security through home ownership. Moreover, the high unemployment rates brought by the economic crisis, which rose to 12.4 percent among Latinas/os in late 2010 (U.S. Bureau of Labor Statistics 2010), put home ownership further out of reach for many Mexican Americans.

A strong conservative reaction growing against the Obama administration further threatened to restrict initiatives of the administration to address housing and neighborhoods issues affecting racial minorities. Led primarily by white political figures, the reaction circulated to state and local governments to promote restrictions against undocumented immigrants (mainly Latina/os), such as ordinances to screen out undocumented immigrants from neighborhood rental properties and labor markets. While the Obama administration sued Arizona in 2010 to stop the most stringent of the state measures passed in the country against immigrants, the efforts of the new conservative movement seem far from over. A number of states are lining up to pursue new restrictions against undocumented immigrants. These measures ultimately will affect the larger Latina/o population, especially in new immigrant settings where all Latina/os become suspect.

Studies of racial-ethnic development in the United States have tended to highlight the social relations of oppression and inequality in the making of minority group status. Theories of internal colonialism and racial-capitalist exploitation take this approach. Yet these theoretical approaches have failed to address adequately the significance of spatial relations in the social construction of racial minority groups, and in doing so they have mirrored the neglect of the spatial dimension in social science in general (M. Smith 1988). Racial minority-group status of Latina/os, African Americans, and others indeed results from economic and political exploitation and repression, but also from unequal spatial relations. Ultimately, the barrio is identified as a socio-spatial unit within a broader underlying socio-spatial system. Within the urban spatial system, the social space of the barrio becomes a convenient marker for identifying Latinas/os and demarcating unequal social distributions. Moreover, the very capitalist logic of the spatial system in U.S. cities produces pressures and dislocations for the barrio. From this perspective, the chances for a policy of rigorous urban redevelopment in the barrio are practically nonexistent. Even under the Clinton administration in the 1990s, which was one of the most liberal administrations in the past twenty-five years, the federal government failed to demonstrate so much as a minimal interest in the redevelopment of U.S. cities, much less minority communities such as barrios.

There is, however, a major process of social redevelopment currently under way in many barrios in the country. The cause is massive immigration. New immigrants are arriving from diverse Latin American backgrounds (Columbians, Guatemalans, Peruvians, Salvadorans, etc.) and contributing their cultural resources to the social reproduction of barrios in ways that redevelop their cultural infrastructures. These immigrants who are settling in barrios are converting baseball parks to soccer fields, adding Central American foods to Mexican American menus, and changing musical preferences from Mexican American *Tejano* to *norteño*, *salsa*, and *merengue*, to say nothing of major linguistic changes from Mexican American bilingualism to Spanish monolingual styles. The impacts of this unabated migration, and subsequent transnational development, are changing the content of the Mexican American barrio; yet this does not necessarily amount to a subtraction. To the contrary, it functions as a de facto redevelopment of the Latin American base of the barrio, which was severely diminished with the prior decomposition of earlier *colonias*.

Finally, it is important to note that barrios are flourishing across major U.S. cities, even without public policy support for the redevelopment of

Latina/o communities. Today, the U.S. Latina/o population has reached 48.4 million (U.S. Census Bureau 2010). This population growth has led to a substantial increase in the formation of Latina/o settlements. The urban spread of new immigrants is contributing to this urban regeneration and rapid cultural evolution. The displacement of Latina/os from barrios located near downtowns is also a major issue in cities. When displaced residents relocate to other neighborhoods, they often reestablish Latinized social spaces in their new settings. Intermixed with existing households, these newcomers may not develop the same ethnic density as in the old barrios left behind, but they nonetheless re-create a cultural milieu sufficient to maintain their Latina/o subculture (which has become the mainstream culture in numerous local areas). This development is especially important when associated with improvements in transportation and communication that support Latina/o social and spatial reproduction. The Latina/o dispersion of second- and third-generation households, along with the influx of new immigrants, has resulted in the Latinization of regional cultural and spatial environments throughout the United States.

NOTES

1 Data for the discussion in this analysis were generated from my many years of living and conducting research in U.S. barrios and from the numerous works cited. Some of my past research on the U.S. Latina/o community includes Rodriguez (2000, 1993, 1987), and Rodriguez and Hagan (2004, 1992). For an extensive review of monographs on the history of Mexican American barrios, see DeLeon and Cuéllar (1996).

2 Some Mexican Americans sought to participate in the new political order immediately after southwestern areas became detached from Mexico, but the new white settlers erected social and political barriers to stifle Mexican American political interests (e.g., see De León 1989). By the beginning of the twentieth century, with a few notable exceptions, large segments of the Mexican American population had been politically disenfranchised as whites took control of government bodies. Yet Mexican Americans remained significant participants in labor organizing across many communities (Acuña 1972).

3 In his observation of Mexican-origin communities in the United States in the 1930s, Gamio ([1930] 1971) states that this was truer of intellectual culture than of material culture. Yet in southern Texas a few elements of Mexican rural, material culture (e.g., culinary implements) have survived through the twentieth century.

4 Simmons (1970) reports that this condition is more prominent among lower-class Mexican Americans than higher-status Mexican Americans.

5 De León (1982) describes how in the mid-1850s whites in the town of Seguín, Texas, drafted resolutions to prohibit Mexican peons from entering the area, and

in Austin a citizens' committee "exiled" twenty Mexican families. In the lower regions of southern Texas, the Ku Klux Klan also acted to maintain rigid boundaries for *colonia* residents.

6 For an illustration of this concern in California in the 1930s, see Governor C. C. Young's Fact Finding Committee ([1930] 1974). "These [Mexican] settlements are sources of constant annoyance to the localities, and only by constant inspection and vigilance on the part of the health authorities can the menace of widespread disease be held in check" (68).

7 Cleaver (1979) summarizes analyses of the social factory by such Marxist and critical theorists as Friedrich Pollock, Herbert Marcuse, and Mario Tronti, including critical analyses of the penetration by capital into the sphere of cultural consumption.

8 For further information on Union de Vecinos and Comité Pro Uno, see www. uniondevecinos.org/.

9 The U.S. Commission on Civil Rights, established by Congress in 1957, became an important federal organ used by Mexican Americans to voice their complaints of unfair treatments by institutions of the larger society (e.g., see U.S. Commission on Civil Rights 1970).

10 Rodolfo Acuña adopted the model of internal colonialism in the first edition of *Occupied America* (1972), but in a later edition he rejected it for the interpretation of Chicano history in the twentieth century.

11 This is not to omit the concrete community accomplishments of Chicano activists. A significant number of Mexican American community-oriented organizations that emerged in the 1960s and 1970s involved personnel with experiences in the Chicano movement. Meléndez (1998), for example, cites Mexican American activists as an important source of organizational development to resist corporate intrusion in the Mission District in San Francisco. Chicano activists also played a critical role in the establishment of Chicano studies centers in universities in the Southwest.

12 See "Housing" and "History of LULAC" at www.lulac.org/ (accessed February 26, 2005).

13 See Association for the Advancement of Mexican Americans, "AAMA History," www.aamainc.us/en/cms/?63 (accessed February 26, 2005).

14 See the COPS website, "Communities Organized for Public Service USA," www. iisd.org/50comm/commdb/desc/d19.htm (accessed February 27, 2005).

15 A general sense of the history of this development in the past decades can be found in studies of residential segregation and desegregation, such as Massey and Denton (1993, 1987) and Massey (1979).

REFERENCES

Acuña, Rodolfo. 1972. *Occupied America: The Chicano's Struggle toward Liberation.* New York: Harper and Row.

———. 1981. *Occupied America: A History of Chicanos.* 2nd ed. New York: Harper and Row.

Alvarez, Rodolfo. 1973. "The Unique Psycho-Historical Experience of the Mexican American People." In *Chicano: The Evolution of a People,* edited by Renato Rosaldo,

Robert A. Calvert, and Gustav L. Seligman, pp. 45–55. San Francisco: Rinehart Press.

Balderrama, Francisco E. 1982. *In Defense of La Raza: The Los Angeles Mexican Consulate and the Mexican Community, 1929 to 1936.* Tucson: University of Arizona Press.

Bardhan, Pranab. 2010. *Awakening Giants, Feet of Clay: Assessing the Economic Rise of China and India.* Princeton: Princeton University Press.

Barrera, Mario. 1979. *Race and Class in the Southwest: A Theory of Racial Inequality.* Notre Dame: University of Notre Dame Press.

Bender, Steven W. 2010. *Tierra y Libertad: Land, Liberty, and Latino Housing.* New York: New York University Press.

Blauner, Robert. 1972. *Racial Oppression in America.* New York: Harper and Row.

Braudel, Fernand. 1984. *The Perspective of the World.* Vol. 3 of *Civilization and Capitalism, 15th–18th Century.* New York: Harper and Row.

Broder, John M., and Charlie LeDuff. 2005. "In Los Angeles, the 'Un-Arnold' Mayor Battles to Keep His Job." *New York Times,* February 21, A10.

Bullard, Robert D., and Beverly Wright, eds. 2009. *Race, Place, and Environmental Justice after Hurricane Katrina: Struggles to Reclaim, Rebuild, and Revitalize New Orleans and the Gulf Coast.* Boulder, CO: Westview Press.

Camarillo, Albert. 1979. *Chicanos in a Changing Society: From Mexican Pueblos to American Barrios in the Santa Barbara and Southern California, 1848–1930.* Cambridge, MA: Harvard University Press.

Carmichael, Stokely, and Charles V. Hamilton. 1967. *Black Power: The Politics of Liberation in America.* New York: Vintage Books.

Clark, John E. 1999. *The Fall of the Duke of Duval: A Prosecutor's Journal.* Austin: Eakin Press.

Cleaver, Harry. 1979. *Reading Capital Politically.* Austin: University of Texas Press.

Davis, Mike. 1990. *City of Quartz: Excavating the Future of Los Angeles.* New York: Random House.

De León, Arnoldo. 1982. *The Tejano Community, 1836–1900.* Albuquerque: University of New Mexico Press.

———. 1989. *Ethnicity in the Sunbelt: A History of Mexican Americans in Houston.* Monograph 7. Houston: University of Houston, Mexican American Studies Program.

De León, Arnoldo, and Carlos E. Cuéllar. 1996. "Chicanos in the City: A Review of the Monographic Literature." *History Teacher* 29, no. 3 (May): 363–78.

Domhoff, William. 1983. *Who Rules America? A View for the 80's.* Englewood Cliffs, NJ: Prentice-Hall.

Dosh, Paul. 2007. "Incremental Gains: Lima's Tenacious Squatters' Movement." *NACLA* 40 (4): 30–33.

Dworkin, Anthony Gary. 1970. "Stereotypes and Self-Images Held by Native-Born and Foreign-Born Mexican Americans." In *Mexican-Americans in the United States: A Reader,* edited by John H. Burma, pp. 397–409. Cambridge, MA: Schenkman.

Feagin, Joe R. 1988. *Free-Enterprise City: Houston in Political and Economic Perspective.* New Brunswick: Rutgers University Press.

Feagin, Joe R., and Clairece Booher Feagin. 2010. *Racial and Ethnic Relations.* 9th ed. Englewood Cliffs, NJ: Prentice-Hall.

Feagin, Joe R., and Robert E. Parker. 2002. *Building American Cities: The Urban Real-Estate Game*. 2nd ed. Englewood Cliffs, NJ: Prentice-Hall.

Friedland, Roger. 1982. *Power and Crises in the City*. London: Macmillan.

Friedman, Milton. 1962. *Capitalism and Freedom*. Chicago: University of Chicago Press.

Gamio, Manuel. [1930] 1971. *Mexican Immigration to the United States: A Study of Human Migration and Adjustment*. New York: Dover Publications.

Gilbert, Alan. 1998. *The Latin American City*. 2nd ed. New York: Monthly Review Press.

Goldfarb, Zachery A. 2010. "Obama's Next Focus of Reform: Housing Finance." *Washington Post*, July 21.

Gómez-Quiñones, Juan. 1990. *Chicano Politics: Reality and Promise, 1940–1990*. Albuquerque: University of New Mexico Press.

Gonzales, Rudolfo. 1973. "Chicano Nationalism: The Key to Unity for La Raza." In *A Documentary History of the Mexican Americans*, edited by Wayne Moquin with Charles Van Doren, pp. 378–82. New York: Praeger.

Gottdiener, M. 1985. *The Social Production of Urban Space*. Austin: University of Texas Press.

Governor C.C. Young's Fact Finding Committee. [1930] 1974. "Health, Relief, and Delinquency: Conditions among the Mexicans of California." In *An Awakened Minority: The Mexican Americans*, 2nd ed., edited by Manuel P. Servín, pp. 64–79. Beverly Hills, CA: Glencoe Press.

Grebler, Leo, Joan Moore, and Ralph Guzmán. 1970. *The Mexican American People: The Nation's Second Largest Minority*. New York: Free Press.

Griswold del Castillo, Richard. 1979. *The Los Angeles Barrio, 1850–1890: A Social History*. Berkeley: University of California Press.

Hartman, Chester. 1974. *Yerba Buena: Land Grab and Community Resistance in San Francisco*. San Francisco: Glide Publications.

Harvey, David. 1982. *The Limits to Capital*. Chicago: University of Chicago Press.

Heller, Celia S. 1966. *Mexican American Youth: Forgotten Youth at the Crossroads*. New York: Random House.

Kowarick, Lúcio. 1994. *Social Struggles and the City: The Case of São Paulo*. New York: Monthly Review Press.

Logan, John R., and Harvey L. Molotch. 1987. *Urban Fortunes: The Political Economy of Place*. Berkeley: University of California Press.

Madsen, William. 1973. *Mexican-Americans of South Texas*. 2nd ed. New York: Holt, Rinehart and Winston.

Marx, Karl. 1967. *Capital: A Critique of Political Economy*. Vol. 1. *The Process of Capitalist Production*. New York: International Publishers.

Massey, Douglas S. 1979. "Effects of Socioeconomic Factors on the Residential Segregation of Blacks and Spanish Americans in U.S. Urbanized Areas." *American Sociological Review* 44 (6): 1015–22.

Massey, Douglas S., and Nancy A. Denton. 1987. "Trends in the Residential Segregation of Blacks, Hispanics, and Asians: 1970–1980." *American Sociological Review* 52 (6): 802–25.

———. 1993. *American Apartheid: Segregation and the Making of the Underclass*. Cambridge, MA: Harvard University Press.

McDougall, Harold. 1998. "San Antonio: A Multicultural Community." In *Boundary Crossers: Case Studies of How Ten of America's Metropolitan Regions Work,* edited by Bruce Adams and John Parr. College Park: Academy of Leadership, University of Maryland. www.academy.umd.edu/publications/Boundary/CaseStudies/bcssan-antonio.htm.

Meléndez, Edwin. 1998. "The Economic Development of El Barrio." In *Borderless Borders: U.S. Latinos, Latin Americans, and the Paradox of Interdependence,* edited by Frank Bonilla, Edwin Meléndez, Rebecca Morales, and María de los Angeles Torres, pp. 105–28. Philadelphia: Temple University Press.

Mindiola, Tatcho, Yolanda Flores Niemann, and Nestor Rodriguez. 2002. *Black/Brown Relations and Stereotypes.* Austin: University of Texas Press.

Montejano, David. 2010. *Quixote's Soldiers: A Local History of the Chicano Movement, 1966–1981.* Austin: University of Texas Press.

Morales, Rebecca. 1982. "Transnational Labor: Undocumented Workers in the Los Angeles Automobile Industry." *International Migration Review* 17 (4): 570–96.

Morris, Earl W., Sue R. Crull, and Mary Winter. 1976. "Housing Norms, Housing Satisfaction and the Propensity to Move." *Journal of Marriage and the Family* 38 (2): 309–20.

Rodriguez, Nestor. 1987. "Undocumented Central Americans in Houston: Diverse Populations." *International Migration Review* 21 (1): 4–26.

———. 1993. "Economic Restructuring and Latino Growth in Houston." In *In the Barrios: Latinos and the Underclass Debate,* edited by Joan Moore and Raquel Pinderhughes, 101–28. New York: Russell Sage.

———. 2000. "Hispanic and Asian Immigration Waves in Houston." In *Religion and the New Immigrants: Continuities and Adaptations in Immigrant Congregations,* edited by Helen Rose Ebaugh and Janet Saltzman Chafetz, 17–30. Walnut Creek, CA: Rowman and Littlefield.

Rodriguez, Nestor, Noelia Elizondo, David Mena, Frank Yeverino, Adolfo Vasquez, and Ricardo Rojas. 1994. "Political Mobilization in Magnolia." In *Barrio Ballots: Latino Politics in the 1990 Election,* edited by Rodolfo de la Garza, Louise DeSipio, and Marta Manchaca, pp. 83–114. Boulder, CO: Westview Press.

Rodriguez, Nestor P., and Jacqueline Hagan. 1992. "Apartment Restructuring and Immigrant Tenant Struggles: A Case Study of Human Agency." *Comparative Urban and Community Research* 4:164–80.

———. 2004. "Fractured Families and Communities: Effects of Immigration Reform in Texas, Mexico, and El Salvador." *Latino Studies* 2 (3): 328–51.

Romo, Ricardo. 1983. *East Los Angeles: History of a Barrio.* Austin: University of Texas Press.

Rubel, Arthur J. 1973. "Two Sides of the Tracks." In *Chicano: The Evolution of a People,* edited by Renato Rosaldo, Robert A. Calvert, and Gustav L. Seligman, pp. 361–71. San Francisco: Rinehart Press.

Saenz, Rogelio, and Cynthia Cready. 1997. "The Southwest-Midwest Mexican American Migration Flows, 1985–1990." Research Report No. 20, Julian Samora Research Institute, Michigan State University.

Sassen, Saskia. 1994. *Cities in a World Economy.* Thousand Oaks, CA: Pine Forge Press.

Simmons, Ozzie G. 1970. "The Mutual Images and Expectations of Anglo-Americans and Mexican Americans." In *Mexican-Americans in the United States: A Reader*, edited by John H. Burma, pp. 383–95. Cambridge, MA: Schenkman.

Smith, Barton. 1986. *Handbook on the Houston Economy*. Houston: Center for Public Policy, University of Houston.

Smith, Michael Peter. 1988. *City, State, and Market*. New York: Blackwell.

Taylor, Paul Schuster. [1934] 1971. *An American-Mexican Frontier: Nueces County, Texas*. New York: Russell and Russell.

Telles, Edward E., and Vilma Ortiz. 2008. *Generations of Exclusion: Mexican Americans, Assimilation, and Race*. New York: Russell Sage.

Texas Low-Income Housing Information Center. 1998. "Postscript: Allen Parkway Village Today." www.texashousing.org/txlihis/phdebate/post.html.

Tirado, Miguel David. 1974. "Mexican American Community Political Organization: 'The Key to Chicano Political Power.'" In *La Causa Politica: A Chicano Politics Reader*, edited by F. Chris Garcia, pp. 105–27. Notre Dame: University of Notre Dame Press.

U.S. Bureau of Labor Statistics. 2010. "Employment Status of the Hispanic or Latino Population by Age and Sex." Database. www.bls.gov/news.release/empsit.t03.htm (accessed October 27, 2010).

U.S. Census Bureau. 2010. "American Community Survey, 2009." Custom tables. http://factfinder.census.gov/servlet/DatasetMainPageServlet?_program=ACS&_

U.S. Commission on Civil Rights. 1970. *Mexican Americans and the Administration of Justice in the Southwest: A Report of the United States Commission on Civil Rights*. Washington, DC: U.S. Government Printing Office.

Wallerstein, Immanuel. 1974. *The Modern World-System: Capitalist Agriculture and the Origins of the European World-Economy in the Sixteenth Century*. New York: Academic Press.

A Pair of Queens

La Reina de Los Angeles, the Queen City of Charlotte, and the New (Latin) American South

José L. S. Gámez

Latin American immigrants and their children, perhaps more than any other element in the population, exult in playgrounds, parks, squares, libraries and other endangered species of US public space, and thus form one of the most important constituencies for the preservation of our urban commons.

—Mike Davis, Magical Urbanism: Latinos Reinvent the US Big City (2000)

There is one question which has remained open in the past because it has never been asked: what exactly is the mode of existence to social relationships? Are they substantial? natural? or formally abstract? The study of space offers an answer according to which the social relations of production have a social existence to the extent that they have a spatial existence; they project themselves into a space, becoming inscribed there, and in the process producing space itself. Failing this, these relationships would remain in the realm of "pure" abstraction—that is to say, in the realm of representations and hence ideology: the realm of verbalism, verbiage and empty words.

—Henri Lefebvre, The Production of Space (1991)

In 2003, Latina/os surpassed African Americans as the largest minority population in the United States. In fact, Latina/o population growth, which is fueled by a combination of migration flows and baby booms, stands to influence U.S. cities in ways that will radically alter many existing urban landscapes. Latina/os are *reinventing the U.S. city,* and researchers such as Roberto Suro (Pew Hispanic Center) and Audrey Singer (Brookings Institution Center on Urban and Metropolitan Policy) have detailed the statistical reality behind the spatial phenomena that Mike Davis addresses in the quote listed above. For example, the largest one hundred metropolitan areas averaged a 145 percent increase in their Latina/o populations in the years between 1980 and 2000. In several cases in the southeastern

United States, those figures are easily doubled for the years between the 1990 and 2000 census surveys alone. Additionally, as this population has increased, four distinct metropolitan types have emerged that reflect both established and new Latina/o settlement patterns. First, sixteen established Latina/o metropolises continue to serve as primary growth centers, but their rates of growth have been characterized as slow (think: Los Angeles). Second, fifty-one new Latina/o destinations have emerged as supercharged growth centers, with Latina/o population increases ranging from 147 to 1,180 percent—and eighteen of these metropolitan areas averaging over 300 percent increases (think: Charlotte, North Carolina). Third, eleven metropolitan areas have emerged as fast-growing Latina/o hubs. Fourth, twenty-two metropolitan areas have emerged as small Latina/o places (Suro and Singer 2002). The 1990s were the decade not only of J-Lo and Ricky but also of an emerging Pan-American nationality (CEPAL 1998; U.S. Census Bureau 2004).[1]

While these figures are somewhat difficult to comprehend, the spatial conditions that they represent have many tangible repercussions. Cities such as Los Angeles and New York (the five boroughs included) remain the homes to the largest Latina/o populations in the United States, with over two million Latina/o residents in the two cities combined (as of the year 2000). And despite their designations as the cities with the highest numbers of newly arrived migrants, the sheer local demographic volume of each population easily absorbs even high rates of newcomers—thus long-established migration centers such as L.A. (originally known as El Pueblo de Nuestra Señora La Reina de Los Angeles de la Porciuncula) demonstrate patterns of slow Latina/o growth. This scenario contrasts greatly with the relatively low Latina/o demographic pools in the southeastern United States into which comparatively high numbers of migrants have jumped. The largest percent increases in Latina/o growth have occurred in what Suro and Singer have called "new Latino destinations"—cities such as Atlanta, Orlando, and Charlotte, North Carolina (also known as the Queen City or the QC) (Guzmán 2001). This spatial shift has made virtually the entire United States below Interstate 40 an emerging Latin heartland, with significant Latina/o populations both in major cities and, increasingly, in many small town and rural areas. In a sense, the border between the United States and its Latina/o *Other* has now shifted well beyond the line of demarcation established by the 1848 Treaty of Guadalupe Hidalgo.

The impacts of this demographic wave can be felt on both coasts in often related but differing ways. Los Angeles, for example, remains a

Latina/o core, and its successive layers of Latina/o residents (from both sides of the border) have helped to establish a variety of unique cultural landscapes. In this sense, East Los Angeles in particular serves as a cultural homeland and is, in some ways, a modern-day Atzlán—"East Los" serves as both a physical and an imagined geography to which the roots of a particular hybrid American identity are tied. The Southeast, by contrast, exhibits a fluid landscape in which the seeds of a Pan-American cultural identity are only now beginning to become established in what is proving to be very fertile land indeed. Cities such as Charlotte now play host to a growing and significant Latina/o population, but this presence has yet to physically transform the city in ways similar to those found in East L.A. In the QC, one has to seek out and identify the spatial practices of an emerging *Latinidad* in order to understand how changing migration patterns have begun to transform new Latina/o destinations. In fact, it is in the invisible geographies of the city that one often finds the Latina/o metropolis; it is in the heterotopic landscapes of contemporary cities—in the margins, the in-between and the often leftover spaces of the city—that one finds the ties between cities like Charlotte, North Carolina, and Los Angeles, California (Foucault 1986). Therefore, this chapter will examine two cases of invisibility—one in the Queen City and one in L.A.—as a way of identifying how the border is now inhabited in places far from geopolitical demarcations, highlighting the role of invisible landscapes as central to the cognitive maps of migrant identities, and identifying urban characteristics that hold promise for the design of public spaces while escaping the narrow confines of representational practices. In a sense, exploring an emergent *Latinidad* may help identify practices that may produce a spatiality that escapes ideology and enact a more democratic form of public culture than might be achieved through prevailing urban policy agendas.

Mi Reina, Mi Casa

The settlement once known as El Pueblo de Nuestra Senora La Reina de Los Angeles de Porciuncula has been transformed into an internationally recognized acronym, and this transformation has roots in both a cultural and a spatial divide that emerged after the annexation of California in 1850. When American settlers sought to re-create a Mexican pueblo in the image of a U.S. midwestern town, they established a clear line between L.A.'s Anglo/Self and its Latin/Other. This self/other split eventually came to be marked by the Los Angeles River, which was less a geographic chasm than a cultural fault line. As the area urbanized, this divide was symbolically inscribed into the space of the city through zoning codes that restricted industrial development on the western side of Los Angeles while allowing it on the east side (Spalding 1992, 107).

This persistent cultural divide now manifests itself through the contrasting spatialities found on either side. East-side communities like Boyle Heights and East Los Angeles are homes to the largest concentrations of Mexicans, Mexican Americans, and Latina/os in the United States. They have served as centers of Mexican and Mexican American social life in Southern California since the early 1900s. In fact, East L.A. is home to over a million of the five-million-plus Latinas/os in the greater Los Angeles area (Herzog 1999). The presence of successive generations of Latina/os and the influence of continued in-migration have been contributing factors in the development of an urban landscape reflective of the cultural preferences of these groups. Therefore, as one moves east from downtown across the Los Angeles River, one finds a "Latina/o City" whose residents share a "more 'classical' way of living in the city based on gregarious, communitarian uses of markets, boulevards (and) parks" (Davis 1992a, 36). Here streets, sidewalks, yards, and parking lots bristle with activity—often in contrast to the almost nonexistent public life of many contemporary suburban communities.

The cultural vibrancy found in Latina/o Los Angeles has now been well documented, and the residential fabric of East L.A. has provided our most salient vision of an urban *Latinidad*. However, the power of Latina/o urbanism is not limited to East L.A. alone. It can be found in the cognitive maps that have shaped Chicana/o literary landscapes as well. For the Chicana author Mary Helen Ponce, the *casitas* of her childhood in Pacoima, California, embodied an ingenuity and resourcefulness that can come only from cultural determination—a determination in which junk, for example, became something much more: "While the homes on our street were different in color, shape, and size, they each had one thing in common: each had a junk pile in somewhere in the backyard. . . . El yonque was important for folks who were short on money but full of ingenuity. The junk pile held the necessary parts to wire a car together or replace rusted pipes, and it helped keep folks from spending hard-earned cash at the hardware store in town. . . . The junk pile was an accepted part of a Mexican household" ([1993] 1995, 3).

However, the landscapes of established Latina/o communities are not often mirrored in those of new arrivals, and, in fact, these two groups can easily inhabit worlds that rarely collide. Migrants are rarely home owners and therefore cannot transform their residences physically, which limits their culturally expressive abilities. Additionally, many of L.A.'s migrants find their first point of entry into the United States through the euphemistically labeled informal economy—an economy that relies upon a disorganized and poorly paid labor force. Economic differences aside, many recent migrants hold regional, ideological, and cultural backgrounds that differ from those of previous generations, and these differences often make it difficult to forge connections between the various Latin communities that make up Latino L.A. For example, unlike previous generations of Mexicans who traveled to L.A., contemporary migrants are more likely to come from beyond northern Mexico or from Central and South America; they are less tied to the politics of the capitalist corporate state; rural migrants are more likely to identify with their pre-Columbian, rather than Spanish, heritage; many urban migrants have industrial and manufacturing work experience. Lacking the financial resources and the social networks available to established Latina/o communities, these newer migrant groups find their access to the city limited and therefore often find themselves inhabiting an L.A. disconnected from both East L.A. and the greater city as a whole.

A case in point: an unassuming house in the Boyle Heights section of East Los Angeles is now home to eight migrant households constituting twenty-three people, all of whom came from (at differing times) the town of Magdalena in the state of Puebla, Mexico.[2] Given the number of residents, the social space of this typical suburban single-family house (a two-story house with a basement) has been transformed into a series of private social settings. Each room within the house—two on the first floor, three on the second floor, and three in the basement—acts as a home unto itself, thereby transforming bedrooms and living rooms into the entire private spaces of a single household.[3]

The kitchen remains the only communally shared space, as it might once have been in an earlier era. However, rarely is it occupied by more than one household at a time; in this sense, the various occupants of the house engage in a domestic form of "hot-desking" in which each household rotates in and out of the kitchen to share a private family meal in the midst of an overcrowded living situation. In a sense, this house in Boyle Heights is rather like those that urban scholar Mike Davis has described as "rent plantations," in which tenants crowd together to afford the often exorbitant rents charged by landlords willing to overlook conventional rental agreements (1992b, 62). Forced to contend with a restrictive residential market, these households have "doubled up" to combine their meager resources and make ends meet (Conquergood 1992).

As each room within the house has become a home unto itself, the driveway and rear parking area have taken on the public functions of the house. Here the men of the house unwind after work or sometimes operate an informal auto repair yard, and children play. In the evenings and on weekends, the parking area is primarily a masculine space where the men of the house trade stories or drink beer. The presence of cars helps to support this gendered spatial practice, as car-related activities are seen as the domain of men; therefore, women are relegated to activities located primarily within the house. From the kitchen window, for example, they overlook outside activities while monitoring the children and attending to household chores.

Unlike the semipublic *yarda* found in much of East Los Angeles, which serves to personalize and extend the space of the house into the public realm of the city, the domestic landscapes of many migrants do not publicly project a sense of the residents' identity (Rojas 1999, 1991).[4] In the case of the Magdalenan households, the social life and activity of the house have been relocated from the front to the rear, thereby leaving the edge of the residential site that would engage the sidewalk untouched. This is partly because little space remains for socialization inside the house, and the former living room, which once overlooked the porch and street, now serves as the home of a small family. Therefore, public access from the street no longer connects the front yard and house, as one might expect. Rather, all access to the house is now gained via the driveway, which leads to the rear kitchen entrance. Thus the front facade of the house projects an anonymous image, and the resultant privacy serves to keep the residents out of sight—lending a form of invisibility that actually affords the residents a modest amount of psychological security.

The social landscape within this house also differs from that of East L.A. in general. For example, the extended-family model often described as characteristic of East Los Angeles, in which "privacy is rare, but not particularly valued," is not replicated here (Crawford and ADOBE LA 1999). The Magdalenan households seem to not only value but also seek to maintain specific moments of privacy within their domestic spheres. This is partly because this collection of households does not represent a conventional extended-family structure; in this case, one does not find several generations of a single family living under one roof. Rather, what one finds is a subset of a Mexican community—some of the Magdalenan migrants are siblings with their respective families, while others are connected only through an extended community—living together, pooling resources, and attempting to branch out into greater Latina/o L.A. As such, these households function along parallel paths with the intent of living out distinctly separate private lives despite their inherently urban situation, in an ironic twist on what sociologist David Halle (1993) has called the suburbanization of North American social life.

As migrants with few resources or services at their disposal, these residents have found support within a loop centered more on Puebla than on Los Angeles. They rarely utilize the public and commercial spaces of East L.A.; their most traversed paths are those leading to places of employment. This is partly because of economic constraints (eating out or going to a club is out of the question) and, partly because of a lack of connection to the greater social life of the east side. In this sense, the social ties of this group of migrants lead generally back to Mexico. This is not to say that the Magdalenan households don't socialize in an urban or civic manner; public socialization does occur, but often in makeshift and temporally determined spaces out of the view of greater Los Angeles. For example, the removal of the cars and occasional addition of a tent or several tables to the parking area in the rear of the house make it possible for special events meaningful to the larger L.A.-based Magdalenan or Pueblan community to take place. Birthdays, weddings, receptions, and *pueblo* parties transform a nondistinctive utilitarian space into a festival site complete with roasted meats, music, and dancing. On one such occasion, fellow migrants from Magdalena, who now live in various parts of Los Angeles, descended upon the house for a public celebration of the marriage of two members of this community. Though this space was only temporarily transformed, the lived experience of the event—the spatiality of cultural expression—clearly *took place* by marking a communal social space. In a real sense, the *zocalo* had migrated from the Mexican *pueblo* to L.A. along with this extended community, and, within this cultural logic, it provided a public realm for a group who might otherwise not have had this type of socially bound space. The migration of both culture and spatial practice that is represented by this house in Boyle Heights helps to illustrate how places once thought disparate are now deeply intertwined. The house and its corresponding semipublic social spaces serve as ports of entry for both new and returning migrants and help to anchor a loop not unlike what geographer Roger Rouse has called a *transnational circuit*. Displacing notions of unidirectional movement, Rouse (1991) points out that migration is now a circular phenomenon that links single communities across several disparate sites. Immigrants, in this sense, do not leave one place for anther; they move—they migrate—between two or more disparate but interconnected places while remaining within a single social network.

It should be noted that Rubén Hernández-León, a sociologist based at the University of California Los Angeles, suggests that this type of international migratory circuit is shaped not only by economic and cultural incentives (potential employment in one area and social or familial networks in another that provide access to employment and information) but also by the distinct national and political spheres. Given the inability of migrants to influence the state practices on either side of the border that they may cross, the circuit that emerges is one that sheds light upon a "border-spanning process, not a border-blurring phenomenon" (Hernández-León 2008, 11). Hernández-León's emphasis upon the sociopolitical dimensions of international migratory circuits highlights the roles that, in this case, U.S. and Mexican immigration and emigration policies play in shaping the socio-spatial worlds of migrants.

In a post-Bush era now belabored by a sluggish U.S. economy still ailing from a financial crisis, President Obama's campaign promises of immigration reform remain unfulfilled. Such reforms would certainly affect migratory flows not only between the United States and Mexico but also between the North and South American continents. However, recent legislation in many states, including North Carolina, that have been influenced by Arizona's recent immigration-related policies has contributed to a climate that is increasingly polarized and decidedly anti-immigrant.[5] Policies such as these present both legal and spatial challenges to migrants as the landscapes that constitute their transnational circuits become increasingly polarized.

Howdy, Vecinos! Welcome to the Queen City

While Los Angeles has achieved a minority plurality in which Latinas/os figure prominently, Charlotte remains dominated by a deeply engrained black-white dynamic. However, recent migration trends have broadened the metropolitan multicultural map, and in this sense the Queen City has gained a lot of new *vecinos*.[6] In an effort to introduce these neighbors to the city at large, Catalina Kulczar, a Venezuelan-born photographer based in Charlotte, recently exhibited a collection of photographs documenting the local Latina/o community at the Charlotte Museum of History (Kulczar 2005).[7] As mentioned at the opening of this essay, the southeastern United States has experienced some of the county's most explosive Latina/o booms in the years between the 1990 and 2005, during which Latina/o demographic growth rose into the triple digits: 394 percent in North Carolina alone by some accounts and well over 100 percent growth in the Carolinas, Georgia, Tennessee, and Arkansas (Martin 2002; Suro and Singer 2002). This type of intensified growth within local Latina/o communities has produced some tensions, and, given this context, one of the goals of the *Vecinos* exhibit was to remind viewers of the struggles Latina/os have encountered on their way to becoming Charlotteans. More importantly, this exhibit serves as a reminder that the Queen City is now confronting a new world border (to borrow the words of Guillermo Gómez-Peña [1993]) and that this confrontation is affecting historical binaries that have long characterized the South. In this sense, the Solid South is (yet again) melting into the air of multicultural modernity; states such as North Carolina are now confronting the "complex nature of race relations in a post-civil rights era" in which biracial frameworks are "unable to grasp the patterns of conflict and accommodation among several increasingly large racial/ethnic groups" (Omi 1993).

Despite their impressive statistical percentages, the actual numbers of Latina/os that have moved to Charlotte over the 1990s may seem less dramatic. According to official Mecklenburg County census figures (Charlotte's metropolitan surrogate), the city's Latina/o population grew from 6,693 in 1990 to 44,871 in 2000 (out of a total county population of 695,454, or 6.5 percent)—a 570.4 percent increase in only ten years. Official figures for the city's Latina/o population are only marginally higher at 7.4 percent (39,800 of 540,828) (Mayor's International Cabinet 2002). Other estimates hold that this populace is at least double what the official record claims, given the endemic undercounting in census reporting (Ortega 2004). This recent growth, which has helped push the total Latina/o population up to about 4 percent statewide, has also contributed to an emerging and visible *Latinidad* in several parts of the city. Charlotte has become a new Latina/o destination, serving both as a point of entry and as a stop within a broader multistate and transnational circuit. Charlotte's formerly strong economy, like that of the state in general, was kept buoyant by a growing service employment sector and a booming residential and commercial construction market—a sector of the economy now dominated by Spanish-speaking labor (El Pueblo 2002).[8]

The impacts of the national financial crisis have been felt in Charlotte in profound ways. For example, Charlotte became emblematic of the larger economic crisis as the national press focused upon foreclosures in Windy Ridge, a neighborhood in the northwestern part of the city. In an article titled "The Next Slum" (Leinberger 2008), the *Atlantic Monthly* pointed out that of the 132 homes in the neighborhood, 81 were in foreclosure; this assessment contributed to other national profiles, such as that in *Fast Company* (Cannell 2009) describing the neighborhood as a soon-to-be ghost town that might foreshadow the "end of suburbia." For migrants in Charlotte, this meant that much of the economic base that had provided employment throughout the 1990s and early 2000s had, by late 2008, largely disappeared. This has tempered the demographic growth that drew national attention between 1990 and 2000, and it remains to be seen how the 2010 census will be affected (Taylor 2010). With slowed transnational traffic, local migrants have become less visible, but their landscapes remain.

Prior to the economic downtown, which arrived in Charlotte in late 2008, several middle-belt or midcity suburban areas had become destinations in a transnational migratory circuit. This pattern differs from conventional models of migration in which central cities serve as initial homes to ethnic enclaves; Charlotte's recent migrants helped generate new life in several aging semisuburban landscapes (dating from the late 1940s to the early 1960s) now locked within successive rings of urban growth. This transition has led to several emerging "enacted environments" showing patterns of spatial expression that mirror those found in places like East Los Angeles while differing in others (Rojas 1991).

Similar to many urban cores that underwent significant cultural and financial reinvestment during the urban renaissance of the 1990s, Uptown Charlotte (as the central business district is known) has become a landscape of power not unlike that described by the urban theorist Sharon Zukin—a landscape in which downtown areas become "synonymous with the city itself" primarily through the assertion of mainstream cultural and economic values (1991, 180). The central city, in this paradigm, is often reinvented as the seat of not only economic capital but also regional cultural capital; and Charlotte has followed this pattern by becoming the second-largest financial center outside New York City and by developing a strong regional cultural infrastructure that includes various galleries and museums, performance spaces, and two new professional sports arenas. Thus real estate values in Uptown Charlotte have skyrocketed, and this has left only a limited range of housing options for an increasingly affluent urban class.

In Charlotte's case, then, the central city lacks a residential fabric into which migrants might weave. Further, much of the new suburban hinterland is often far removed from places of employment (with the notable exceptions of construction and landscape services), organized around life-style neighborhoods (golf-community development, for example), and often out of the reach of most migrant pocketbooks. This has left the former suburban fringes from the late 1940s through the 1960s as the primary port of entry for many local migrants.

These landscapes are accessible for several reasons: midcentury residential developments are now facing a stage of succession as elderly residents, who represent the first home owners in such neighborhoods, slowly transition out; many of the homes in these areas are now in the hands of absentee landlords, thereby creating a large pool of rental units; these areas have a lower percentage of family growth than other parts of the city and therefore less competition for residential structures; and the commercial components of these areas are also aging, thereby providing affordable spaces for migrant entrepreneurs. In three such areas (along the North Tryon, Central Avenue, and South Boulevard corridors), Latina/os are rapidly approaching a significant threshold of 13 percent of the local residential population, which is considered a tipping point that will lead to an increasingly concentrated Latino landscape (Smith and Furseth 2003).[9]

Central Avenue in eastern Charlotte presents a telling case study. Prior to the recent economic downturn and recent local legislation, what one found was an aging auto-oriented landscape no longer attractive to middle-class communities that had become a space of opportunity for many migrant communities. This area remains home to one of the city's most diverse populations, but Latina/os became, over the 1990s and early 2000s, an increasingly visible and dominant cultural force. In this sense, Central Avenue represented an emergent Latina/o Main Street indicative of the economic impacts of recent demographic shifts. For example, Charlotte's Latina/o purchasing power has been estimated at $311 million, and this has manifested itself in the approximately four hundred Latina/o-owned businesses that have sprung up in this neighborhood and other areas of the city (Mayor's International Cabinet 2002).

From a socio-spatial perspective, it is noteworthy that the aging auto-oriented area represented by Central Avenue has provided evidence of an emerging Latina/o public realm rather like those found in established Latina/o landscapes such as those of East Los Angeles. For example, taco trucks have often occupied nondescript urban spaces in ways that actually help to articulate a new form of public social space. They might occupy an edge of a typical suburban shopping strip, thereby creating an active boundary to a formerly ill-defined urban space. In this sense, they have not only created a new edge condition, which helps to formalize and support a social space, but also activate that edge through the introduction of culturally focused commerce that attracts both pedestrians and motorists. Lured by an inexpensive meal, Latina/o patrons on the site has signaled an insurgent form of urbanism like that described by anthropologist James Holston—an urbanism that establishes place via grassroots occupation rather than through top-down planning or urban design initiatives (Holston 1996).

However, recent immigration debates have begun to affect local social and municipal policies. In the case of Central Avenue, mobile vendors, as represented by the various taco truck entrepreneurs in the area, have now been banned from selling their wares within four hundred feet of any residential structure or within any existing setback or required buffer.[10] This local ordinance was passed in response to complaints made by residents within areas that connect to the Central Avenue commercial corridor. The complaints ranged from those associated with excessive noise, litter, and congestion to those that explicitly pointed to the clientele; but Charlotte is not alone in this effort. Nationally, Charlotte is one of many municipalities, including Los Angeles and Des Moines, that have passed ordinances limiting the activities of mobile vendors at a time of increased anti-immigrant sentiments (Gottlieb 2009). The impact of this local ordinance has been the displacement of much of the emergent public life along Central Avenue to other areas of the city. This, coupled with the rise in unemployment among many local migrants in the area, has dampened the vitality of Central Avenue.

Despite the commonalities that Latina/o shopping streets such as Central Avenue may hold with those in other established Latina/o landscapes, Charlotte's residential landscapes fail to exhibit characteristics often associated with Latina/o domestic spaces. For example, the "housescapes" described by Daniel D. Arreola (1988) and the "East Los Angeles vernacular" delineated in the work of scholars such as James Rojas (1991) have yet to develop in Charlotte, and it is unclear that they will develop. This is, partly a consequence of Charlotte's relatively new experiences with Latina/o migration and lifestyles and partly a consequence of the nature of migration itself. Many of the Queen City's newest Latina/o neighbors represent a traditional model of first-wave immigrants—that is, men who are establishing a stakehold in the region and who may at a later date bring friends and family along. This group has yet to articulate a residential landscape reflective of their presence because they have not had the time or the resources to do so—like the households described in the previous section, many of Charlotte's migrants are not home owners, and they often keep a low profile to evade the attention of a variety of prying eyes.

However, the lack of a tangible Latina/o residential landscape may also be a consequence of the material landscape itself or of the housing stock that has become available within this middle belt of development rings. Specifically, the material fabric of these neighborhoods differs from that of places like California and the southwestern United States, making the adaptation of typical housing stock more difficult. Brick, a material of choice for developers in this region during the mid-twentieth century, is not easily painted, and this makes the addition of color (a vehicle of personal and cultural expression) difficult. Additionally, much of the housing stock from this era represents a spatial typology that proves difficult to physically transform without significant financial investment. The typical suburban models of this era were often small split-level homes averaging 1,500 square feet; the split-level home, or a home with essentially three levels separated by a combination of half and full flights of stairs, limits incremental home owner-built additions because level changes within the house often restrict the extension of any one level. This coupled with landscape changes—these house types were often placed on residential sites with significant slopes or elevation changes—creates a rigid house type.

These factors do not imply that there are no parallels between the Queen City and parts of L.A. In fact, many migrant households find themselves crowded into residential spaces not unlike those of the Magdalenan households described earlier. The doubling up of multiple families in a single residence is a survival strategy employed by many migrants that provides for a form of financial and psychological security. Doubling up allows migrants to pool financial resources for rent, food, and transportation, among other things. This practice allows migrants to create a type of familial stability despite the instability associated with travel. In this sense, these residential spaces are not viewed by many migrants as overcrowded and, therefore, undesirable; rather, the increased numbers of residents provides for social cohesion and a sense of security that comes from being a part of a group or community. Additionally, this sense of community often stems from a collective identity tied to an alternate geography that connects a new migrant landscape to an established cultural home.

L.A./Q.C.: Hybridity and Proto-Urbanism

Latina/o migration into southern states such as North Carolina represents a challenge to the structure of regional cultural politics, which has been tied to the historically rooted black/white binary that has long characterized the southeastern United States. However, the challenge that Charlotte now faces is one that will put it into play with other cosmopolitan centers and will necessarily reshape traditionally insular cities into more globally integrated and more culturally pluralistic urban nodes. Therefore, Charlotte is not just the Gateway to the New South (a title often cited in local civic booster and travel literature)—it is also rapidly becoming a gateway into the new Latin American South. By contrast, Los Angeles has now become a postminority city. When Latinas/os became L.A.'s largest minority group during the 1990s, the city crossed a threshold into a landscape of cultural pluralism that foreshadowed trends soon to affect many U.S. urban centers. Though East L.A. is over 90 percent Latina/o, the city overall has no dominant statistical demographic group—L.A. is now a minority-majority city.

While on the surface these two queen cities may not appear to have much in common, the view from the streets provides a different perspective. Latina/o L.A. has established itself culturally and spatially, and a similar presence is now emerging in places like Charlotte, albeit more slowly because of recent economic cycles. However, migrants in both contexts tend to occupy invisible terrains that seemingly belong simultaneously to both sides and to neither side of the U.S./Mexican border. Migrants often poach urban remnants left behind as majority and middle-class populations move on in search of greener pastures and newer suburban amenities. Despite the vibrancy exhibited by these landscapes, the spatial transformations that migrant communities initiate are often overlooked at best and resisted at worst—civic officials, local professionals (planners, urban designers), for example, often view the emergence of ethnic landscapes as evidence of urban decline or nonconforming urban practices (Mendez 2004).[11] In many ways, the recent ordinance regulating mobile vendors in Charlotte is evidence of how the socio-spatial practices of migrants have been perceived as problematic. When viewed through the lens of middle-class values, Latina/o cultural landscapes are all too easily characterized as spaces that meet only a narrow interpretation of what Michel Foucault defined as heterotopias (1986, 23-24).

For Foucault, heterotopias were spatial moments in which the whole of society could be seen at play in singular and exaggerated conditions. In other words, Foucault posited heterotopias as counterspaces to the imagined but unattainable perfection of utopias—those spaces that "present society itself in a perfected form" but are "fundamentally unreal spaces" (1986, 24). Utopias, in this sense, are *representational spaces* conceived by architects, bureaucrats, scientists, planners, and urban designers whose goals include the ordering of both social and spatial life (Lefebvre 1991). Heterotopias, on the other hand, are "something like counter-sites, a kind of effectively enacted utopia in which the real sites, all the other real sites that can be found within the culture, are simultaneously represented, contested, and inverted" (Foucault 1986, 24). Historically, those in the seat of power have marked these sites of contestation as places of social deviance or crisis.[12] And the cultural landscapes of Latina/o communities (both established and migrant) are often also categorized as spaces of crisis and/or deviance.

Though Foucault's terminology was undertheorized, the promise of the countersite proposed by Foucault can be found more clearly articulated the work of the cultural theorist Homi Bhabha.[13] Bhabha's search for the *location of culture* is a search that, in many ways, begins in the heterotopic realms of which Foucault wrote. For Bhabha, such spaces provide moments (both spatial and temporal) in which the grid of dominant norms is disordered and a new hybrid spatiality comes into being; these are spaces, therefore, that offer a view into an *other* space: "All forms of culture are continually in a process of hybridity. But for me the importance of hybridity is not to be able to trace two original moments from which the third emerges, rather hybridity to me is the 'third space' which enables other positions to emerge. . . . The process of cultural hybridity give rise to something different, something new and unrecognizable, a new area of negotiation of meaning and representation" (Bhabha 1994, 198).

The in-between spaces and urban zones often defined as marginal by many professional standards are in fact quite the opposite; such places provide openings in the urban fabric for new social realms to be enacted—for new, hybridized forms of a Pan-American urbanism to take shape in precise places at specific moments in time. For example, by certain standards a gathering of individuals in a space can be viewed as loitering, or the marking of an urban landscape can be viewed as graffiti; from another vantage point, these same actions can be viewed as the social production of a place—as the public articulation of a culture that reorganizes the space of the city by opening up a new place of community negotiation. These spaces become nodes in an emergent urban landscape of contestation, resistance, and dialogue, extending the landscapes from which migrants travel into new settings. This spatial extension forms not only a transnational network—a network that spans more than one nation-state or is occupied by migrants from multiple countries of origin—but also a hybrid urbanism rooted in the performance of a traveling, translated, and transformed set of cultural expressions.[14] As such, these places might best be seen as *prototopias* rather than heterotopias—as only initial and emergent socio-spatial zones that point to ways the aging auto-oriented landscape might be made more vibrant.

These spaces offer strategies by which a civic dimension might be reinstated in landscapes that often were built without this crucial component of public infrastructure. However, they also challenge conventional notions of a public realm. As emergent and hybrid spatial entities, prototopias share in both local conditions and a global circuit while simultaneously remaining apart from each; they are deeply ingrained within a border-spanning culture that belongs to both the North and the South and neither at the same time. In part, this has to do with microscale economies rooted in migrant entrepreneurship and the microcommunities that they serve. However, this dimension of commerce also originates in the traditional urban and social fabric of many Latin American cities and towns, where culture is implicitly a part of the public action that takes place in the street, the plaza, and in the market. Though in the United States this kind of Latin cultural life lacks the physical urban fabric to support it, it persists and begins to transform local spaces that have been based on global cultural interests (Herzog 1999). In this sense, the cultural location of public life is hybridized through the transformation and performance of public culture.

This is not to romanticize the plight of many migrants or to minimize the degree to which mainstream societies limit accessibility of the city in general. However, migrant social life has begun to rearticulate the meaning of the urban landscape in many places through spatial occupation, and such occupation helps determine the value and meaning of places for specific groups of people. By extension, social occupation can and does *take place* through the performance of culture and through the enactment of daily social rituals. Culture takes place in two primary ways. First, as a performative expression, it occurs in time and space—it *takes* place, it happens. Second, as a dimension of social occupation, it articulates, appropriates, and activates space—it *takes* a part of the urban realm and redefines it as a specific site within a network of social relations located within an often invisible and imagined cultural geography.

In this sense, the cultural location of many migrant landscapes straddles the local and the global, and this illustrates a need for an expanded notion of the public realm—one that does not center on the values of a dominant or mainstream culture but rather supports a plurality of cultures equally situated as public actors. In other words, singular notions of the public and of the public realm no longer suffice; migrant landscapes demonstrate that urban space is made up of multiple publics who often occupy competing public realms. However, mainstream urban design and planning practices often fail to confront the complexities of an era marked by multiple publics, favoring instead the spatial narratives of a post-Seaside era—the narratives of traditional urban structures and a singular definition of the public realm.

Traditional urbanism is not problematic in and of itself: New Urbanism, for example, offers many useful alternatives to the often ill-planned or nonplanned development now ringing many U.S. cities. What is problematic is the way culture itself is irrationally abandoned within such a framework. Culture, as a component of traditional civic or urban identity, is often framed by social norms and behaviors of mainstream or dominant society and by images rooted in the urban nostalgia for a bygone era. In this sense, the post-Seaside era has ushered in a now dominant model of urbanity in which a particular notion of public culture is envisioned—it is "an elaboration of a distinctive culture of civil society and of an associated public sphere" not unlike that which "was implicated in the process of bourgeois class formation" (Fraser 1994, 78). Under this framework, culture itself is involved in the formation of social realms, often through practices that lie outside the realm of the rule of law but that nonetheless shape public actions, beliefs, and images. The implied model of the public is one that eliminates difference by discounting views that conflict with those of the mainstream; this model of the public seeks "zero-degree" cultural zones that veil social and material inequalities behind screens of shared values (82). This model overlooks structural inequalities that at best maintain migrant landscapes (among others) as invisible or at worst label them as deviant. In this sense, the public realm is not neutral; in the words of legal scholar Nancy Fraser, "Public spheres themselves are not spaces of zero-degree culture, equally hospitable to any possible form of cultural expression. Rather, they consist in culturally specific institutions—including, for example, various journals and various social geographies of urban space. These institutions may be understood as culturally specific theoretical lenses that filter and alter the utterances they frame" (86).

The migrant landscapes explored in this essay represent the possibility of a hybrid public realm that may mitigate the pressures of many recent trends in planning and urban design and may point to a location of culture that lies outside conventional frames. While invisibility may be a particular consequence of often-indeterminate legal, economic, and social status, such an invisibility can be both beneficial and tactical: tactical in the sense that invisibility allows for a form of spatial occupation that is fluid and dynamic, and beneficial in the sense that invisibility provides a form of refuge—a *homeplace*, if you will—that affords a measure of safety, of resistance, and of invention (hooks 1990). From this perspective, one of the most promising attributes of the emergent *Latinidad* often found in migrant landscapes is that they manifest a counterurbanism that is not contingent upon physical representation in an aesthetic sense. Rather, the *Latinidad* of the prototopias explored earlier is tied to spatial expression as a dimension of a critical imagination (Appadurai 1994) and to the practice of a border-spanning culture that helps articulate a "new cartography: a brand new map to host the new project" of a transcultural spatiality (Gómez-Peña 1993).

The articulation of a prototopia is, therefore, difficult to manifest under the auspices of conventional urban design or planning practices that privilege images of the past over the spatiality of the present. Migrant landscapes are evidence of reclaimed existing spaces that have been imbued with new transnational, transcultural, and spatial expressions. In this sense, such spaces redeploy, or "reconvert," in the words of Néstor García Canclini (2005), the cultural dimensions of a homeland in an expanded borderland, and this redeployment results in a hybridization of cultural attributes that draw from the past and present. However, this spatial practice is not rooted in nostalgia for some lost condition; rather, it fundamentally engages the present. As Homi Bhabha puts it, the spatiality of a border condition is fundamentally a spatiality of the moment: "The borderline work of culture demands an encounter with 'newness' that is not part of a continuum of past and present. It creates a sense of the new as an insurgent act of cultural translation. Such art does not merely recall the past as social cause or aesthetic precedent; it renews the past, refiguring it as a contingent 'in-between' space, that innovates and interrupts the performance of the present. The 'past-present' becomes part of the necessity, not the nostalgia, of living" (1994, 7).

The tactical and strategic reuses of space in both established and emerging Latina/o landscapes provide models for the rebuilding of our urban and suburban landscapes generally. By reassessing the ideology through which culture is spatialized and performed and the ways past and present are recombined, and by identifying the emergent qualities of a new form of public realm, one can begin to learn from the locations of the cultures now present in our cities. The Latina/o landscapes examined in this essay, both emergent and established, are evidence that culture has a powerful influence over space—that place can be taken over, reconfigured, rewritten, and revitalized through the simple act (performance) of cultural expression (Lefebvre 1991). In capitalizing upon the opportunities that this type of grassroots urbanism holds for the city, the public realm itself must be reclaimed as a multifaceted forum. In a sense, this requires a reconfiguration of the past that can interrupt the present. It requires us to remember that "public life has always combined three characteristics: a common-wealth for the common good or benefit, open to general observations by strangers, and involving a diversity of people and thus engendering a tolerance of diverse interests and behaviors" (Brill 1989, 20).

Urban spaces should be viewed as encompassing a wide and diverse set of publics that, when taken comprehensively, create a multifaceted public realm. The spatiality of many Latina/o landscapes offers proof that such diversity can actually prosper in spaces otherwise thought inadequate by mainstream or middle-class standards. As such, this urban *Latinidad* should be nurtured and allowed to generate a form of the public realm that reflects the lived realities of a contemporary transnational condition. The uses of the public domain that both emergent and established Latino landscapes represent help illustrate how the city itself can be revived as a space of public engagement. They do so through the debates they spawn, the cultural values they promote, and the mental maps they help establish. In this sense, the space of the city is enacted as the open geography of transnational culture—of a border culture that is now a fundamental part of North American metropolitan settings.

NOTES

1 The thirty-nine million Latino residents in the United States already constitute the fifth-largest concentration of Latinos globally, and this population is projected to increase to 102.6 million by the year 2050, thereby making U.S. Latinos the third-largest Latin American concentration after those of Brazil (250.1 million) and Mexico (146.7 million).

2 This research began in the late 1990s with a series of interviews and observational visits with both residents of the house in question and members of the family

who own the property; the precise location of the house has been withheld at the request of the interviewees.

3 I am using the term *household* to describe a group of people sharing one dwelling unit within the larger house. Within the context of this house, a household may be a couple, a couple with a young child, or a group of single men.

4 Public extensions of personal and family identity through the physical articulation of front yards (*yardas*) can be found throughout the established Latino neighborhoods on the east side of Los Angeles, but many migrant landscapes remain unaltered.

5 For example, in May of 2010, North Carolina became the eighteenth state in the United States to introduce legislation similar to that of Arizona, which requires all immigrants to carry documents verifying their legal status in the states and authorizes police to question people suspected of being in the state and/or country illegally; see Bash, Hornick, and Keck (2010).

6 The city of Charlotte takes its name from Queen Charlotte, wife of King George III of England, and therefore has acquired the nickname of the Queen City.

7 The *Vecinos/Neighbors* exhibit represents a body of work dating back to 1997, when Kulczar first began photographing members of the Latino community in Charlotte.

8 As the Latino advocacy and policy organization El Pueblo, Inc., has pointed out, Spanish is now a required job-site skill, as over 90 percent of the labor pool on construction sites in the Raleigh-Durham-Chapel Hill triad and the Charlotte-Mecklenburg metropolitan regions is now migrant Latino; additionally, over 95 percent of the state's "guest" agriculture workers and over 50 percent of the labor found in the state's meat-processing industry are Latinos.

9 Smith and Furseth's research also points out that over the decade of the 1990s Latinos became increasingly segregated from white Charlotteans while simultaneously becoming more integrated with local blacks.

10 See Charlotte City Code, Part 5: Special Requirements for Certain Uses, Section 12.510 (Petition No. 2008-79, 12.510), adopted December 14, 2008.

11 Several California municipalities have attempted to enact local legislation aimed at suppressing the spatial expression of Latino cultural interests, and this has led some state policy makers to consider the relationship between Latino cultural landscapes and urban policy.

12 I use the past tense in this case because Foucault's work on spatiality took a historical perspective, as did his overall body of work, and it was from this that a lineage of heterotopias could be mapped—a lineage that included spaces marked by states of crisis such as those associated with rites of passage in pre-modern societies or those associated with patterns of behavior marginalized by dominant societies (psychiatric hospitals or prisons would fit this bill).

13 Foucault's essay detailing heterotopias was published after his death in what appears to be draft form. This was a topic that he did not develop in any detail, despite the important position that space held in his body of work.

14 While I am crafting a specific definition here for the term *transnational network*, my need to define the term reflects the changing nature of research in the area; for a concise discussion of transnationalism, see Hernández-León (2008).

REFERENCES

Appadurai, Arjun. 1994. "Disjuncture and Difference in the Global Cultural Economy." In *Colonial Discourse and Post-Colonial Theories: A Reader*, edited by Patrick Williams and Laura Chrisman, 324-39. New York: Columbia University Press.

Arreola, Daniel D. 1988. "Mexican-American Housescapes." *Geographical Review* 78 (3): 299–315.

Bash, Dana, Ed Hornick, and Kristi Keck. 2010. "What Does Arizona's Immigration Law Do?" *CNN Politics*, April 23. www.cnn.com/2010/POLITICS/04/23/immigration.faq/index.html.

Bhabha, Homi. 1994. *The Location of Culture*. New York: Routledge.

Brill, Michael. 1989. "Transformation, Nostalgia, and Illusion in Public Life and Public Place." In *Human Behavior and Environment: Advances in Theory and Research*, vol. 10, *Public Places and Spaces*, 7-30. New York: Plenum Press.

Canclini, Nestor Garcia. 2005. *Hybrid Cultures: Strategies for Entering and Leaving Modernity*. Minneapolis: University of Minnesota Press.

Cannell, Michael. 2009. "R.I.P. Suburbia." *Fast Company*, March 10. www.fastcompany.com/blog/michael-cannell/cannell/suburbia-rip.

CEPAL. See Comisión Económica para América Latina y el Caribe.

Comisión Económica para América Latina y el Caribe. 1998. "America Latina: Proyecciones de población, 1970-2050." *Boletín Demográfico* 62 (July).

Conquergood, Dwight. 1992. "Life in Big Red: Struggles and Accommodations in a Chicago Polyethnic Tenement." In *Structuring Diversity: Ethnographic Perspectives on the New Immigration*, edited by Louise Lamphere, 95-144. Chicago: University of Chicago Press.

Crawford, Margaret, and ADOBE LA. 2004. "Mi casa es su casa." *Assemblage* 24 (August): 12-19.

Davis, Mike. 1992a. "*Chinatown*, Revisited? The Internationalization of Downtown Los Angeles." In *Sex, Death and God in LA*, edited by David Reid, 19-53. Berkeley: University of California Press.

———. 1992b. "The Empty Quarter." In *Sex, Death and God in LA*, edited by David Reid, 54-74. Berkeley: University of California Press.

El Pueblo, Inc. 2002. "2002 Latino Legislative Agenda." www.elpueblo.org.

Foucault, Michel. 1986. "Of Other Spaces." *Diacritics* 16 (1): 22–27.

Fraser, Nancy. 1994. "Rethinking the Public Sphere: A Contribution to the Critique of Actually Existing Democracy." In *Between Borders: Pedagogy and the Politics of Cultural Studies*, edited by Henry A. Giroux and Peter McLaren, 74-100. New York: Routledge.

García Canclini, Néstor. 1995. *Hybrid Cultures: Strategies for Entering and Leaving Modernity*. Translated by Christopher L. Chiappari and Silvia L. López. Minneapolis: University of Minnesota Press.

Gómez-Peña, Guillermo. 1993. *Warriors for Gringostroika*. St. Paul, MN: Grey Wolf Press.

Gottlieb, Jeff. "Taco Trucks Are Feeling the Crunch across the U.S." *Los Angeles Times*, May 20, 2009. http://articles.latimes.com/2009/may/20/local/me-tacotrucks20.

Guzmán, Betsy. 2001. *The Hispanic Population: Census 2000 Brief.* May. Washington, DC: U.S. Census Bureau.

Halle, David. 1993. *Inside Culture: Art and Class in the American Home.* Chicago: University of Chicago Press.

Hernández-León, Rubén. 2008. *Metropolitan Migrants: The Migration of Urban Mexicans to the United States.* Berkeley: University of California Press.

Herzog, Lawrence A. 1999. *From Aztec to High Tech: Architecture and Landscape across the Mexico-United States Border.* Baltimore: John Hopkins University Press.

Holston, James. 1996. "Spaces of Insurgent Citizenship." *Architectural Design* 66 (11/12): 54-59.

hooks, bell. 1990. *Yearning: Race, Gender, and Cultural Politics.* Boston: South End Press.

Kulzcar, Catalina. 2005. *Vecinos/Neighbors.* Charlotte Museum of History, Charlotte, NC, January 15 to August 21.

Lefebvre, Henri. 1991. *The Production of Space.* Oxford: Blackwell.

Leinberger, Christopher B. 2008. "The Next Slum?" *Atlantic Monthly,* March. www.theatlantic.com/magazine/archive/2008/03/the-next-slum/6653.

Martin, Karen. 2002. "A City Transformed." *Planning* 68 (July): 14–19.

Mayor's International Cabinet, City of Charlotte, North Carolina. 2002. *The Economic Impact of the International Community in the Charlotte Area: A Report Issued by the Economic Impact Task Force of the Mayor's International Cabinet.* February 15.

Mendez, Michael. 2004. "Latino New Urbanism: Building on Cultural Preferences." *Opolis: An International Journal of Suburban and Metropolitan Studies* 1 (1). http://repositories.cdlib.org/cssd/opolis/vol1/iss1/art5.

Omi, Michael. 1993. "Out of the Melting Pot and into the Fire: Race Relations Policy." In *Policy Issues to the Year 2020: The State of Asian Pacific America—A Public Policy Report.* Los Angeles: LEAP Asian Pacific American Public Policy Institute/UCLA Asian American Studies Center.

Ortega, Angeles [Director of the Latin American Coalition, Charlotte, NC]. 2004. Interview by author. Fall.

Ponce, Mary Helen. [1993] 1995. *Hoyt Street: Memories of a Chicana Childhood.* New York: Anchor Books/Doubleday.

Rojas, James T. 1991. "The Enacted Environment: The Creation of Place by Mexicans and Mexican-Americans in East Los Angeles." Master's thesis, Massachusetts Institute of Technology.

———. 1999. "The Latino Use of Urban Space in East Los Angeles." In *Urban Latino Cultures: La Vida Loca en L.A.,* edited by Gustavo Leclerc, Raul Villa, and Michael Dear, 131-38. Thousand Oaks, CA: Sage Publications.

Rouse, Roger. 1991. "Mexican Migration and the Social Space of Postmodernism." *Diaspora* 1 (1): 8–23.

Smith, Heather, and Owen J. Furseth. 2003. "Exploring the Geography of Hispanic Settlement in Charlotte, North Carolina 1990-2000," Unpublished report, Department of Geography and Earth Sciences, University of North Carolina, Charlotte.

Spalding, Sophie. 1992. "The Myth of the Classic Slum: Contradictory Perceptions of Boyle Heights Flats, 1900-1991." *Journal of Architectural Education* 45 (2): 107–19.

Suro, Roberto, and Audrey Singer. 2002. "Latino Growth in Metropolitan America: Changing Patterns, New Locations." Survey Series, Census 2000. Brookings Institution, Washington, DC. www.brookings.edu/~/media/Files/rc/reports/2002/07demographics_suro/surosinger.pdf.

Taylor, Marisa. 2010. "Fear, Economy Slow Rise in Undocumented Immigrants." *Charlotte Observer,* May 2. www.charlotteobserver.com/2010/05/02/1410504/fear-economy-slow-rise-in-undocumented.html.

U.S. Census Bureau. 2004. "Interim Projections by Age, Sex, Race, and Hispanic Origin: 2000-2050." www.census.gov/population/www/projections/usinterimproj/ (accessed March 18).

Zukin, Sharon. 1991. *Landscapes of Power: From Detroit to Disney World.* Berkeley: University of California Press.

Fostering Diversity

Lessons from Integration in Public Housing

Silvia Domínguez

During the late 1980s, Boston became one of the many cities that were court-ordered to integrate public housing. Up to that point, the Boston Housing Authority (BHA) had ignored legislation prohibiting racial discrimination in the provision of public housing and had relentlessly continued to systematically discriminate against African Americans, clustering them in poor, typically African American neighborhoods and simultaneously reserving housing developments in white areas for European American applicants (Vale 2000). For instance, Irish Americans went to projects in the Irish American neighborhoods of Charlestown and South Boston, and Italian Americans went primarily to East Boston, an Italian American area. In 1988, however, a class action lawsuit by the NAACP forced the BHA to integrate.

In 2000, the minorities who were integrated into the Maverick Gardens housing project resided adjacent to Maverick Square, a busy Latin American enclave in East Boston with retail establishments and human service organizations. In contrast, minorities integrated into Mary Ellen McCormack Housing Development in South Boston (Southie) were clustered and isolated by an antagonistic Irish American population. While conducting fieldwork in these two neighborhoods in 1999, I expected that the Latin American women in Maverick Gardens would experience improved economic conditions and greater access to needed services. Not only did the women in Maverick Gardens have access to co-ethnics in the surrounding neighborhood, but my memories of televised images of Southie residents reacting violently to African American individuals in opposition to forced busing led me to expect continuing racial intolerance there. Nevertheless, after several months of fieldwork I started to view a distinct pattern: the Latin American women in South Boston were improving their economic situation and residential mobility.[1]

Based on a conceptual framework centered in neighborhood-based racial relations and social capital, this study examined the consequences of forced integration in two public housing developments. Particular focus was placed on historical developments and resulting neighborhood cultures, tenant task forces, and demographic changes to both neighborhoods and public housing. Two research questions were key: What dynamics influenced the consequences of forced integration? And what was the role of neighborhood-based services and tenant organizations in the process of integration? I utilized data from archival records, participant observation, and longitudinal ethnographic interviews with public housing residents over two years in South Boston and East Boston.

This comparative ethnography explored the way South Boston's ethnic-based, tightly knit community bonds contributed to a violent reaction against the pioneer African American families that was reminiscent of Boston's infamous Busing Crisis in the 1970s, when African American students were bused into the neighborhood via court-mandated school integration and encountered violence and brutal racism. A decade later, South Boston's reluctance to integrate public housing resulted in outside intervention by local, state, and federal authorities who sought to democratize the tenant task forces at Mary Ellen McCormack and to substantially improve professional services through linkages to human service organizations in South Boston as a method to reduce the violence and successfully integrate these developments.

The Irish Americans in South Boston were historically prepared to fight, with cognitive frames for struggle informed by several decades of conflict between them and African Americans (Ignatiev 1995). Instead, the area was diversifying away from the white-black dichotomy and introducing Latin American immigrants as a key element in the transition (Domínguez 2008). There were no cognitive frames for struggle against them, and they effectively became cultural buffers to the existing interaction. Last, gentrification refocused residents' concerns from ethnic relations to the skyrocketing cost of housing.

Latin Americans were also integrated into East Boston's Maverick Gardens Housing Development. Here the reaction from the Italian American population was subdued, but the Italian American "minority" maintained undemocratic control of the task force with the assistance of BHA through patronage-based relations that fostered the deterioration of Maverick Gardens, thus setting the stage for HOPE VI qualification. Social service institutions were reacting to the heavy influx of Latin American immigrants. Inadequate outreach from tenant organizations meant that they did not effectively serve public housing residents. Gentrification and value differences fractured opposition against Latin American immigrants; thus those who lived and worked outside public housing resented public housing residents, viewing them as "getting a free ride." The Latin American residents who constituted the majority at Maverick Gardens were isolated, lacking services, and struggling within a regressive social milieu.

This study found that integration of distinct populations was significantly bolstered by diversity—in this instance through the migration of different minorities onto a previously black-white social stage. When Latin Americans and Asian Americans moved into the area, they buffered the racial antagonisms. Along with issues in housing integration research, this ethnographic study constitutes an important theoretical contribution to social capital theory, network theory, and ethnic and racial integration debates by focusing on how Latin Americans are changing relations, expanding knowledge, and challenging notions of race relations and neighborhoods that are transcending a dated black/white dichotomy.

In this essay I initially review the influences of neighborhood cultures and integration of public housing developments from a historical perspective. Following this analysis I examine the role of the tenant task forces and make recommendations for future policy.

Interpersonal and Institutional Social Capital: The New Multiculturalism

Pierre Bourdieu (1985) expanded the economic concept of "capital" to include social, cultural, and symbolic as well as economic resources. This framework enhances the understanding of the stratification process at individual and aggregate levels. At the interpersonal level, social capital explains how social ties (networks and/or associations) promote social support and status attainment (Briggs 1998). Alejandro Portes has defined it as the "ability of actors to secure benefits by virtue of membership in social networks or social structures" (1998, 3). The concept of social capital has been used in the study of how neighborhood social organization can decrease youth violence (Sampson, Raudenbush, and Earls 1997) and the study of civic and regional performance in the maintenance of democracy (Putnam 1993). I will use Putnam's approach to examine the consequences of forced integration of public housing by applying the concept of social capital at the neighborhood and institutional levels. The literature describes how social capital can function as a source of social control, family support, and benefits from relations beyond the family (Portes 1998). Two of these functions are relevant to this study: social capital as a means of social control and as a source of family-external benefits.

In homogenous immigrant communities, social control evolves through the formation of tight-knit networks that render formal controls unnecessary by creating culturally bounded solidarity and enforceable trust (Zhou and Bankston 1996, 207). These networks serve parents, teachers, politicians, and police authorities, who seek to maintain control and promote conformity. Cultural linkages can act as "leveling norms" with negative results: discouraging Latinas from getting an education and thus reducing their chance of achieving social mobility (Domínguez and Watkins 2003); fostering dynamics that reduce employability among young African American women (Fernández-Kelly 1995); promoting substance abuse and recycling regressive practices among immigrant men (Menjívar 2000); and resulting in the loss of community members who migrate to less restrictive environments (MacDonald 1999). Leveling norms also increase friction in defended neighborhoods where discrimination and intrusion lead communities to be on the "defense," a factor that tends to further tighten the close-knit relations of social networks (Rieder 1985). A case in point is MacDonald's (1999) book on growing up white in public housing in South Boston. He demonstrates how the tight-knit relations and social solidarity encouraged students to boycott schools in protest against integration. These youths left school and in the process ultimately curtailed their prospects for moving out of poverty.

Ethnic neighborhoods with histories of supporting political access to the mainstream offer residents resources through extrafamilial relationships and political machinery based on ethnic identity and allegiance. The Irish in Boston and other cities responded to overt discrimination by the Protestant establishment by struggling through the political process to gain direct control over government. Political patronage-based relations opened opportunities in civil service in exchange for political support (Auyero, Lapegna, and Poma 2009; Blau and Elman 2002). Thus social capital functioned as a source of social control and leverage-producing extrafamilial networks that enhanced the power of ethnic neighborhoods (O'Connor 1998).

Institutional social capital can lead to neighborhood social organization and an increase in previously denied government services through linkages between different institutional service providers. This is particularly influential in low-income communities where the demand for services is substantial. In fact, institutions that have linkages with others play an important role in increasing the social capital of their clients and reducing inequality (Small 2009). Nevertheless, in immigrant neighborhoods language and cultural differences are particularly challenging to service providers, who must provide linguistic and culturally responsive services to improve the quality of life (Alegria et al. 2010; Waters 2001). In the absence of bilingual and bicultural services, immigrant and minority families remain isolated and without resources to meet a range of survival demands (Domínguez 2004; Domínguez and Watkins 2003).

The Role of Ethnic Relations in Housing Segregation

One of the most prevalent and insidious aspects of U.S. society is rampant segregation of cities. Segregated housing patterns started with industrialization, which created densely clustered worker housing and a segregated workforce (Drake and Cayton 1945; Greenberg 1981). The real estate industry and neighborhood "improvement associations" strove to maintain racial boundaries by restricting interracial sales in the 1920s (Bauman 1987). These strict racial divisions were reified by federal legislation and policies adopted between 1934 and the mid-1940s. The government subsidized suburbs and lending programs that facilitated home ownership. Millions of European American GIs benefited, but African Americans and Latinos were structurally denied similar housing opportunities in suburbs. Rapid suburbanization led to "white flight" from the cities and shifted financial, cultural, employment, and institutional resources to the suburbs. Cities became predominantly African American and lower income. Minorities were redlined (a term derived from the practice of marking a red line on a map to delineate the area where banks would not invest) from the financial benefits of federal housing subsidies and programs. Despite the 1968 Civil Rights Act, which made it illegal to discriminate on the basis of race, racial and ethnic discrimination in the real estate and lending industries has not abated. As Michael Maly states, "Discriminatory practices retain high levels of isolation and segregation, stack the deck against racially mixed communities, and perpetuate the assumption that mixed communities are not viable" (2005, 12).

Although much of the literature on segregation has focused on the separation of African Americans and European Americans, Latin Americans have experienced the same discriminatory dynamics. As a result they have often come to occupy "buffer" zones between black and white areas that maintain structural segregation (Frey and Farley 1996). Maly (2005), however, argues that the influx of Latino immigrants can stabilize integrated black-white neighborhoods by alleviating white residents' fears that blacks will "take over" the neighborhood; the presence of more than two ethnic groups breaks down the black-white opposition.

The Field Research Environment and Methodology

The ethnographic data in this analysis were collected through my participation as a family and neighborhood ethnographer in the Welfare, Children and Families Three-City Study and my personal field research agenda. The Three-City Study examined work, welfare, family, money, intimate relationships, and social networks among low-income families, as well as institutional resources available to them at the neighborhood level, in Boston, Chicago, and San Antonio. As a Boston-based ethnographer, I conducted participant observation and longitudinal ethnographic interviews during 2000-2003 with Latin American immigrant women living in public housing in South and East Boston. In addition, I conducted fieldwork in these neighborhoods, attended meetings and other events, and interviewed subjects. These two neighborhoods (which were forcibly integrated at the same time) were selected for this study because they offer a rich comparison based on the different ethnic populations. I recruited women through service providers familiar with public housing residents, and personally by identifying mothers with children in parks and outside areas. Neighborhood informants were long-term merchants, neighborhood activists, and social service providers who were identified through observation and inquiry. I also relied on newspapers, policy papers, needs assessments, and other publications for historical and contextual information. The analysis is based on fifty-five intensive in-person interviews (sometimes repeated) and extensive field notes from over two years of participant observation in various community events.

Interviews and observations were documented in field notes and then analyzed using QSR N6 qualitative software and a modified grounded theory approach. The methodology examines events and patterns over time. The longitudinal ethnographic fieldwork assessed the dynamics related to different impacts of forced integration. This study supplements the literature on integration by concentrating on how neighborhoods have been shaped by previous waves of immigrants and by the level of discrimination against immigrants in prior eras. Finally, this study addresses a critical gap in the literature on desegregation by addressing the dynamics of forced integration.

Public Housing and Neighborhood Types

Historical differences have resulted from distinct neighborhood trends related to the introduction of public housing and its subsequent racial integration: South Boston as a defended neighborhood (Lukas 1985; O'Connor

1998; MacDonald 1999; Lehr and O'Neill 2000; Domínguez 2011) and East Boston as a "receiving zone" for new immigrants who often stayed there only transitorily (Pulio 2007; Borges-Méndez et al. 2006; Domínguez 2011). In South Boston, John McCormack obtained a commitment for public housing from President Roosevelt. By 1949, South Boston had close to three thousand apartment units in three large developments: Old Harbor Village in 1938 (later renamed Mary Ellen McCormack, this was the first public housing development in the nation); Old Colony in 1939; and West Broadway in 1949. As Lawrence Vale noted, this was a "vastly disproportionate share of the city's total allocation achieved at a time when public housing was widely considered to be a highly desirable housing resource" (2000, 176). The institutionalized political power of the Irish in South Boston to gain access had paid off. But although the mayor delivered federal funds to the neighborhood, residents felt harassed by the conditions that federal agencies imposed, an ambivalence that would later lead to conflict.

Initially public housing developments reflected the ethnicity and race of the adjacent neighborhoods. Italians were placed in Maverick Gardens in East Boston when it opened in 1942, and the Irish went to the newly built South Boston and Charlestown developments. When upwardly mobile residents left the projects, the economic status of those who remained declined, and along with it the image of public housing. By the end of the 1950s, Euro-American "worthy poor" had stopped applying for public housing, seeing it only as a last resort.[2] As Vale (2000) explains, Boston housing and development officials were no longer able to fill public housing with the two-parent white families that they had always preferred, so they turned their attention to housing for the elderly and urban renewal projects, neglecting public housing as its population became increasingly poor and nonwhite.

Through the Irish American patronage system, the BHA controlled the assignment of residents and resources well into the 1980s, reinforcing a two-tiered system that led to racial segregation and differences in housing stock quality. African American applicants were kept on separate lists until units in segregated low-income neighborhoods became available. Euro-American applicants were advanced in the waiting lists for openings in more advantageous neighborhoods. The developments in South and East Boston benefited from this, since they were maintained as homogenous zones. Ultimately, the Massachusetts Commission against Discrimination challenged this segregation as discriminatory through the courts.

Meanwhile, Boston's segregated schools had also reached the courts, and in 1974 Judge Garrity ordered their integration. This process, which bused children from one neighborhood to schools in another, became known as "forced busing." South Boston residents viewed integration as outsider infringement on their sovereignty. Mafia leaders and politicians, headed by James L. Bulger, who was one of America's Most Wanted, and his brother William M. Bulger, who rose to be the president of the Massachusetts State House, used their overt political influence to manipulate the poorest residents—those in the public housing developments—to "defend" South Boston through violent means (Rieder 1985). The virulent protests by South Boston residents against school integration reached a fever pitch and placed Boston on the national map as a racist city.

The Integration of Public Housing

By the late 1980s the BHA was attracting persistent complaints of racial discrimination. White neighborhoods with public housing developments struggled to come to terms with the need to integrate given applicant lists that were more than 80 percent African American. But as late as 1988 the patronage-based system continued, and there were almost no African Americans or Latin Americans in South and East Boston housing developments.

My research (Domínguez 2011) has shown, the presence in a neighborhood of similar ethnic populations inside and outside public housing is a significant factor affecting social mobility out of public housing and into market-rate housing, since friends and family in the neighborhood can help residents with the transition and reinforce a future orientation. This traditional mobility was threatened by integration. Ironically, the issue was never part of the narrative against integration, but disruption of the traditional pattern nevertheless significantly reduced mobility among European American low-income families, who then were more likely to remain as third- and fourth-generation immigrants in public housing.

In 1988, the threatened loss of at least $75 million in annual federal aid forced Mayor Flynn and the BHA to develop a program of integration in the all-white public housing developments. Once again, through strong leadership based on ethnic identity and community pride, South Boston politicians urged the community to staunchly oppose federal intervention. Residents began to call the impending influx of minorities "forced housing." In a January 12, 1988, WGBH news broadcast, Christopher Lyden reported on a neighborhood meeting of Old Colony residents and Mary

Ellen McCormack residents held at the Santa Monica Church: "City Coun-
cilman Jimmy Kelly stirred things up tonight by linking this year's housing integration to the raw memories of school busing in South Boston a
decade ago. He seemed to suggest that violence is all but unavoidable. The
crowd cheered. The crowd jeered at Flynn as he made the case for a fair
and equitable housing policy" (qtd. in Domínguez 2011, 58). Jimmy Kelly
had played a similar role in stirring up opposition to school integration
in the seventies. This controversy provided him with the political power
necessary to build political capital and advance his public stature. Federal courts found in both 1987 and 1989 that the BHA was practicing overt
discrimination (*New York Times* 1989). A BHA study in 1990 found that a
majority of verified incidents of racial discrimination and harassment in
public housing citywide since the beginning of forced integration in 1988
had occurred in the three projects in South Boston (Marantz 1990). The
first African American families who had moved into these developments
had been driven out by racist violence. By 1992, however, six hundred minority families had moved into South Boston developments. Mayor Flynn
revived a Civil Rights Cabinet following the shooting of a black man by a
white man in the Old Colony project. Facing another lawsuit by the National Association for the Advancement of Colored People (NAACP), the
BHA pledged to end its discriminatory practices and paid $1.8 million to
approximately eight hundred families who had been discouraged from living in the predominantly white developments (Rezendez 1992).

The South Boston community continued to protest integration. In
1994, led by Jimmy Kelly, they held "a flag-waving protest demonstration
through downtown South Boston and attended a 'raucous' meeting [at
Santa Monica Church], where outsiders [African Americans] were blamed
for making their streets more dangerous" (Hart 1994). With political and
Mafia influence, racial attacks persisted as Irish Americans felt embold-
ened by the perception that police and city officials, along with area residents, were not sympathetic to integration (Levin and McDevitt 1993).
This is consistent with a power-differential hypothesis, which states that
when members of minorities are greatly outnumbered in a region the
perpetrators of intolerance have no fear of reprisal (Levine and Campbell 1972). In the context of persistent racial problems, minority tenants
in two predominantly white developments, charging that the BHA had
failed to adequately respond to complaints of racial harassment by white
tenants, filed a federal class action suit against the BHA and the city. Another Housing and Urban Development (HUD) investigation found that

the BHA had downplayed "systematic discrimination" against nine minority families living in South Boston developments between 1990 and 1996. HUD secretary Mario Cuomo termed this bias suit the most serious discrimination case ever brought against a local agency. Meanwhile the BHA had to institute severe penalties against civil rights violations, and this action further fueled animosity against the newcomers.

A HUD investigation in 1995 revealed systematic discrimination against nonwhites at Mary Ellen McCormack Housing Development, where 152 desirable townhouse units were reserved for whites. Vale states, "Within the BHA, a system within the system continued to operate" (2000, 378). In a final move toward integration, resources were utilized by reformers within the BHA to develop and professionalize the tenant task forces. The BHA developed a policy that resulted in 40 percent of the McCormack townhouse units becoming occupied by minority residents by 2000. This level of integration caused severe antagonism when whites on the waiting lists perceived themselves as being passed over by a policy that favored minorities.

That antagonism was evidenced one morning when I walked along the path that followed the boundary between the three-story brick buildings and the townhouses, which had separate entrances and front yards. On this street was a man planting in his new front yard. In front of me, two Irish American residents stopped and yelled, "Why don't you go plant where you came from?" I anticipated a confrontation, but instead the man looked up with a smile and said, "Buenos días, señores" (Good morning, gentlemen). The two men looked surprised and kept walking.

Nonwhites integrating the East Boston projects met with fewer problems than the "pioneer" families in South Boston had. As noted earlier, East Boston had developed into a "receiving zone" where immigrants could land, a place that could become a stepping-stone in a socially mobile context. Jews, Irish, and finally Italians had made East Boston their home. This neighborhood and its social service institutions were used to dealing with the transformation of immigrant communities. And although the Italian Americans had historically competed for low-wage jobs with African Americans and Irish Americans in East Boston, they had flourished and racial tensions had decreased. When asked about the integration of Maverick Gardens, a long-term African American female resident active in the Maverick Tenants Organization commented: "When I came in, like in the early eighties, the racial turmoil was winding down. But sporadically there were issues with families and old-timers that were turf oriented and felt that people with different cultures were invading their space. Then kids started to play together. There were teams of soccer ball and softball and badminton and basketball, and then they all went and got their jackets. Everyone was a 'Maverick Hound Dogger.' Those are the things that I really liked about Maverick" (Domínguez 2011). This relative lessening of racial tensions in the project was due to the diffusion of the Italian close-knit community into the surrounding neighborhood. They were replaced by a continuous influx of immigrants from Colombia and El Salvador. Further, the potential for conflict was mediated and defused by a strong network of institutionalized nonprofit agencies, like the East Boston Ecumenical Center, that served the needs of different waves of immigrants.

Demographic Changes

Demographic changes in the two neighborhoods and public housing developments are the key independent variables in this ethnographic study. East and South Boston began the 1990s with overwhelmingly white populations (75.8 percent and 95.5 percent respectively). But by 2000, the white population in East Boston had decreased to 49.7 percent, while the Hispanic population had grown from 17.6 percent to 39 percent and the African American population from 2.1 percent to 3.1 percent. In South Boston, the percentage of whites changed less dramatically, from 95.5 percent to 84.8 percent, with Hispanics going from 1.5 percent in 1990 to 7.6 percent in 2000 and African Americans from .09 percent to 2.3 percent. While the increase in the Latin American population occurred throughout East Boston (i.e., both inside and outside public housing), it was almost entirely limited to public housing in South Boston (Boston Foundation 2007a, 2007b).

By 2002, Latin American immigrants had become the majority population in Maverick Gardens in East Boston and in Mary Ellen McCormack in South Boston. In fact, Latin Americans are currently the largest population in Boston public housing developments (Domínguez 2011). This rapid demographic transition changed the racial dynamics in both public housing and neighborhoods as Latin Americans assumed the place of the anticipated African Americans as the majority-minority population.

The Tenant Task Forces

In the context of mass social movements and citizen empowerment, particularly of low-income minorities, tenant task forces were created to counterbalance the absolute power of "traditional" development managers. In 1968, the BHA's director of social planning initiated the task forces to increase resident involvement (Vale 2000, 326). With increased tenants' participation, the influence of BHA patronage gradually weakened, though my own study, like Vale's (2000, 327), found the announcement of its ending to be "premature." The tenant task forces function as social service organizations governed by a board of directors made up of tenants and, at times, institutional players like representatives from neighborhood health centers. The boards set the goals and objectives of the programs. The director of services applies for funding through federal and state initiatives and private foundations. The tenant task forces are institutionally supported by the BHA's Office for Family and Community Services and are monitored by an oversight entity, the Committee for Public Housing. One of the findings of the fieldwork was that tenant task forces in the public housing developments of Boston differ on the following dimensions:

- Level of professionalism of program
- Quality and quantity of programs delivered
- Quality and quantity of links to social services in the surrounding neighborhood
- Success of yearly Unity Day celebrations
- Dissemination of information
- Availability of forums for the ventilation of grievances
- Level of democratization of the board of directors
- Reputation among the residents in the development and in community organizations

Mary Ellen McCormack Tenant Task Force

On a late August afternoon in South Boston, a yearly Unity Day celebration brought together black, white, and brown residents, area social service representatives, Irish American politicians, and BHA personnel. I walked around following Laura, a dynamic woman in her late twenties who directed the programs at the Mary Ellen McCormack Tenant Task Force. Laura was busy with food, photographs, and entertainment. Residents remained for several hours, some with barbeques and plenty of family and friends around. The music transitioned between salsa, hip-hop, and oldies. There were clowns, mimes, and various organized games for the children. Anabel, the employment advocate for the task force, had her family with her while monitoring the schedule for the clowns and mimes.

The 2001 Mary Ellen McCormack Unity Day celebration brought different Irish American politicians seeking support, including several former mayors of Boston, state representatives, and police commissioners. It was significant yet customary to see such political representation at most events held at the development. Laura and Anabel were tired but very content with the turnout.

The Mary Ellen McCormack Tenant Task Force was housed in a separate building that included a large community room, a kitchen, a bathroom, and two small offices. Elaine, a Euro-American resident volunteer, sat at the front desk. There was one office for Laura, and Anabel and Ana, the community organizer, occupied the other, larger office. The large room was where all programs and meetings occurred. There was also a library and a video room.

Early in my fieldwork, I was informed about the existence of the tenant task force by Maria, a first-generation Puerto Rican (a woman in the study), who was being recruited by the task force board. It became evident that the task force workers were desperately trying to integrate the board but had had limited success with African Americans; thus they were now focusing on recruiting Latin American residents. This outreach to and courting of Latin American women went on throughout the period of my research. All the women in the sample in South Boston had dealt with the task force at some point and were familiar with its services.

The staff's level of education was a key factor leading to the success of outreach activities. The director, Susan, a young Euro-American, had an MSW and a MBA from Boston College. Laura had studied anthropology and had an MPH in health education from the University of South Carolina. She managed a team of four: two college professionals and two residents with high school educations. One college-educated worker, Anabel (a Latin American), was in charge of employment services. When asked to describe her job, Anabel stated:

> Employment advocate . . . it just kind of entails that a person is going to come here and I am going to get them employed, and what happens is that there are many other issues that arise, social issues and concerns like child care, welfare, needing skills, trying to motivate people to remain in training, and then there are immigration issues . . . it's not just employment. I do an assessment and try to orient people to take steps, but you have to give me something to

work with, the motivation, desire to kind of achieve, in order to get employed, otherwise it's not going to work.

As a bilingual and bicultural single mother and a public housing resident, Anabel was highly effective. She understood the needs and realities of her caseload. Not only was she culturally responsive, but she also had a welcoming and warm disposition.

Laura managed six different social service grants at Mary Ellen McCormack. In addition, she had worked to establish the task force as a not-for profit corporation. Another responsibility was to run and diversify the board of directors. The task force printed a monthly publication in English and Spanish that included the board meeting minutes and advertisements for programs and services.

The tenant task force also provided a forum for grievances. On July 30, 2001, the task force organized a meeting on public safety. The meeting's objective was to reduce racial tensions following the death of an elderly Irish American resident who apparently had had a heart attack during the city's Puerto Rican Festival. The Irish American residents blamed the Latin Americans who were becoming the majority population. Among the people on stage were two members of the task force board; Jim Kelly, the state representative from South Boston; James Hussey, the superintendent-in-chief of the Boston Police; George McGrath, the housing manager at the development; Bill McGonagle, deputy administrator of the BHA; and several Boston and BHA police force officials. Around two hundred residents were present, all Irish American except for eight African Americans and three Latin Americans who could not speak English.

In a fashion similar to that chronicled by other ethnographies of defended neighborhoods (Suttles 1972; Rieder 1985; De Sena 1990), the Irish Americans exaggerated their fears, complaining about a loss of their distinctive way of life, including "loud music that is different," "thirteen to fifteen people living in apartments," and the tendency of the new residents to "break all the rules," with nobody doing anything about it. Kelly spoke about how he himself had come from the adjacent Old Colony Public Housing Development. Instead of invoking a divisive "us" and "them," he complained that "we need a consistent police presence. Where is the police presence? Where is it?" The crowd cheered. A female resident got up and said loudly, "Look at this hall. It is full of white people. They are not here. They are not here because they are guilty and they know it. Where are they? They are not here because they are guilty." Again the crowd cheered.

The African American board member yelled for clarification: "Who are 'they'? Who are 'they'?" Laura calmed down the crowd by explaining that minority families associated with the task force had the same concerns as the Irish American families did.

The Latin American women asked me to translate for them and used this opportunity to voice their own complaints about public safety issues. "This is getting really bad. There are kids out all day and they are just bothering people," stated a participant. Another person added, "We need more police presence. The neighborhood is changing for the worse." These women had the same concerns as the Irish Americans. However, most attendees were not open to hearing about Latin Americans' issues, which, though shared, were not accorded equal importance. The Latin American women wore nice dresses and had their hair done, whereas the rest of the crowd looked very much disheveled. Yet, it was the Latin Americans who were being accused of disorderliness. In addition, at no time did the Latin Americans become defensive even though they were the targets of the complaints. They seemed to focus on the commonality of the issues related to quality of life and security rather than racial differences. "We are all in this place together, and neither is better than the other. We are in the same situation." The social framework of racial battles between African Americans and Irish Americans that had developed over centuries was not relevant to the Latin Americans' experience. Their different history, language, and culture had established a capacity to absorb the aggressiveness. Although "forced busing" and "forced housing" had been set up as Irish American versus African American fights, the influx of Latin American residents dramatically changed the community's social dynamic. Additionally, by providing a forum for the ventilation of grievances, the tenant task force was able to defuse racial tensions in the neighborhood.

In the following days I asked residents about the meeting, and while the Irish Americans continued to complain about the lifestyles being brought in by the influx of Latin American immigrants, the Latin American women whom I spoke with could not understand why the Irish Americans did not see them, and other ethnic and racial groups, in terms of what they all shared. Josefa, a first-generation Honduran woman, said, "What is all that about anyways? Why do those two [whites and blacks] fight so much? Aren't we all in the same situation here?" Isabel, a second-generation Honduran girl, stated, "We have the same concerns they have, and we have the same problems they have, but they act like they love this place and not like they want to move on to better housing. . . . We are all in the same situation."

From the late 1990s into the mid-2000s home values in South Boston increased and many low-income residents were forced out of their previously affordable rental homes. Many were friends and family of the Irish American residents of Mary Ellen McCormack, who had previously played the role of providing a bridge into market-based housing in South Boston. Once they migrated out, many Irish American residents were left stranded in public housing. While Anabel was an effective advocate with Latin Americans and African Americans, few Irish Americans ever asked for services.[3] Constance, the director of services of the neighboring West Broadway Tenant Task Force in South Boston, explained, "The whites here have nowhere to go now. They used to be the friends and family of those who lived in the surrounding area here in Southie. Now those people have moved with the high rents, and those high rents do not allow these residents the ability to move on like they used to. If you ask me, they are the ones who are really doing badly here. They have nowhere to go, they are trapped . . . and they see blacks and Latinos moving on and they can't stand it."

The Mary Ellen McCormack Tenant Task Force was well organized. The professional and educated staff provided culturally responsive services from which many of the women in the study benefited. Staff espoused tolerance and commonality of needs, and even previously divisive politicians avoided divisive language during meetings. During the process of integration, opponents did not move out in the sort of "white flight" documented in previous research (Green, Strolovitch, and Wong 1998). Instead, they were forced out by gentrification, and the phenomenon of "yuppies" moving into the neighborhood became the focus of contention in the early 2000s, displacing the neighborhood's concern with racial/ethnic integration. Laura, a young woman who was employed at Head Start and whose family had resided in South Boston for many generations, told me, "I am really happy to work with the women in my group [her racially and ethnically diverse coworkers at Head Start]. Everyone is really nice, and we help each other all the time. Sometimes I need to change schedule with another and it is never a problem . . . What is really a problem is that all these yuppies are moving in, and we are having to move out of South Boston because rents are going through the roof. I am really angry about this because my family is from South Boston and I can't live here anymore." Laura represented Irish Americans living outside public housing who were being threatened by the rising rents. The integration of Latin Americans and to a lesser extent Asians into public housing was successful primarily because they were not the anticipated African Americans and because their styles of interaction were inconsistent with the contentious white-versus-black racial conflict models that had previously dominated the neighborhood. Further, the professionalism of the staff acted to defuse conflict. Third, the close-knit ties, social control, and enforceable trust of the traditional Irish American community were weakening as the political and cultural climate was becoming less charged. Gentrification was rapidly becoming the most significant problem, since it threatened the capacity of the Irish, with generations of dominance in South Boston, to remain in that neighborhood.

The Maverick Gardens Tenants Organization

One morning in July, I walked from Maverick Square to the shore, while looking across the bay in appreciation of the skyline of Boston. The sun was radiant and the view across the Boston Harbor was incredible. I was wondering who the lucky residents were that lived here and enjoyed the view when I spotted the plaque for the Maverick Gardens Tenants Organization. This task force was based in an apartment that had been remodeled as an office. When I walked in, Jenny, a woman sitting behind a brand-new corporate-style desk, directed me to another office, where six Latin American women were complaining in Spanish that they kept being placed in jobs that taught them nothing useful for employment. Later on, Isabella, the director of the task force, said that those women were assigned to that office as part of workfare (welfare reform) requirements. Isabella had grown up in Maverick Gardens and talked fondly about the past when residents had all been Italians and "there were no differences between us and the people in the neighborhood." Isabella introduced me to Rose, a lifetime resident of Maverick Gardens who assisted Isabella in the office. The tenant organization operated two programs, one to train women without employment skills in retail sales, through work in a thrift shop, and the other to provide mental health services for families. These two programs were valuable in meeting the employment skill training and mental health needs of low-income communities. Cheryl, one of the psychologists working in the program, explained, "The purpose of the program is to bring in-house user-friendly counseling with goals of self-sufficiency by professional clinicians." This mental health service was available at no charge, and although it was a program that other task forces desired there were no bilingual or culturally responsive clinicians. This lack of bilingual, bicultural services was a critical problem in a context where the majority of residents were Latina/o.

From further fieldwork I discovered that only two newsletters had been printed in the last ten years and that these were available only in English. I was never able to verify the existence of a board of directors for the tenant organization. The Unity Day celebration in 2001 at Maverick Gardens was a "disaster," according to Eliana (a woman in the study), who reported that only Boston Legal Aid representatives had attended.[4] In fact, Eliana was the only woman in the study who knew that the task force existed. This meant that the tenant organization had not been able to recruit any neighborhood institutions, residents, or services and programs outside East Boston to participate. The acute lack of outreach was especially problematic because social service organizations were extremely busy with the influx of immigrants and were not likely to specifically target services to the public housing developments without continual outreach from the task force.

Latina/os at Maverick Gardens were also isolated from the immigrant population in the surrounding neighborhood. Many immigrants in Maverick Gardens had been in the United States for several years, and of these, many were second-generation immigrants. Recent immigrants, who worked several jobs and lived in congested apartments, resented the public housing residents, whom they viewed as "getting a free ride." Father Wilson, pastor of the Holy Redeemer Church across from Maverick Gardens, told me, "It [Maverick Gardens] is its own separate community. Before, when it was all Italian Americans here, they were considered neighbors, family members that would eventually move into the larger East Boston community. But now, they are not seen as neighbors by anybody." He talked about Maverick Gardens being an "island" inside a neighborhood. "It is so cut off, to get to the harbor you have to go around the development. There is an insular mentality brewing there. I do not know how many people, but I would say the majority have never experienced life in any other way." Father Wilson said that Latin Americans living in the larger community exhibited animosity toward their "same people" living at Maverick Gardens. "Many of the immigrants are not eligible for any benefits, and they see residents of public housing not advancing or moving on in any way."

Gentrification also affected East Boston but did not cause the amount of low-income flight that was occurring in South Boston. Instead, recent immigrants tended to double up in apartments, while others bought houses to be shared among two or three families. Neighborhood of Affordable Housing (NOAH) and other institutions in East Boston galvanized residents to maintain affordable housing as a long-term reality. The process of gentrification and the efforts to resist it deflected neighborhood attention away from Maverick Garden residents.

Why were these task forces so different in terms of programs delivered to residents, professionalism of the staff, programs linked outside the developments, quality and success of the Unity Day celebration, dissemination of information, level of democratization of the board of directors, and reputation among the residents of the development? Information gathered from interviews by representatives of the BHA's office with residents, community service providers, and the Committee for Public Housing offered some explanations.

Supporting Actors: The Committee for Public Housing and BHA Operatives

Down a spiraling street in the Mission Hill neighborhood of Boston, I found the hidden entrance into a warehouse-type building of the Committee for Public Housing office. This was a very small space with few employees. It was evident that it lacked resources. Two young women, both Latin American, met with me in a small room that served as a conference room. The committee is a watchdog organization focused on democratizing the task forces and improving the living conditions of residents in all the public housing developments in Boston. One of their efforts to democratize the boards of directors is the provision of task force election materials in several languages. During our conversation, they reported the Maverick Tenants Organization among the task forces that were "dysfunctional," with little participation by residents or connection to the surrounding neighborhood. Lucy stated, "It is not a fully functioning board. It has about four people involved." She added that "those that stuck it out over the years have gotten all the power, and this has made it into a one- or two-person rule and leaving out all African Americans and Latinos." When asked how this was possible, Lucy explained, "BHA favors those leaders who have been around for a long time and can be mobilized for specific purposes. It is a lot easier for [a board member] to pick up a phone and get things done if [he or she] has a relationship with the chair of the tenants' task force. In exchange, chairs can ask for special favors like moving people ahead of others in the waiting lists or evicting somebody who is causing them problems . . . This is how these boards work, and this is why we have such a difficult time democratizing the process."

When I spoke with John D., a manager of Family Services at Boston Housing Authority, he told me that Unity Days had begun with the start of the Drug Elimination Grants twelve years ago. These grants provided seed money for local tenant task force development and youth workers. To enhance Unity Days, "We get service providers on board because they need clients, and we['ve] got the clients who need the services." Some task forces have been successful in developing positive relationships with area providers. Others are problematic, and the agency steps in to assist them to improve service delivery. "I can evaluate how organized one development is by how successful their Unity Day is," he said. Among the task forces he mentioned as organized and viable was Mary Ellen McCormack. "We don't have to help them at all . . . They have worked everything out and they have excellent Unity Day celebrations." On the other hand, he numbered Maverick Gardens among the developments with poor Unity Day celebrations that showed how "nonviable those task forces are."

A very different response came from the BHA's most senior liaison to the tenant task forces. When asked about Maverick Gardens, he stated that Isabella "did an incredible job . . . Look, they are getting Hope VI!" I asked him why he thought that Hope VI was a good thing, and he explained that "this would bring money and services" that the BHA could not afford. Hope VI is available only to developments that are considered to be "severely distressed" structurally and socially. These are developments that housing authorities like the BHA have ceased to maintain around the nation. When a "severely distressed" development becomes a community problem for several years, it qualifies for HOPE VI funding. In the process, the old buildings are torn down and neighborhood areas are revitalized, but the actual supply of subsidized housing units is significantly decreased. Residents are forced to relocate. In numerous instances they are isolated and not well informed, which serves the BHA by blunting any vigorous protest against the policy. In fact, none of the women I was following knew about the upcoming changes.

What Lucy said was consistent with the patronage that BHA was infamous for and that is well documented in Vale's (2000) book. Tenant task forces were initially developed to break up the entrenched patronage relationships between the BHA and the housing managers by providing tenants with a voice in decisions. It appears that BHA maintained systemic patronage with long-term task force members who supported the Hope

VI destruction of Maverick Gardens. In the meantime, Latin Americans and other residents were not offered services that would help them move out of their state of economic vulnerability.

The information developed in fieldwork at the Maverick Gardens Tenants Organization demonstrates that racism against non-Italian Americans was systematic but that unlike South Boston's racism was not publicly recognized. As a result, it continued without outside interference. Consequently, the tenants' organization did not grow or develop supportive social services for the community or link with surrounding institutions that could address the needs of low-income women struggling to survive. Maverick Tenants Organization did not show leadership by disseminating information or by democratizing the board of directors. Therefore, they were not well perceived by BHA administrators and the Committee for Public Housing. Isabella and Rose's longevity as residents at Maverick Gardens only served to further facilitate the continuation of a legacy of politically based patronage between the tenant organization and BHA. Meanwhile, the tenant task force at Mary Ellen McCormack functioned according to a more professional dynamic. This arrangement facilitated access to resources to all the residents but primarily Latin Americans, the largest ethnic group.

Institutional versus Interpersonal Social Capital

In confrontations over integration, institutional and interpersonal social capital can function as either integrative or exclusionary. Interpersonal social capital in conjunction with political institutional players drove the struggle against integration in South Boston. This type of social capital was extremely effective through community pressure in manipulating the poorest residents to act violently. This resulted in local, state, and federal policy involvement that consequently neutralized the effects of interpersonal, exclusionary social capital. I had expected high levels of interpersonal social capital after integration in East Boston, where class and ethnic-based homophily existed. Yet as we experienced, value differences between the residents in the housing project and the recently arrived immigrants in the neighborhood and a lack of institutional linkages to outside the project hindered the development of that integrative social capital and left the families in public housing isolated and abandoned by public housing authorities. Conversely, in South Boston after integration, institutional social capital in the form of linkages between social service agencies and service providers who became bridges to the Latin American community was key in providing linguistically and culturally responsive services and helping families at Mary Ellen McCormack to survive and improve economic conditions. Here interpersonal social capital was more likely to be exclusive, whereas institutional social capital was more integrative.

Policy Lessons

These neighborhood-based case analyses of the consequences of forced integration and its accompanying dynamics lead to important policy recommendations. The historical background of immigrants in East Boston and South Boston resulted in different levels of governmental influence and public policy for each neighborhood. South Boston has a long history of racial antagonism. The perception of Boston as a racist city is grounded in South Boston and Charlestown (also an Irish American enclave), and famous media images of violent, racist demonstrations against busing and housing integration (Lukas 1985). The city, state, and federal governments lost key court decisions that resulted in substantial financial settlements awarded to minority families who had experienced discrimination and persecution in public housing developments. Time and time again, the federal government excoriated the City of Boston for having a housing authority that continued patronage-based relationships and discrimination against minorities. In this respect, South Boston is an embarrassment for a city that is otherwise a bastion of intellectualism, culture, and liberalism.

In South Boston, the strong sense of community led to a violent reaction against integration. The eventual public policy response was to ensure that minority families obtained the services needed to prevent further lawsuits and civic embarrassment. The BHA's institutional response was to (1) *democratize* the boards of directors and the tenant task force of Mary Ellen McCormack; and (2) *professionalize* the task force's service delivery. Through these steps, patronage-based relations were virtually eliminated and social service delivery for public housing residents in South Boston improved in quality and quantity. The improvements were exemplified both by Laura's professionalism and ability to obtain grants to increase the services and by the hiring of Anabel, another Latin American immigrant who demonstrated to women that their experiences and bilingual and culturally responsive services could lead to successful careers and community empowerment. Through their leadership, these professionals also established linkages with area service providers, maintained political capital, and defused racial conflict by offering forums for the ventilation of grievances.

While relations based on patronage ended in South Boston, they continued in East Boston. The thought that the establishment of tenant task forces would break up patronage-based relations was indeed premature. The lack of overt racism and violence in East Boston did not create a demand for reform; instead, it protected and characterized the racial patronage that persisted in East Boston between the Maverick Tenants Organization and the BHA. In this instance, patronage-based relations reinforced existing unequal power relations and social capital and structured social control. When the Latin American population expanded at Maverick Gardens, the lifelong Italian American residents maintained total power with the aid of the BHA. Efforts by the Committee for Public Housing to democratize the board failed. Services and linkages to neighborhood social services did not develop. In the absence of violence, policies that allowed for the ventilation of grievances could have served the same purpose of creating demand for reform, but East Boston had no violence and no forums for ventilation of resident's complaints, so Maverick Gardens was slated for demolition. Residents were isolated and struggling for survival, factors of structural and institutional neglect that facilitated HOPE VI funding and neighborhood destruction. Concurrently, the existing network of neighborhood service institutions continued to meet the needs of arriving immigrants, while limiting efforts to reach the Maverick Gardens residents.

The key strategy facilitating integration in public housing developments in South Boston was the fostering of diversity through admission of Latin American and Asian immigrants in place of the fearfully anticipated African Americans. The struggle against busing was a struggle against African Americans. The cognitive framework of confrontation was based on the legacy of antagonism between African Americans and Irish Americans. The appearance of Latin Americans caused a dramatic change in the social dynamics of South Boston. They buffered the confrontation by absorbing Irish Americans' aggressiveness instead of reacting impulsively to racist attacks, as in the case of the man working in his front yard who responded to racial slurs with a civil greeting. In addition, they were different, representing the hope of first-generation immigrants, as exemplified by the three Latin American women who had their hair done and wore pretty dresses to the meeting at Santa Monica Church where Irish Americans expressed hostility against Latin Americans.[5] In addition Latin

American women often responded to the "us and them" rhetoric of the Irish Americans by focusing instead on the commonality between the two groups, in such statements as "After all, we are all living in public housing" and "Why do they love this place so much? Don't they want to move on like us?" This difference led to different ways of establishing solutions to successfully address community problems.

While homogenous networks recycle the same information, heterogeneity brings different ideas. Latin Americans, the majority ethnic populace, eroded the strong sense of community entitlement intrinsic to the Irish American identity. This identity was based on a history of perceived discrimination and homogeneity and manifested itself in the defended nature of the South Boston neighborhood. Latin Americans provided a critically influential social and cultural buffer between African Americans and Euro-Americans. They all collectively shared the same objective of housing mobility (Frey and Farley 1996). The major lesson of this study is that diversity can be employed as an effective mechanism in the resolution of racial conflict. While diversity is frequently described as a desirable goal, it can also be a valuable tool in catalyzing positive outcomes in social dynamics. The underlying mechanism is the deactivation of preexisting cognitive frameworks of narrow cultural and ethnic racism in defense of Eurocentric dominance, which developed historically in this society and is not unique to Boston's regressive legacy of overt discrimination in public housing.

NOTES

1   At the time of the study, public housing applicants were given two choices in terms of apartments in developments. If they did not take the first one in one development, they had to take the second one in another development. Therefore, the resident population was randomly selected in terms of educational, employment, and human capital variables.

2   The differentiation between "worthy" and "unworthy" has been a historical feature of social welfare benefits that has determined who deserved and did not deserve to be aided via public monies (Katz 1990).

3   Another factor in the declining condition of the Irish American residents left in public housing can be attributed to their being third- and fourth-generation immigrants living in poverty and as such having lost, through the generations, the motivation and capacity to get ahead.

4   Boston Legal Services was present throughout the fieldwork in these public housing developments. They were available for housing issues but mainly as part of welfare reform and the struggles regarding eligibility for benefits, disabilities, and other needs.

5 The largest part of the congregation of Santa Monica Church is now Latin American (2007).

REFERENCES

Alegria, M., M. Atkins, E. Farmer, E. Slaton, and W. Stelk. 2010. "One Size Does Not Fit All: Taking Diversity, Culture and Context Seriously." *Administration and Policy in Mental Health and Mental Health Services Research* 37:48-60.

Auyero, J., P. Lapegna, and F. P. Poma. 2009. "Patronage Politics and Contentious Collective Action: A Recursive Relationship." *Latin American Politics and Society* 51:1-31.

Bauman, John. 1987. *Public Housing, Race, and Renewal.* Philadelphia: Temple University Press.

Blau, J. R., and C. Elman. 2002. "The Institutionalization of US Political Parties: Patronage Newspapers." *Sociological Inquiry* 72:576-99.

Borges-Méndez, Ramón, Brandynn Holgate, Carlos Maynard, Robin Reale, and Jennifer Shea. 2006. "Latino Business Owners in East Boston." Gastón Institute Publications. Paper 119. http://scholarworks.umb.edu/gaston_pubs/119.

Boston Foundation. 2007a. "Geography-at-a-Glance: East Boston, 1990 and 2000." In *A Time Like No Other: Boston Indicators Report, 2004–2006.* Boston: Boston Foundation.

Boston Foundation. 2007b. "Geography-at-a-Glance: South Boston, 1990 and 2000." In *A Time Like No Other: Boston Indicators Report, 2004–2006.* Boston: Boston Foundation.

Bourdieu, Pierre. 1985. "The Forms of Capital." In *Handbook of Theory and Research for the Sociology of Education*, edited by John G. Richardson, 241-58. New York: Greenwood.

Briggs, Xavier de Souza. 1998. "Brown Kids in White Suburbs: Housing Mobility and the Many Faces of Social Capital." *Housing Policy Debate* 9 (1): 177-221.

De Sena, Judith N. 1990. *Protecting One's Turf: Social Strategies for Maintaining Urban Neighborhoods.* Lanham, MD: University Press of America.

Domínguez, Silvia. 2004. "Estrategias de movilidad social." *Araucaria* 5: 92-128.

———. 2008. "Race Relations and Immigration in Boston." *Footnotes: A Publication of the American Sociological Association* 36, no. 6: Front page.

———. 2011. *Getting Ahead: Social Mobility, Public Housing and Immigrant Networks.* New York: New York University Press.

Domínguez, Silvia, and Celeste Watkins. 2003. "Creating Networks for Survival and Mobility: Social Capital among African American and Latin-American Low Income Mothers." *Social Problems* 50:111-35.

Drake, St. Clair, and Horace Cayton. 1945. *Black Metropolis.* New York: Harcourt, Brace.

Fernández-Kelly, Maria P. 1995. "Social and Cultural Capital in the Urban Ghetto: Implications for Economic Sociology and Immigration." In *The Economic Sociology of Immigration: Essays on Networks, Ethnicity, and Entrepreneurship*, edited by Alejandro Portes. New York: Russell Sage Foundation.

Frey, William, and Reynolds Farley. 1996. "Latino, Asian, and Black Segregation in U.S. Metropolitan Areas: Are Multiethnic Metros Different?" *Demography* 33 (1): 35-50.

Green, Donald P., Dara Z. Strolovitch, and Janelle S. Wong. 1998. "Defended Neighborhoods, Integration, and Racially Motivated Crime." *American Journal of Sociology* 104 (2): 372-403.

Greenberg, Stephanie. 1981. "Industrial Location and Ethnic Residential Patterns in an Industrializing City." In *Philadelphia: Work, Space, Family, and Group Experience in the Nineteenth Century*, edited by Theodore Hershberg, 204-32. New York: Oxford University Press.

Hart, Jordana. 1994. "Three Women Assaulted near South Boston Project." *Boston Globe*, July 11.

Ignatiev, Noel. 1995. *How The Irish Became White*. New York: Routledge.

Katz, Michael. 1990. *The Undeserving Poor: From the War on Poverty to the War on Welfare*. New York: Pantheon Books.

Lehr, Dick, and Gerard O'Neill, G. 2000. *Black Mass: The Irish Mob, the FBI, and a Devil's Deal*. New York: PublicAffairs.

Levin, Jack, and Jack McDevitt. 1993. *Hate Crimes: The Rising Tide of Bigotry and Bloodshed*. New York: Pantheon Press.

Levine, Robert A., and Donald T. Campbell. 1972. *Ethnocentrism*. New York: Wiley.

Lukas, J. Anthony. 1985. *Common Ground: A Turbulent Decade in the Lives of Three American Families*. New York: Vintage Books.

MacDonald, Michael Patrick. 1999. *All Souls: A Family Story from Southie*. New York: Ballantine.

Maly, Michael T. 2005. *Beyond Segregation: Multiracial and Multiethnic Neighborhoods in the United States*. Philadelphia: Temple University Press.

Marantz, Steve. 1990. "Racial Data Given by BHA: Most Complaints Are in South Boston." *Boston Globe*, August 23.

Menjívar, Cecilia. 2000. *Fragmented Ties: Salvadoran Immigrant Networks in America*. Berkeley: University of California Press.

New York Times. 1989. "Housing Drive for Blacks Ordered in Boston." June 28.

O'Connor, Thomas. 1998. *South Boston, My Hometown: A History of an Ethnic Neighborhood*. Boston: Northeastern University Press.

Portes, Alejandro. 1998. "Social Capital: Its Origins and Applications in Modern Sociology." *Annual Review of Sociology* 24:1-24.

Pulio, Stephen. 2007. *The Boston Italians: A Story of Pride, Perseverance, and Paesani, from the Years of the Great Immigration to the Present Day*. New York: Beacon Press.

Putnam, Robert. D. 1993. "The Prosperous Community: Social Capital and Public Life." *American Prospect* 4 (13): 35-42.

Rezendez, Michael. 1992. "Shots at Black Man Lead Flynn to Revive Civil Rights Cabinet." *Boston Globe*, December 3.

Rieder, Jonathan. 1985. *Canarsie: The Jews and Italians of Brooklyn against Liberalism*. Cambridge, MA: Harvard University Press.

Sampson, Robert J., Stephen Raudenbush, and Felton Earls. 1997. "Neighborhoods and Violent Crime: A Multi-Level Study of Collective Efficacy." *Science* 277:918-24.

Small, M. L. 2009. *Unanticipated Gains: Origins of Network Inequality in Everyday Life*. New York: Oxford University Press.

Suttles, Gerald D. 1972. *The Social Construction of Communities*. Chicago: University of Chicago Press.

Vale, Lawrence. 2000. *From the Puritans to the Projects: Public Housing and Public Neighbors*. Cambridge, MA: Harvard University Press.

Waters, Mary C. 2001. "Second Generation Assimilation Experiences in a Majority-Minority City." Paper presented at the Host Societies and the Reception of Immigrants Conference, Weatherhead Center for International Affairs, May 10-12, Cambridge, MA.

Zhou, Min, and Carl L. Bankston III. 1996. "Social Capital and the Adaptation of Second Generation: The Case of Vietnamese Youth in New Orleans." *International Migration Review* 28:821-45.

161

Fostering Diversity

Mexican Americans and Environmental Justice

Change and Continuity in Mexican American Politics

Benjamin Marquez

The three decades after World War II were a period of unparalleled economic growth. Income, production, and consumption increased at a rapid pace along with the problems of hazardous waste disposal. By the 1970s, a full-fledged environmental movement emerged in response to the dangers posed by pollution to human health and the ecosystem. Thousands of groups across the country worked to eliminate, clean up, and prevent toxic pollution, but there was little discussion of the possibility that racial and ethnic minorities might bear disproportionate environmental burdens (Rhodes 2003, 52). The United Church of Christ's Commission for Racial Justice sounded the alarm over disproportionate exposure to environmental hazards in 1987 with the publication of *Toxic Wastes and Race in the United States*. The massive national study found that unequal environmental burdens existed and that racial and ethnic minorities were shut out of the decision-making process for environmental policy. When the first environmental cleanup campaigns led by people of color took place in the 1980s, a new strand of environmental activism had emerged, one that considered environmental pollution to be a form of racial discrimination. Built upon the ideals of the civil rights movement, environmental justice activists argued that people of color suffered disproportionate exposure to environmental hazards because of racist dumping practices and the economic vulnerability of their communities. Like racism in housing, education, or employment, the harm minorities suffered from environmental pollution was linked to racial inequalities in power and wealth (Bullard 1990; Lee 1992; Szasz 1991).

The growing militancy of environmental justice activists set the new movement on a collision course with Anglo-dominated environmental groups, most of which ignored the question of race and the environment (Cole and Foster 2001, 30). In early 1990, disagreements between the two camps erupted into a highly publicized conflict. That year, Mexican American environmental activists joined their African and Native American counterparts in a rebuke of the environmental establishment. In a widely circulated letter, environmental justice activists accused groups like the

Sierra Club, the Audubon Society, the Wilderness Society, and the National Resources Defense Council of racism and complicity with the country's worst polluters (Moore et al. 1990; Martinez 1992). They further charged that America's largest environmental groups had evolved into staff-based organizations with no meaningful grassroots accountability.[1] They argued that the traditional environmental movement was little more than groups of white middle-class people more interested in maintaining pristine outdoor recreational areas than tackling the problems people of color faced in their own homes. Pesticide use on commercial farms, illegal dumping in inner-city neighborhoods, mining tailings on Native American reservations, and lead paint poisoning in aging homes rarely caught the attention of the environmental establishment. These Anglo-dominated organizations, according to the letter, were instead accepting money from the country's worst polluters, thereby legitimating their practices in minority communities. Finally, the letter charged that Anglo-dominated environmental organizations were oblivious to the cultural significance of the land and water to Native and Mexican Americans, and to their theft and contamination, accompanied by and resulting in "the murder of innocent people" (Moore et al. 1990).

A firestorm of controversy followed the break with white environmentalists, but the split was inevitable, for environmental justice advocates were already at work building new organizations and communication networks. The process culminated in the 1991 First National People of Color Environmental Justice Leadership Summit, which brought seven hundred activists together to formulate strategies for combating environmental dangers in their communities (Cole and Foster 2001, 31–32). Mexican Americans were key players at the summit, as they had been in the formation of their own regional network of environmental justice organizations. A year earlier, the South West Organizing Project in Albuquerque, New Mexico (SWOP), had convened the Regional Activist Dialogue, a gathering of minority environmental activists from Asian, African American, and Native organizations to discuss the creation of a network to serve their common interests (Moore 1992). The meeting attracted 141 activists representing fifty-seven environmental groups, labor unions, and Native American tribes from all five southwestern states as well as Utah, Nevada, and Oklahoma. The discussions held at the gathering convinced them of the need to formalize their ties by creating the Southwest Network for Environmental and Economic Justice (SNEEJ) (Moore 1992; SNEEJ 1992a, 1992b). The idea was to create an information clearinghouse, build the capacity of existing organizations, and, eventually, coordinate their work. To create a base upon which the network could grow, SNEEJ established a central office in Albuquerque. By 2000, the network had a paid staff and a membership of eighty independent organizations that regularly met to exchange information and utilize SNEEJ training facilities.

A new kind of political entity had been created, but one deeply rooted in the civil rights movement. Indeed, SNEEJ's founders were veteran activists who had fought for equal civil rights during the Chicano movement in the 1960s. They understood the environmental threat faced by Mexican Americans as a heightened and continuing problem. SNEEJ's executive director, Richard Moore, argued that the ideology and disruptive tactics of the Chicana/o movement were necessary to solve the environmental hazards facing people of color. The same structure of power that produced police brutality, lack of affordable health care, low-quality education, poverty, and Anglo cultural hegemony brought environmental hazards and people of color in close proximity (Moore and Head 1994). Another lesson drawn from the civil rights movement was the concept of coalition building among people of color. The new, multiracial network that came together in the 1990s was not an alliance of convenience but the expression of the belief that people of color stood apart from the rest of American society. The details of each group's history were different, but racism and economic exploitation were common elements, as manifested by the concentration of environmental hazards in minority communities. Populations affected, according to a SNEEJ statement, included "immigrant communities fighting the placement and operation of dangerous incinerators and landfills, farm workers being poisoned by pesticides, garment workers impacted by plant closings, communities poisoned by industrial pollution, Native Americans threatened with or already paying the costs associated with uranium mining and militarism, Asian/Pacific Islander, Latina, and Mexicana, 'high tech' workers being poisoned on the job, and Chicano and African American communities suffering from severe lead poisoning" (SNEEJ n.d.).

SNEEJ politics has been couched in a deep distrust of Anglo-dominated institutions. For these activists, the problems facing Mexican Americans in the Southwest are a continuation of the first European colonialists' plan to exploit the people of the Southwest and the land's resources. Thus the demand for environmental justice rests, in part, on their collective identity as indigenous people who were colonized by European settlers (Perez 2002; Sierra 2003). SNEEJ affiliates mobilize around other issues, such as pollution in the semiconductor industry, unemployment, garbage collection, public health delivery, and transportation. They have lobbied to ensure governments' and corporations' accountability for their actions, but harbor few illusions that they will be treated fairly (Quiroz 1999). They argue that people of color suffer under long-standing, racist land use policies designed to segregate Mexican Americans in polluted industrial areas. Any gains they realize through interest group lobbying are perceived as small relative to the damage inflicted on indigenous people (Sierra 2004).

Some observers thought that SNEEJ's attacks on white environmentalists were unnecessarily antagonistic to potential allies, especially because groups like the Sierra Club responded to the criticisms by initiating the hiring of minority staff and filing legal briefs on behalf of minority plaintiffs. But the problem as perceived by southwestern environmental leaders was that mainstream groups refused to form partnerships based on mutual respect and accountability and thus perpetuated racial inequality (Moore and Head 1994). Ultimately, differences arose because of the assumptions each held about life and politics in the United States. According to environmental justice activists, mainstream environmentalists abstracted the ecosystem from economic and racial hierarchies. They argued that mainstream groups saw humanity as "as a homogeneous mass: if one benefits, all benefit. To judge by the literature of mainstream environmental organizations, there are no poor or rich, no black or white, just polluters and defenders, land or fauna to protect, a single, generic humankind to consider" (Rhodes 2003, 30). SNEEJ's activists pointed out that their work revolved around environmental problems that rarely affect white, middle-class families: illegal dumping, slaughterhouses, sewage treatment plants, lead paint poisoning, commercial pesticide use, and dangerous working conditions.

The SNEEJ activists argue for a more radical, politically comprehensive understanding of race, poverty, and the environment. Operating in urban and rural communities, Mexican American environmental activists have affiliates in every southwestern state. Rejecting conventional notions about coalition building around neutral, non–racially specific issues, the network brings race and culture to the center of its organizing strategy (Alinsky 1971; Wilson 1990). SNEEJ activists have concluded that race, nationality, and class are the central determinates of social stratification in the United States, an argument with a long history in Mexican American politics (Marquez 2000). However, SNEEJ activists are the first significant group of Mexican American activists to expand this notion by building a multiracial, transnational network of organizations. This innovative understanding of community places race and culture at the center of their political strategies, a position long advocated by leading organizers of color (Delgado 1994; Sen 2003).

Origins of the Mexican American Environmental Justice Movement

One of the first Mexican American organizations to launch an environmental justice campaign in the post–civil rights era was SWOP. Founded in 1981, SWOP was created by activists who cut their political teeth during the Chicano movement and saw the need to organize along a broad spectrum of interrelated issues. Their goals were "racial and gender equality and social and economic justice." To that end, the organization worked on projects such as voter registration drives, after-school care, housing, and cultural preservation. However, in 1986, SWOP won its most significant victory. That year the group organized residents of Northwest Albuquerque against Ponderosa Products, a local particleboard plant. Community members had long complained about noxious odors, contaminants in the water supply, and loud noises generated by the plants' saws and heavy machinery. Rebuffed by the company's management, SWOP activists worked with neighborhood residents to monitor the plant's emissions and bring their case to the larger public. SWOP activists also pursued the case in the courts, where they demonstrated that Ponderosa Products had violated multiple state and federal environmental laws. Within a year, SWOP, Ponderosa Products, and the State of New Mexico reached an accord whereby the corporation agreed to clean up the groundwater contaminated with formaldehyde, nitrate, and nitrogen. The company also agreed to install air and noise pollution control devices so that they would comply with New Mexico environmental standards (Kimball 1987, 1989; P. Robinson 1989).[2]

In the late 1980s and early 1990s, Mexican American environmental justice organizations emerged in other parts of the country. In 1991, a landmark environmental justice campaign took place in East Austin, Texas, a poor Mexican and African American community. The local environmental justice group People Organized in Defense of the Earth and Her Resources (PODER) initiated a drive against the East Austin Tank Farm, a fifty-two-acre gasoline distribution system where ten million gallons of gasoline were stored. Fuel piped in from nearby refineries was picked up by truck and then distributed to service stations throughout the Austin area. At issue was the air and water pollution created by the gasoline and chemical spills as well as the traffic hazard generated when large amounts of gasoline were trucked through the neighborhood every day. Area residents suffered from headaches and nausea because of the fumes. Others claimed that their well water was not fit to drink and, in some cases, killed the grass in their yards. PODER drew skeptical responses when its activists announced that the only solution they would accept was complete disassembly and removal of the tanks. PODER was a small, underfunded community organization, while the offending facilities were owned by some of the largest oil companies in the world: Chevron, Star Enterprises, Mobil, Exxon, Citgo, and Coastal Refining and Marketing had storage tanks on the East Austin site. Moreover, because the facilities had been in the area since World War II they were exempt from many environmental statutes.

The sequence of events that led to the eventual removal of the East Austin Tank Farm presented a model of successful environmental justice activism. PODER activists began by thoroughly researching the practices at the fuel storage area and enumerating the health risks the tanks posed. They kept careful records of the deadly chemicals released at the facility and studied laws governing their use (Almanza and Diaz ca. 1994). They launched a public relations campaign and brought groups of public officials and representatives from sympathetic organizations to tour the area and see the environmental damage firsthand. Finally, the group launched a legal strategy that proved to be indispensable to their success. After documenting instances where the oil giants had violated state and federal environmental laws, PODER pressured the Texas Water Commission and Air Control Board to investigate the oil companies' storage practices. Tests conducted on area groundwater found contamination in 71 of 116 area test wells, with one well having seven hundred times the acceptable limit for benzene (Shattuck 1998). It was further revealed that the oil companies had violated state and federal laws by illegally expanding the capacity of their tanks and failing to report chemical and gasoline spills. The negative publicity, PODER's political pressure, and the threat of substantial fines finally forced all the oil giants to leave (Ward 1992a, 1992b; Enos 1992; Johnson and Ward 1992; Wright 1992; Ward and Wright 1993).

Other groups pursued similar strategies and enjoyed comparable successes in the 1990s. In Arizona, Tucsonians for a Clean Environment (TCE) successfully sued Hughes Aircraft and the U.S. Air Force. Over a period of twenty-five years Hughes Aircraft had dumped over 1,250,000 gallons of toxic fluids into thirty-three acres of unlined holding ponds and evaporation beds in the desert (Fillipi and Zuroski 1988, 3, 12). The chemicals were linked to unusually high occurrences of cancer, multiple sclerosis, systemic lupus, liver disease, and central nervous system damage among barrio residents. The uncontrolled dumping was conducted on such a vast scale for so long a period that the connection to the health problems in the community was clear. In a suit initiated by TCE, 1,620 victims of the Hughes Aircraft waste disposal practices received an $85.5 million settlement for their suffering (*Arizona Star* 1992; Bodfield-Mandeville 1992; Bagwell 1991).

In another struggle that spanned more than a decade, African and Mexican American activists fought to eliminate a lead poisoning hazard in West Dallas, Texas. Residents organized under the West Dallas Coalition for Environmental Justice successfully sued the RSR Corporation, which had been recovering lead from used automobile batteries and other materials since 1934. The lawsuits brought by the coalition and the Texas attorney general resulted in the closing of the plant and a multi-million-dollar cleanup in 1986 (Bullard 1990; R. Robinson 1994). With the discovery of high lead blood levels in community residents, the West Dallas Coalition brought a class action suit against the RSR Corporation that recovered $20 million in damages linked to the company's smelting and dumping practices (Colquette and Robertson 1991; MacLachlan 1992).

PODER added to its list of accomplishments in the late 1990s the removal of a Browning Ferris Incorporated (BFI) glass and newspaper recycling plant from the east side of town. The plant was targeted as a hazard because it scattered paper for miles, attracted vermin, and once erupted into flames. Through direct negotiation with BFI and local officials, the Austin City Council changed the zoning designation of the land surrounding the plant, thus forcing it to move. That struggle took seven years (Staff 1998).

Finally, the Mothers of East Los Angeles (MELA) had a steady stream of environmentally related successes that protected area residents from increased traffic and environmental pollution. They successfully stopped the construction of a new prison, toxic waste incinerators, chemical processing plants, and an aboveground oil pipeline in East Los Angeles (Colquette and Robertson 1991; Pardo 1990).

The Dual Agenda

Mexican American environmental activists successfully overcame tremendous obstacles when shaping environmental policy. However, the obstacles to achieving greater economic equality were formidable. In 1991, the SNEEJ network launched what would become its longest and most bitterly contested campaign, the Electronics Industry Good Neighbor Campaign. The campaign called for a greater scrutiny of the industry's production techniques and a redistribution of its profits (Paterson 1991; Franco 1992). Centered in Austin, San Jose, Phoenix, and Albuquerque, it targeted primarily companies like Sematech, Intel, Advanced Micro Devices, Applied Materials, and Motorola for their pollution of the environment. Moreover, activists pointed out that these large corporations were enriching themselves at the expense of the poor by receiving generous subsidies from the state. States were subsidizing the electronics industry even as few of its high-paying jobs went to local residents and little of its profits was reinvested in community projects. The demand was for the electronics industry to behave in a socially responsible manner. In practical terms, activists in Austin and Albuquerque wanted the industry to invest in neighborhood development, pay its production workers higher salaries, and provide job training for residents with few skills (Walsh 1993).

The expansion of the electronics industry in the Southwest has been particularly irksome to environmental activists in New Mexico. In their minds, the industry epitomizes everything indigenous people have struggled against since the first European settlers arrived. Like the first North American colonizers, electronics firms have come to New Mexico in search of cheap land, resources, and labor. However, this new wave of colonialism is also an unprecedented assault on indigenous culture. The production of computer chips requires a large amount of one highly symbolic resource—water. Water is scarce in New Mexico, and the cooperative arrangements of water usage that native people created to survive in a harsh climate became part of Hispano culture. The computer industry's demand for substantial levels of water resources infuriated SWOP's activists when it was revealed that the Intel Corporation would consume so much water that the water table would be lowered to the point where the wells on small ranches and farms might run dry (Moore and Head 1994). According to SWOP, "More recently, multi-national corporations like Intel and Royal Philips have come to New Mexico promising jobs in exchange for government subsidies, weak environmental laws and scarce resources. New Mexico communities gain little from these investments. The state continues to become poorer" (SWOP 2002). To dramatize their critique, SWOP announced a yearly "Corporate Welfare Award" to recognize politicians and corporations who have demonstrated "leadership in obtaining or approving subsidies and tax abatements." In 1998, the computer giant Intel was awarded their "Lifetime Achievement Award" for its accomplishments (Marquez 2003, 40).

The Electronics Industry Good Neighbor Campaign is an ongoing project with ambitious goals, but thus far it has gained little political traction. Similiar to their previous campaigns, PODER and SWOP have faced united opposition from industry when they have called for community investment. This time, however, opposition has come from groups that sided with environmental justice activists in the past. Local official leaders have feared that the firms under attack would migrate to areas of the country with fewer environmental restrictions and a less politically active population. Conservative Mexican American leaders have added to the chorus of opposition by citing the employment opportunities generated by the electronics industry. Albuquerque and Austin high-tech firms have also been adept at public relations campaigns that tout their contribution to the local economy. In contrast to past successful fights, this one has featured no legal avenues for environmental activists to pursue. The corporations targeted by SNEEJ affiliates have accepted subsidies approved by local officials or public referendum. Finally, the targeted electronics companies have become more careful about violating environmental statutes that might render them vulnerable to attack by activist groups. This strategy, along with a determination to vigorously resist claims of bias in the courts, has undermined one of the environmental justice movement's most powerful tools.

Future of the Mexican American Environmental Justice Movement

Mexican American environmental activists can look back on their first decade of work with pride. They were proactive, arguably as effective in their campaigns as mainstream environmental organizations. They utilized existing statutes and regulatory processes to their advantage to halt the construction of waste dumps and reprocessing plants near minority neighborhoods, remove existing environmental threats, and hold powerful industrial polluters accountable for their actions. In some instances they consolidated their gains into a lasting presence in community politics. Some Mexican American environmental justice organizations are now a mainstay in local politics. For example, after MELA handed the governor of California and the waste disposal industry a surprising defeat in 1990 by stopping the construction of a string of waste disposal incinerators, the group moved to consolidate its gains. MELA is now part of an alliance of elected officials, black community organizations, and environmental groups like Greenpeace and the Sierra Club that monitor environmental politics in their community. It has also expanded the scope of its work by becoming involved in campaigns for improved educational opportunities, accessible health care, water conservation, and increased police protection (*Precinct Reporter* 2003; Pleasant 2002; *Los Angeles Sentinel* 1998; Pardo 1998).

Affiliate members of SNEEJ have demonstrated a remarkable tenacity. After the initial splash of activism, environmental justice work has become part of the political landscape in many southwestern communities. In New Mexico, SWOP is still monitoring Intel to hold the corporation accountable for chemicals it releases into the air and demanding compensation for negative health impacts (SWOP 2002). The group works with individuals living in rural small towns to organize, conduct surveys, monitor local polluters, and establish working relationships with local officials (Rodriguez 2001). More recently it has conducted voter registration drives in an attempt to elect public officials more sympathetic to its values (Fraire 2004). In Austin, PODER has worked on such issues as removal of recycling plants and prevention of the construction of unwanted facilities like a horse track or condominiums that would gentrify the neighborhood. More recently, the group eliminated another East Austin environmental hazard, an electrical power plant. (Almanza 2003; PODER 2007).

But social change does not proceed along a steady, predictable path, and more recently, with some exceptions, there have been few dramatic, high-profile victories comparable to those in the 1990s. Some important political developments of the new millennium have made the work of environmental justice activists far more difficult. The first is the fact that industries have become more careful about avoiding bad publicity and litigation. Corporations conducting business in poor, minority neighborhoods now take the necessary legal and public relations steps to avoid any legal vulnerability and to insulate themselves from the public relations damage that comes from an environmental racism accusation (Pitney Hardin 2002; Spiesman 2003). The most significant environmental justice wins came about through corporate arrogance and the assumption that minority communities would remain passive receptacles of hazardous waste. While more conscientious corporate behavior is a desired goal, a drop in blatant violations of environmental regulations deprives environmental justice groups of the leverage many used against wealthy and powerful polluters (Cole and Foster 2001, 1-9).

A second, related development is the loss of some important legal tools. Recent Supreme Court rulings have made it extraordinarily difficult for environmental justice activists to pressure or force polluters to alter their behavior through civil rights litigation. Section 602 of Title VI of the Civil Rights Act of 1964 provides that "no person . . . shall on the ground of race, color, or national origin be excluded from participation in, be denied the benefits of, or be subjected to discrimination under any program or activity receiving Federal financial assistance." Since this act was adopted the Supreme Court established some limitations against claiming discrimination in environmental cases, in that plaintiffs must prove intent to discriminate. The Third Circuit Court of Appeals used similar reasoning in 2002 to strike down almost thirty years of Environmental Protection Agency disparate-impact regulations (McNamara 2002).

Legal action can be brought under Title VI against an entity to prevent the granting of a construction permit or to prevent permit renewal, but it cannot be used to compensate communities for past injuries of exposure to pollutants. Minority communities suffering from a history of exposure to environmental hazards will have to pursue common-law claims of negligence and nuisance. Industry cannot be subject to litigation or sanctions unless damage can be proven to be deliberate and systematic. Charges of intentional discrimination may be admissible in court if the record reveals that a company's facilities were located only in minority communities (Yamada 1998; Dickerson 1999). The reality is that now most environmental justice claims will have to be conducted in the courts within the constraints of existing laws and court actions (Harding and Mehan 1998).

Environmental racism continues to be a potent political argument against the construction or operation of hazardous facilities in minority communities, but fewer and fewer of those claims have succeeded in the courts. Thus environmental justice activists find it much more difficult to win restitution for those harmed by pollution. Although the charge of disparate impact is not the only effective strategy environmental justice activists can pursue, a powerful legal tool was eliminated when the courts began demanding proof of intentional discrimination in the siting of hazardous waste facilities. As of 2003, no plaintiffs had succeeded in establishing discriminatory intent in an environmental justice case (Gerrard 2003, 3). Environmental justice activists can pressure state or local government to investigate claims of systemic discrimination. However, many find this strategy less productive as the current conservative atmosphere renders local officials increasingly uncooperative (Egan 2004; Guzzi 2004;

Viederman 2004). Even the Environmental Protection Agency has a long-standing bureaucratic culture hostile to environmental justice claims. As Rhodes (2003) observed, the EPA is still "dominated, regardless of the party in power in the White House, by professionals who come from a culture that is wanting in sensitivity to social justice. To incorporate a concept such as environmental justice into the EPA's operational reality, its leaders may have to first recognize the internal institutional and cultural barriers working against this change" (90). The legal and administrative obstacles to claims about disproportionate risk are daunting but not insurmountable. Numerous legal theories can be applied in such cases, and important precedents have been set. Nevertheless, each new case will require expert counsel, ample resources, and time (Gerrard and Foster 2008).

Finally, environmental activists have to contend with the barriers of class. Corporate entities can wear down activists in long-term struggles or, as in the case of the Electronics Industry Good Neighbor Campaign, ignore them altogether. As SNEEJ activists themselves state, they are struggling against a vast array of environmental and economic problems facing communities of color. Thus the stunning victories of the 1990s may have masked a larger disadvantage facing their communities. For example, the success of Mexican and African American activists in West Dallas in ridding their neighborhood of a lead poisoning threat was, in light of the total environmental threat, merely a first step. In their analysis of the campaign against lead poisoning in West Dallas, Macey and Susskind (2001) credit the sustained efforts of local organizers for the removal of a major environmental hazard from their neighborhood: "For decades a symbol of neglect by industry and agency officials, the RSR smelter smokestack [in addition to smelter site buildings] has finally been removed, brick by brick, from the West Dallas skyline." However, they go on to observe that removing the factory and its contaminated soil was only one small step, since "countless industries remain in operation in West Dallas, scattered among single-family homes."

SNEEJ is an important network of social movement organizations, and Mexican Americans are key players in its work. Mexican American environmental justice advocates are rooted simultaneously in a long history of cultural nationalism and in contemporary multiracial American society. They claim an indigenous identity and call for racial solidarity, two themes common to many Mexican American organizations. At the same time, they have been theoretically and organizationally innovative the way they have interwoven Mexican American cultural and political goals with those of other people of color. The SNEEJ coalition is first and foremost a united front of African Americans, Asian/Pacific Islander Americans, Latino Americans, and Native Americans. Significantly, they envision a coalition that includes poor, working-class Anglos, but it is incumbent upon people of color to organize their communities independently of those working relationships. The coalition also includes workers of Mexico, Latin America, and the Third World. The problems faced by people of color are racism, the threat of culture loss, and world capitalism's relentless demand for cheap labor and raw materials.

These problems require a change in the organization of the workforce and the distribution of profits, an imposition of new terms and conditions under which local industry will operate in Mexican American communities. As a condition for utilizing indigenous resources and labor, local communities should be guaranteed job training for individuals, well-paying jobs, and a clean and safe workplace. Ultimately, solutions to the adverse conditions under which people of color live must be community based. Successful resistance to Spanish and later Anglo-American colonialism hinged on community solidarity, a phenomenon made possible by a shared culture and deep attachments to the land (Prindeville 2004). Today, Mexican American advocates for environmental justice continue to argue that increased air and water pollution, unemployment, and the disruption of community are the by-products of the free market and racism. In the end, social justice cannot be achieved where white privilege persists and institutionalized racial hierarchies distort power relations between groups.

The near-term prospects are not good for SNEEJ activists even as evidence mounts that people of color suffer disproportionately from exposure to hazardous waste and toxic storage and disposal facilities (Pastor, Sadd, and Hipp 2001; Atlas 2002; Pastor, Sadd, and Morello-Frosch 2004; Mohai and Saha 2006; Campbell, Peck, and Tschudi 2010). The rightward drift of American politics, sophisticated tactics utilized by industry, and a diminished set of legal tools will continue to hobble their work in the foreseeable future. But although the dramatic victories SNEEJ affiliates scored in the 1990s are unlikely to be repeated, veteran environmental justice activists are committed long-term residents of their communities with a personal as well as a political will to persevere. The senior leadership is made up of veteran organizers who developed their skills during the civil rights era and brought their experience to SNEEJ. Like the younger generation of activists whom they have trained and mentored, the senior leadership argues that today's environmental threat is neither new nor unique. The issue is power and the struggle for control of the environment and control of productive forces. All environmental justice organizing is concentrated at the local level where people live and raise their families. Still, bringing pressure to bear on high-tech firms to comply with existing environmental law is difficult for small, resource-poor community groups. Challenging the power and privilege of business owners to invest, design production, and take profits as they choose will require more political power than environmental justice groups currently possess. SNEEJ's regional network of organizations has set the stage for further organizational capacity, but its task of building regional and eventually national power is daunting, and many feel that people of color face "an uncertain economic and political future (Leon Guerrero 2003).

NOTES

1 A similar critique was made in 1993 by a major PR executive for pesticide makers, E. Bruce Harrison, who described the large environmental organizations as bloated bureaucracies dependent upon mass mailings and the largesse of polluting corporations to fund their day-to-day operations (Rampton and Stauber 2000).

2 The Settlement Agreement between Ponderosa Products, Inc. and the Environmental Health Department of the City of Albuquerque, State of New Mexico, was completed on March 6, 1989.

REFERENCES

Alinsky, Saul D. 1971. *Rules for Radicals: A Practical Primer for Realistic Radicals.* New York: Vintage Books.

Almanza, Susana. 2003. Interview by David Todd. October 16. Transcript. Conservation History Association of Texas, Texas Legacy Project. www.texaslegacy.org/bb/transcripts/almanzasusanatxt.html.

Almanza, Susana, and Antonio Diaz. ca. 1994. "PODER: East Austin Tank Farm Victory." Unpublished manuscript.

Arizona Star. 1992. "Federal Officials to Hear TCE Concerns." July 14.

Atlas, Mark. 2002. "There Goes the Neighborhood: Environmental Equity and the Location of New Hazardous Waste Management Facilities." *Policy Studies Journal* 30 (2): 171-92.

Bagwell, Keith. 1991. "Groups Seek Backers in Push for New TCE Suit." *Arizona Daily Star*, May 25.

Bodfield-Mandeville, Rhonda. 1992. "Environmental Racism Stirs Activism." *Tucson Citizen*, August 1.

Bullard, Robert, D. 1990. *Dumping in Dixie: Race, Class, and Environmental Quality.* Boulder, CO: Westview Press.

Campbell, Heather E., Laura R. Peck, and Michael K. Tschudi. 2010. "Justice for All? A Cross-Time Analysis of Toxics Release Inventory Facility Location." *Review of Policy Research* 27 (1): 1-25.

Cole, Luke W., and Sheila R. Foster. 2001. *From the Ground Up: Environmental Racism and the Rise of the Environmental Movement.* New York: New York University Press.

Colquette, Kelly Michelle, and Elizabeth A. Henry Robertson. 1991. "Environmental Racism: The Causes, Consequences, and Recommendations." *Tulane Environmental Law Journal* 5 (1): 153-207.

Delgado, Gary. 1994. *Beyond the Politics of Place: New Directions in Community Organizing in the 1990s.* Oakland, CA: Applied Research Center.

Dickerson, Steven L. 1999. "Playing the Race Card: Environmental Justice Strengthened by Title VI Civil Rights." *Texas Lawyer*, March 29, 43.

Egan, Maretha. 2004. "Task Force or Task Farce?" *Voces Unidas* 14 (1-2): 6-7.

Enos, Craig. 1992. "30 Protest Exxon in E. Austin." *Daily Texan*, November 24.

Fillipi, Mark G., and Donn Zuroski. 1988. "Ground Water Monitoring Evaluation: Hughes Aircraft, U.S. Air Force Plant No. 44, Tucson, Arizona." U.S. Environmental Protection Agency, Region 9.

Fraire, Celia. 2004. "Mensaje a nuestros lectores: Message to Our Readers." *Voces Unidas* 14 (3): 2.

Franco, Aida. 1992. Interview by author. December 18. Albuquerque, NM.

Gerrard, Michael B. 2003. "The Law of Environmental Justice: Theories and Procedures to Address Disproportionate Risks." *New York Law Journal*, November 28, 3.

Gerrard, Michael B., and Sheila Foster, eds. 2008. *The Law of Environmental Justice: Theories and Procedures to Address Disproportionate Risks.* Chicago: American Bar Association Publishing.

Guzzi, Karina. 2004. "The Intel Pollution Problem." *Voces Unidas* 14 (1-2): 10-11.

Harding, Russell J., and G. Tracy Mehan. 1998. "EPA's 'Select Steel' Ruling: Is a Clearer Picture of 'Environmental Justice' Emerging?" *Washington Legal Foundation Legal Backgrounder* 13 (December 4).

Johnson, Michelle T., and Mike Ward. 1992. "$150,000 OK'd for Tank Farm Probe." *Austin American-Statesman*, May 20.

Kimball, Rene. 1987. "Sawmill Residents Claim Agencies Too Soft on Plant." *Albuquerque Journal*, January 29.

———. 1989. "Plant Reaches Anti-Pollution Pact with City." *Albuquerque Journal*, March 29.

Lee, Charles. 1992. "Toxic Waste and Race in the United States." In *Race and the Incidence of Environmental Hazards*, edited by Bunyan Bryant and Paul Mohai, 10-27. Boulder, CO: Westview Press.

Leon Guerrero, Michael. 2003. "Returning to Basics." *Voces Unidas* 13 (1/2): 8-11.

Los Angeles Sentinel. 1998. "Community Coalition to Discuss Health Care Crisis." October 21, A1.

Macey, Gregg P., and Lawrence E. Susskind. 2001. "The Secondary Effects of Environmental Justice Litigation: The Case of West Dallas Coalition for Environmental Justice v. EPA." *Virginia Environmental Law Journal* 20:431-77.

MacLachlan, Claudia. 1992. "Unto the Third Generation." *National Law Journal* 14, no. 3: S11.

Marquez, Benjamin. 2000. "Representation by Other Means: Mexican American and Puerto Rican Social Movement Organizations." *PS: Political Science and Politics* 33 (3): 541-46.

———. 2003. *Constructing Identities in Mexican-American Political Organizations: Choosing Issues, Taking Sides.* Austin: University of Texas Press.

Martinez, Elizabeth. 1992. "Notes on a Net That Works." *Crossroads* 26:2-3.

McNamara, Patrick J. 2002. "Environmental Justice: Injunction Stopping Issuance of Air Permit Thrown Out on Title VI Grounds." *Environmental Compliance and Litigation* 17 (8): 1.

Mohai, Paul, and Robin Saha. 2006. "Reassessing Racial and Socioeconomic Disparities in Environmental Justice." *Demography* 43 (2): 383-99.

Moore, Richard. 1992. "Confronting Environmental Racism." *Crossroads* (April): 6-8.

Moore, Richard, et al. 1990. Letter to Jay Hair, President, National Wildlife Federation. March 16. http://soa.utexas.edu/work/eaejp/PODER/Document2.pdf.

Moore, Richard, and Louis Head. 1994. "Building a Net That Works: SWOP." In *Unequal Protection*, edited by Robert Bullard, 191-206. San Francisco: Sierra Club Books.

Pardo, Mary. 1990. "Mexican American Grassroots Community Activists: 'Mothers of East Los Angeles.'" *Frontiers* 11 (1): 1-7.

———. 1998. *Mexican American Women Activists: Identity and Resistance in Two Los Angeles Communities.* Philadelphia: Temple University Press.

Pastor, Manuel, Jr., Jim Sadd, and John Hipp. 2001. "Which Came First? Toxic Facilities Minority Move-In and Environmental Justice." *Journal of Urban Affairs* 23 (1): 1-21.

Pastor, Manuel, Jr., James L. Sadd, and Rachel Morello-Frosch. 2004. "Waiting to Inhale: The Demographics of Toxic Air Release Facilities in 21st Century California." *Social Science Quarterly* 85 (2): 420-40.

People Organized in Defense of the Earth and Her Resources. 2007. "Victories." www.poder-texas.org/victories.html.

Perez, Roberto J. 2002. "Piden a Fox a negociar fronteras abiertas." *La Prensa* (San Antonio, TX), October 20, 6A.

Paterson, Kent. 1991. "High-Risk High-Tech." *Texas Observer,* January 29.

Pitney Hardin, Kip. 2002. "Environmental Justice: Meeting the Challenge." *Metropolitan Corporate Counsel*, February, 18.

Pleasant, Betty. 2002. "Hahn-Parks Conflict Picks Up Steam." *Los Angeles Sentinel*, February 21, A1.

PODER. See People Organized in Defense of the Earth and Her Resources.

Precinct Reporter (San Bernardino). 2003. "Parents and Teachers to Protect Smaller Class Size." March 13, 2.

Prindeville, Diane-Michele. 2004. "The Role of Gender, Race/Ethnicity, and Class in Activists' Perceptions of Environmental Justice." In *New Perspectives on Environmental Justice: Gender, Sexuality, and Activism*, edited by Rachel Stein, 93-108. New Brunswick: Rutgers University Press.

Quiroz, Julie 1999. "Tales from Three Cities: Organizing Race into Regionalism." *Colorlines* 2 (2): 19.

Rampton, Sheldon, and John Stauber. 2000. "Silencing Spring: Corporate Propaganda and the Takeover of the Environmental Movement." In *Reclaiming the Environmental Debate: The Politics of Health in a Toxic Culture,* edited by Richard Hofrichter, 157-75. Cambridge, MA: MIT Press.

Rhodes, Edwardo Lao. 2003. *Environmental Justice in America: A New Paradigm.* Bloomington: Indiana University Press.

Robinson, Paul. 1989. "Summary of Groundwater Cleanup Program at Ponderosa Products, April 1989, Sawmill Neighborhood, Albuquerque, New Mexico." Southwest Research and Information Center, Albuquerque, NM. May 2.

Robinson, Ronald. 1994. "West Dallas versus the Lead Smelter." In *Unequal Protection,* edited by Robert Bullard, 92-109. San Francisco: Sierra Club.

Rodriguez, Victoria. 2001. "Nitrates Found in Abo Valley." *Voces Unidas* 11 (3): 3, 8.

Sen, Rinku. 2003. *Stir It Up: Lessons in Community Organizing and Advocacy.* San Francisco: Jossey-Bass.

Shattuck, Jessica. 1998. "Susana Almanza: Putting Big Oil in Its Place." *Mother Jones,* November/December, 20-21.

Sierra, Javier. 2003. "En defensa propria." *Mundo Hispanico* 24 (642): 68.

———. 2004. "A Dirty Injustice." *Hispanic* 17 (May): 80.

Southwest Network for Environmental and Economic Justice. n.d. "History." www.sneej.org.history.htm (page no longer accessible).

———. 1992a. "List of Participants: SW Network 1992 Gathering." September 24-27, 1992. www.sneej.org (page no longer accessible).

———. 1992b. "SW Network for Environmental & Economic Justice Coordinating Council Meeting 6/18-20/92." www.sneej.org (page no longer accessible).

SNEEJ. See Southwest Network for Environmental and Economic Justice.

Southwest Organizing Project. 2001. "What Intel Says: 'We're a Good Corporate Neighbor.' How Intel Acts: Profits before People." *Voces Unidas* 11 (3): 7–8.

———. 2002. "Message to Readers: Another World Is Possible." *Voces Unidas* 11 (4): 2–5.

Spiesman, Thomas. 2003. "Surviving Environmental Justice Attacks." *New Jersey Law Journal,* October 20.

Staff, Jenny. 1998. "Eastside Discontent: Residents Lose Fight to Stop Expansion of Auto Parts Distributor." *Austin Chronicle,* September 18-24.

SWOP. See Southwest Organizing Project.

Szasz, Andrew. 1991. "In Praise of Policy Luddism: Strategic Lessons from the Hazardous Waste Wars." *Capitalism Nature Socialism* 2 (1): 17-43.

United Church of Christ Commission for Racial Justice. 1987. *Toxic Wastes and Race in the United States.* New York: Public Data Access.

Viederman, Steve. 2004. "The Power of Shareholding." *Voces Unidas* 14 (1/2): 16–17.

Walsh, Edward. 1993. "Backyards, NIMBY'S and Incinerator Sitings: Implications for Social Movement Theory." *Social Problems* 40 (1): 25-38.

Ward, Mike. 1992a. "Diesel Fuel Spilled at East Austin Tank Farm." *Austin American-Statesman,* November 17.

———. 1992b. "Regulators: Austin Gas Operators Continue Operating Despite Vapors." Texas Press Association, April 18.

Ward, Mike, and Scott W. Wright. 1993. "Exxon to Move Terminal." *Austin American-Statesman*, February 19.

Wilson, William J. 1990. *The Truly Disadvantaged: The Inner City, the Underclass, and Public Policy*. Chicago: University of Chicago Press.

Wright, Scott W. 1992. "Chevron Plans to Close Terminal in East Austin." *Austin American-Statesman*, August 27.

Yamada, Gerald H. 1998. "A Race Based Waste Case." *Legal Times*, July 1, S35.

After *Latino Metropolis*

Cultural Political Economy and Alternative Futures

Victor Valle and Rodolfo D. Torres

This essay makes a general case for grounding a twenty-first-century critical Latino urbanism in something we shall provisionally call "cultural political economy."[1] It makes that case by attempting to resolve lingering theoretical tensions between socioeconomic (structural) and culture-based (semiotic) approaches to our neoliberal present (Ribera-Fumaz 2009; Jessop and Oosterlynck 2008). This postdisciplinary interpretation reaffirms the centrality of capitalist formations in the study of the Latino urban question by embedding social and cultural categories in the lived spaces of our macroeconomic order. The kind of cultural political economy we posit strives for a theoretically and empirically useful analytic with which to approach the urban question for our changing times.

From the above approach, we sketch a few strategic lines to confront changing class formations and deindustrialization in neoliberal capitalism's period of indefinitely prolonged crisis. Our cursory review then explores the ways the current economic crisis implicates the scholarly projects of Latino and Chicano urban studies and how our interpretations of cultural political economy might reconfigure these projects to answer the continued attacks from the populist Right.

We picked up our critical thread by making explicit the theoretical themes we implied in *Latino Metropolis* (Valle and Torres 2000). This chapter responds to Torin Monahan's insightful review of *Latino Metropolis* (2002) by offering a more explicit statement of what he calls a postmodern political science in our attempt to represent our work in postdisciplinary theoretical terms. Our best recollections of more than a decade ago tell us that we wrote it to explore strategic political and discursive opportunities that Los Angeles offered as it emerged as a majority Mexican and Latino city. We argued then that the context in which the city reached this demographic tipping point was as important as its passage through the socioeconomic minefield of industrial transformation. For us, the maturation of a then hardly noticed transition to a post-Fordist mode of production in the nation's largest manufacturing center spelled the most important element of that irreducible difference. The emergence of a majority Latino immigrant working class in both the new manufacturing enterprises and the growing service sector was a symptom of a wrenching deindustrialization and reindustrialization of the region, a thoroughgoing reorganization of production in which neoliberal globalization imported the maquiladora model to those industrial sectors that were too expensive to relocate to Latin America or Asia. More important to the lived experiences of that emergent Latino working-class majority were the socioeconomic and cultural consequences of that new industrial order, its ever-harsher regime of growing class inequality, misery, and marginalization.

In formulating our argument, we tried to recognize the obvious: that the attainment of a supernumerary status would not guarantee diminished social inequalities so long as the region's symbolic economy continued to racialize, and therefore devalue, Latino immigrant labor. The means of cultural production, in other words, played a powerful role in reinforcing and reproducing the new social relations of post-Fordist production and its disciplinary requirements. We believed we saw, for example, subtle interactions between the recurring moral panics directed against illegal "alien" workers, the postmodern commodification of Mexican cuisine and ethnic tourist enclaves, and a huge restaurant industry that depended on the exploitation of a Latina and Latino immigrant workforce. We did not accept that decade's hegemonic symbiosis as the last word, however.

Instead, we tried to explore the ways in which a confluence of economic, political, and cultural changes meshed with the consolidation of a progressive Latino labor leadership and the day-to-day practices of Latino hybridity as aspects of a contestatory and pragmatic survival strategy in all the arenas of representations, including the practices of place-making. Making sense of these enmeshments, or what Marx called the metabolism of social and material conditions, required a degree of theoretical and methodological experimentation on our parts. Marx, after all, never developed a full-blown theorization of culture deduced from the logics of communicative processes. Instead, he saw the so-called "natural" environment as a seemingly endless, yet two-sided metabolic dialectic with humans, who, in modifying it, evolved new social relations to survive the environment they had changed.

That metabolism cannot function without the coordinating and interpretive cultural membrane through which human societies appraise, modify, and adapt to their environments: an approach to the symbolic order that Marx lacked, but intuited, when he proposed the logic of his biological metaphor. He brushed up against the symbolic order again when he acknowledged the seeming mysteries of the commodity fetish, an object of socially produced value that is nevertheless a bearer of multiple connotative secrets: "A commodity appears at first sight an extremely obvious, trivial thing. But its analysis brings out that it is a very strange thing, abounding in metaphysical subtleties and theological niceties" (Marx 1990, 163). Slavoj Zizek argues that the social relations that produce the commodity "fetish as a solid object" nevertheless carry within them the ideology that hides the social costs of the commodity's creation, a spectral parallel of pure "ideology" that hides the commodity's contradictions in plain sight. He convincingly uses the ways digital technology has taken the "dematerialization" of the money fetish, its transformations from gold bullion to paper currency to the transfer of the digital bank draft, to illustrate the extreme literalness with which these spectral transformations now occur, transformations that Marx would scarcely recognize. Our interpretation of the dematerialized fetish simply translates Zizek's notion of the "spectral aspect of capitalism" as one aspect of the cultural life of capitalism theorized from the more nuanced perspective of discourse and discursive practices (Zizek 2009, 301-2).

Our reading of the contributions of cultural studies has therefore led us to rethink Marx's biological metaphor and to look for the genealogies of social metabolism. Culture, in our version of this trope, functions as a medium and a by-product, a lived neural network and a physical archive of knowledge from which societies formulate and test new social forms and conceptual and material technology. Our formulation of culture does not distinguish between its resemblance to a living organism and its transformations into market commodities or technology. It tries instead to sense the organic life of culture in those moments when lived neural networks and the residues of the symbolic order obey the genetic and viral logics of language mutation. It proposes a conceptual language that tries to detect a dynamic process, namely those instances when the network's residues materialize in the archive of the known and knowable and blur the boundaries with which we try to distinguish the contaminating human trace from our idealized images of nature. The combined, synergistic effect of medium and residue can powerfully influence our social and so-called natural environments by exerting an inertial force that retards social adaptation to new environmental conditions or by generating new knowledge with which to transform those conditions. That the cultural function's dual aspects fill the seemingly minimal interstitial gap that articulates the linkage of the social to the material environment does not diminish its power. Great effects often occur at a seemingly microscopic scale, a subtlety that allows us to envision cultural processes occurring within an ecological model of the biosphere.

We could go further, arguing that living organisms cannot sustain themselves without mediating communicative systems, membranes if you will, through which they interact and do something that resembles learning from the environment. Human society, in such a reformulation, would then emerge in that place where the spheres of culture, political economy, and biology overlap, a triangular arrangement that situates the lived "materiality" of Henri Lefebvre's theorization of "the everyday" within an ecology of human and nonhuman communicative communities. (Lefebvre 2007, 32). Such a reframing would allow us to resituate Marx's notion of metabolism within the most recent theorizations of ecology and evolutionary biology, but that task taxes our theoretical abilities and clearly overstates the intentions we had in mind when we wrote *Latino Metropolis*, which was to slow the slide of cultural studies into irrelevancy.

We were more concerned then with recalibrating its formidable critical tools for a new task: building the conceptual equation that would balance the discursive and the structural material realities of globalized capital accumulation. What could Stuart Hall and Michel Foucault tell us, we asked ourselves, about the cultural-economic metabolism of post-Fordist political economy, and could we extrapolate a category that would fuse political economy and a critical theory of culture, a field since named *cultural political economy?* We tried, that is, to take the critical turn in the global metropolis seriously and to bring cultural critique to power and class relations as they occur in the globalized city, the messy, fluid, and densely meaningful place, and therefore the ideal arena in which to study the processes of globalization. We were also interested in the global city's radical cosmopolitanism, a space of lived hybridity in which the immigrant subject's virtuoso experimentation with that environment's multiple political and cultural codes fosters new ways of thinking and acting around, under, and beyond the nation-state's rigid categories.

That cosmopolitanism underlies the implicit logic of *Latino Metropolis*. We tried to express it by simultaneously running a positivist analytic alongside a critical interpretation in such a way as to give each a reciprocal role within an overarching interpretive construct, which, for us, was L.A.'s entire symbolic and built landscape. We felt that we could no longer talk about Latinos, the city's ethnic majority, without a totalizing theory of the city that could correlate a specific cultural process to every social relation within the context of market capitalism. Doing this required us to redirect cultural studies away from its then customary preoccupation with the subaltern subject and its myriad processes of identity formation. We believed that all subjectivities, including the varieties of "whiteness" embodied by the city's corporate elite, merited the critical gaze of cultural studies. If these critical approaches hold any validity, they should allow us to interpret identity formation for all social classes and racialized ethnicities, and to locate the cultural effects we theorized within the totality of existing social relations of late global capital.

We therefore sought the reciprocal translatability between analytic and critical approaches, between the dialectical and the genealogical, to identify those points of structural articulation where cultural effects were unambiguous. We also strove for an approach that would allow us to plot the intersection of spatial and temporal planes from which indigenous local memories and their subjective spaces erupt from global capital's urban matrix. The genealogical investigation of L.A.'s built environment that Valle explored after the publication of *Latino Metropolis* provided a powerful way to theorize the knowledge strands that construct a cultural political economy.

The City as Narrative Observatory

Michele Foucault's theory of "governmentality," however, provides one method of doing the improbable—identifying the knowledge strands that encode the global city's assembly instructions. Each of its knowledge strands began to be instrumentalized and codified as strains of governmental technology in the fifteenth and sixteenth centuries, when emerging European states used the administrative apparatus of the medieval justice system to organize new governmental offices. These relatively small institutional innovations began to "governmentalize" the state by increments (Foucault [1978] 1991, 102-3). Liberalism's eighteenth-century inauguration stimulated new government innovations to ensure the modern state's survival. Governments rapidly borrowed the new techniques of disciplining the populace it sent to the prisons, the hospitals, the factories, and the military. The new census-taking methodologies established a concrete basis for imagining and implementing a national political economy. Obtaining accurate counts of the population provided a practical way to monitor a nation's demographic wealth and health, and the material conditions and social relations that contributed to or detracted from its productivity.

As inventory-taking methods improved, it also became possible to monitor the lives of individual citizens. Birth and death certificates, school, tax, criminal, and military records, and a growing list of other documentary procedures allowed government to envision a state of perpetual surveillance, one initially devised for controlling prisoners and hospital patients but applied later to the full citizenry. Methods used to contain contagion in cities or reinforce the military chain of command also found their way into rationales for reorganizing government bureaucracies. Innovations in the surveillance and regulation of mental illness, sexuality, and female fertility allowed bureaucracies to narrow the application of that technology from the general populace to discrete social groups until focusing its gaze upon the body of the individual.

The modern state's tendency to apply these disciplinary techniques to different classes of objects led to another innovation: one could more thoroughly manipulate and disseminate the abstract discourse of the state by ascribing to it human corporeal qualities. The state's metonymic association with the body grew from an earlier metaphor—the medieval city as corporate or fictional person (Frug 1999, 31). Each innovation in governmental technology incrementally modified the state's forms and political rationality, a process that expanded the state's power while increasing its dependence on the invention and reorganization of existing governmental institutions to consolidate its gains and neutralize challenges to its authority.

In time, the proliferation of governmental functions and organs not only produced internal contradictions that undermined older governmental functions but revealed that the state did not possess a coherent, essential core of truth upon which it was based, only a collection of different and sometimes incompatible administrative techniques that the populace experienced as the unitary state. Foucault called the state's ever-changing governmental adaptations governmentality, or that "ensemble" of "institutions, procedures, analyses and . . . calculations and tactics that allow the exercise of this very specific albeit complex form of power, which has [the population] as its target, [political economy] as its principal form of knowledge, and [the apparatuses of security] as its essential technical means" (Foucault [1978] 1991, 102).

From the eighteenth century onward, the formerly distinct spheres of "government, population, and political economy" gradually fused into "a solid series" of social practices we today call the economy. Foucault's spectrum of effects theorized the production of wealth, the security of the state, and the control of the population as an integrated whole. However, rather than stress the Orwellian notion of a centralized state under the control of a single, all-knowing entity, Foucault envisioned the state as a field of effects generated by an ensemble of governmental technologies that naturalized that state's political hegemony. His theorization would allow others to more than simply speculate on the vague possibilities of a genealogy of the present. It would give those with sufficiently rich archives the means to identify and disentangle the governmental technologies that shape the state and its inhabiting subjectivities.

A key observation, one half-explained in *Latino Metropolis*, was the role capital plays, via its power to create and implement laws and generate and circulate its necessary truths, in re-creating the governmental technologies that generate the state "effect." (Valle would take the next step and make that formulation of the cultural technologies of capital accumulation explicit in his next book, *City of Industry: Genealogies of Power in Southern California* [2009].)

That was then, the more than a decade-old "then" of *Latino Metropolis*, in which we generally predicted the inevitability of our present economic collapse and resurgent anti-immigrant Latino hysteria. We recognized the potential for that crisis in the contradictions of a U.S. capitalist system that cannibalized itself in successive crisis of financialization rather than reinvest in the production of new wealth. We therefore recommended, given that these conditions were bound to recur and intensify, that Latino urban studies scholars and activist organizers accept coming social dislocation as a certainty they should plan for in their scholarship and praxis. We believe the economic meltdown of 2008 and its effects validate the continued pursuit of the scholarly project we envisioned for Latino urban studies: its interdisciplinarity as a field of study and its focus on interpreting the Latino working class within the totality of an urban landscape and experience.

The city, as the localized arena of global processes and changing class relations, is still the conceptual space in which to continue those experiments. The present-day context of economic collapse and resurgent anti-immigrant hysteria, however, also suggests that we remain vigilant to new possibilities of scholarly activism, that we look to the critical turn for more than monkey wrenches and cultural technologies of discontent. We should also consider using those tools to identify new opportunities of strategic urban intervention and to create moments of emancipatory rupture with which we might free ourselves to imagine another urban future in the space opened up by the social and cultural equivalent of a cosmological singularity.

Genealogy offers another way to revisit our revolutions for the lessons their successes and failures teach, for traces of the singularities that rupture and reset the clock of capitalist hegemony. We are not talking about reviving boring Stalinist hagiographies of worker heroes but of producing cultural genealogies of those settings in which emancipatory subjectivity erupted in specific individuals, social movements, or class formations.

The various genres of narrative art, whether written, performed, or lived, represent one way of observing and exploring the fusion of these spaces and subjectivities. Entering that narrative observatory requires the recovery of the seemingly disconnected stories Latinos and Latinas told themselves when they encountered each other and reinvented themselves in the sweatshops, boulevards, slaughterhouses, and movie houses of the last century, when they dreamed of other radical futures few outside the immigrant and exile communities seemed to hear or see. Making an inventory of revolutionary remembering could be that first step in preparing ourselves to identify, and if possible, cultivate new revolutionary subjectivities in the cities that Latina/o immigrants know best. We could start, in other words, by identifying the low-hanging fruit of an abandoned neighborhood tree, and then making plans for that tree's pruning, watering, and feeding.

Answering Arizona

We borrow from a speech Mao gave on May 29, 1939, as a kind of ideal to which we should aspire in the aftermath of Arizona's recent censorship of the Latino/ethnic studies high school curriculum. "It is good if the enemy attacks us, since it proves that we have drawn a clear line of demarcation between the enemy and ourselves. It is still better if the enemy attacks us wildly and paints us as utterly black and without a single virtue; it demonstrates that we have not only drawn a clear line of demarcation between the enemy and ourselves but also achieved a great deal in our work" (Mao 1939, n.p.). Could it be that they deserved the epithets of the populist Right, especially when they accused our colleagues of fomenting a postcolonial critique of the United States' conquest of the Arizona territory? As we all know, many of the attacks were fevered projections of an ethnic *reconquista* that our colleagues do not teach. We also know that they meant these attacks to distract Arizonans from the ruling majority's failure to prevent the state's fiscal collapse. They instead chose to blame the racialized other they strove to re-create, Mexican and Latino immigrants and their children, who will indeed alter the state's balance of political power, if only modestly.

The Tea-Bagger populists needed to turn the Latino/a immigrant into a terrifying threat. It did not matter to them that the community's integration into the state's electorate, and their attendant acquisition and exercise of civil rights universally accepted for African Americans, has been painfully slow. The symbiotic media-state representations of immigrant border violations had already produced the appropriate intensity of moral sensitization. They targeted teachers who taught the modest virtues of ethnic and racial diversity and the Latino community's well-documented contributions to Arizona's wealth as agents of subversion. The teachers who had had the audacity to urge the next generation of Latina and Latino voters to act as first-class rather than alienated citizens were a terror too good to pass up. Why calmly accept that inevitability, one that would not fundamentally alter the state's neoliberal underpinnings, if you could orchestrate a major distraction? Cultivating a panic was much better than acknowledging that Latino immigration was a symptom, not a cause, of the economic globalization that had destroyed the high-wage manufacturing Arizona had secured during the cold war, or that the low-wage, no-benefit post-Fordist regime that had replaced it depended on a surplus of "unskilled" immigrant labor. Such is the racist logic, Zizek observes, of populist xenophobia: it obsesses over the impure outsider that would threaten the purity of the polis, its innocent "we" of (white) natives, the indispensable ingredient of "whiteness" that the Tea-Baggers presume in their tribal construct of citizenship.

Perhaps it is time to earn their scorn. Perhaps it is time to search our political and cultural memories of failed revolutions, as Zizek recommends, for the antipode of the populist pole, a position around which a viable Left could coalesce and offer a coherent alternative to the populist Right. The students of Latino urbanism have a particular role to play in the search for that new positionality. We hope the next generation of Latino urban scholars will show how a viable Left in the United States cannot emerge if it does not embrace the quintessential "part of no part," the undocumented immigrant, and that inventory of others effectively stripped of citizenship, as its core constituency, the future majority that will embody and express our deepest democratic values and impulses.

Place matters in this continuing enterprise. That was one of the implications we explored in *Latino Metropolis* when we called for a new kind of

Latino politics—a politics of class and workplace. We asserted an emphasis on the places of production to imagine a new politics, one that would cut across districts and working-class neighborhoods: community politics are not principally the politics of neighborhoods but the politics of work, class, and culture. We should advance this line further now and reconsider what the category of class can mean in U.S. cities when the immigrant-dependent restaurant industry scatters the place of production throughout the urban landscape. That same question applies more directly to the Walmart clerks and subcontracted warehouse workers symbiotically connected to Asian manufacturing via that vast trans-Pacific system of commodity distribution known as logistics. Not only does understanding immigrant workers' role in global manufacturing clarify their labor power's strategic significance, it forces us to question the notion that consumption is the new point of production, an implicitly nationalist orientation that tends to privilege the welfare of the "American" worker-consumer over all the others, while ignoring the urgency of building transnational worker solidarity.

The organizers of Warehouse Workers United are, as of this writing, attempting such a recentering of working-class citizenship amid the world's largest concentration of warehouses. Global trade in the Pacific Rim and Southern California's north-south mountain corridors has created a new battlefield clustered around the rail, truck, and air infrastructure of San Bernardino and Riverside Counties. Geography has funneled the huge increases in cargo pulsing from the ports of Los Angeles and Long Beach through the historically depressed region misleadingly named the Inland Empire. The transformation of the logistics industry, which was touted as the cure to the region's chronic job losses and epidemic of housing foreclosures, actually raised particulate air pollution to the world's fourth highest while turning temporary employment agencies into the new growth sector (Hart 2006, 28). These permanently temporary agencies eagerly refined the "sweatshop" subcontracting technologies to the retail industry's specifications. They drastically lowered wages, job security, and safety standards for more than fifty-three thousand workers (most of them undocumented) by creating a barrier of deniability for the warehouse retailers to evade responsibility for creating those conditions (Jamieson 2012).

The Change To Win-supported campaign's answer to the atomizing technologies of outsourcing has been to build an impressive coalition of environmental, labor unions, church groups, and West and East Coast Occupiers in support of immigrant Latino workers battling for union representation, living wages, and safer working conditions (Woodman 2012). It attempts not only to create that tipping point at which Latino immigrant workers can make the transition from racialized minority to empowered working-class majority but also to neutralize the demoralizing effects of labor subcontracting by representing the entire transportation corridor as a continuation of the warehouse. Its strategy is to expose the industry's vulnerabilities to a variety of community actions, from regulatory and legal interventions against safety violations to blockades of key trucking arteries, by revealing its complicity in degrading the region's social and natural ecology (Lifsher 2012; Lydersen 2011).

Obviously, a handful of Latino urban scholars will not lead this constructive political project by themselves. Already a whole bundle of academics of seemingly marginalized tendencies, from critical ethnic studies to postcolonial studies, cultural studies, women's studies, and gender studies, as well as independent scholars, artists, and activists, are asking questions of this sort. As the Occupy movement demonstrates, their numbers will increase as the crisis in the developed economies of the West deepens and as the corporate sector further privatizes the academic organs of social reproduction and promotes a politics that makes it easier to simply externalize those functions.

What lies ahead for this next generation of would-be scholars, and how do they pursue it? We believe that Latino and Latina urban theorists can perform a great service of research and practice that explains to their would-be colleagues, and progressives generally, why they must see their futures in creating class relations based upon complete identification with the emergent urban immigrant majorities. They can also help by excavating the discursive legacy, those genealogies of knowledge and practice that have directly contributed to the recent mass mobilizations of Latino immigrant workers. They can set an example by acknowledging the Latino and Latina radical and revolutionary intellectuals, workers, and scholars who shaped the agenda and narratives that reacquainted organized labor and today's Occupiers with the feasibility of a national general strike by achieving a scale that spoke more loudly than its rhetoric.

Cultural processes were crucial in producing that result. The use of Spanish-language media, above all radio, to mobilize millions validated the importance we gave to that strategic resource in *Latino Metropolis*. The content and forms of their appeal to Latino workers also betrayed a genealogical moment overlooked in the scholarly studies that interpreted the 2006 mobilizations. Immigrant rights organizers formed in L.A.'s Marxist-

Leninist circles of the 1970s led that first push to prevent the passage of HR4437, legislation that would have set the stage for the deportation of millions of undocumented Latino immigrant workers and the prosecution of anyone convicted of sheltering them. That generation's historical formation was especially evident in the year's May Day demonstrations. They had orchestrated a mobilization in which supposedly "conservative" immigrants in immaculate white T-shirts denounced racism, sexism, class inequality, borders, imperialism, and neoliberal globalization—a concise inventory, in other words, of a discursive formation we can call the Latino Left.

Two immigrant rights activists, Jesse Diaz and Javier Rodriguez, deserve recognition for their intrepid leadership in initiating, organizing, and framing that day's unprecedented demonstrations. In addition to the million or so marchers mobilized in Chicago, New York, and dozens of smaller cities across the United States, one million more went to the streets of Los Angeles in two separate marches. The first wave of marches demanded immediate and unconditional amnesty for all undocumented immigrants, an immediate halt to border fence construction, decriminalization of the undocumented, and an immediate cessation of factory raids and deportations. More importantly, the mobilizations emptied the workplace. As many as 75 percent of the Los Angeles industries employing Latino labor shut their doors, while as many as 90 percent of the day truckers hauling goods from the ports of Los Angeles and Long Beach stayed home. "On farms in California and Arizona," Rodriguez said, "fruit and vegetables went unpicked, and across the country, meat-packing and poultry plants, fast-food franchises and other businesses were forced to close. In a lot of cases, employers supported their workers: all over Los Angeles businesses started putting up signs saying they would be closed on May 1" (Diaz and Rodriguez 2007, 99–101).

Those events deserve further study, starting with the so-called mainstream Latino organizations and unions that fragmented and weakened the mobilization's initial message by prematurely supporting the Democratic Party's pragmatic path to immigration reform. A new generation of scholars and organic intellectuals must also give itself permission to question the institutions from which they should expect bolder leadership. Would it be reasonable for them to ask, for example, why the Chicano studies discipline, especially its bureaucratic apparatus, seemed to take such a reticent stance toward the self-organizing immigrant energy recently displayed on the streets? That institutional ambivalence (not the independent scholars who met in the streets) also suggests itself when a few scholars and administrators still try to reconcile the uniqueness of Chicano identity, as asserted in the 1960s, with the growing and by now irreversible immigrant presence, which has transformed Latino communities everywhere. We will not go into all the twists and turns of that reticence here. Suffice it to say that, except for the sober concluding pages of Michael Soldatenko's *Chicano Studies: The Genesis of a Discipline* (2009), only a fraction of works within the discipline seem to have mustered the courage to directly discuss the widening fissures of this ideological debate. Strangely, that silence continues, as Soldatenko observes, even though a growing number, perhaps a majority, of scholars sheltered under the rubric of Chicano studies practice strains of scholarship that have already outstripped the discursive boundaries of its most generous disciplinary definitions. That silence means that the pressure to reradicalize Chicano studies has also come from the students and their sisters and brother academics outside the discipline.

We can hear that prodding to revisit pre-Chicano movement origins in works such as Gilbert G. Gonzalez's *Guest Workers or Colonized Labor? Mexican Labor Migration to the United States* (2007), Mike Davis's *Magical Urbanism: Latinos Reinvent the US Big City* (2000), David R. Diaz's *Barrio Urbanism: Chicanos, Planning, and American Cities* (2005), and William David Estrada's *The Los Angeles Plaza: Sacred and Contested Space* (2008), especially for his masterful recontextualization of the plaza's Magonista, Wobbly, and anarchist synergies. Raul Homero Villa's *Barrio-Logos: Space and Place in Urban Chicano Literature and Culture* (2000) and Ignacio Lopez-Calvo's *Latino Los Angeles in Film and Fiction: The Cultural Production of Social Anxiety* (2011) push upon that reticence from another direction. Both challenge the long-held myths that authentic Hispanic "cultural identity was to be found outside the urban context" and that the early 1970s had somehow birthed a fully formed Chicano literature from the preceding decade's radical protest. Lopez-Calvo's work does an especially effective job of debunking Chicano literature's pastoral image and uncomplicated identitarian origins. Not only does that literature draw from deep indigenous, Hispanic, and African roots, but its late twentieth-century energy is urban and therefore modern in its questioning of imposed or "traditional" tropes of racial, gender, and sexual identity. Its polyvocal, restless, questioning energy will continue in this century, Lopez-Calvo writes, given that "the massive migration of Latinos to Los Angeles has turned this late-capitalist metropolis into a privileged site for Chicano and Latino cultural production. It is no longer the Babylon where Mexican immigrants inevitably lose their 'authentic' national traits and roots" but the imaginary in which they radically remap the city's democratic possibilities (2011, xii, 3).

Ernesto Galarza's cryptic Magonista and Wobbly references in his classic autobiography, *Barrio Boy*, represent another contribution that urges a critical look back to the early Chicano movement's preoccupation with identity formation. Galarza would say as much in a series of interviews he gave in 1977-78 and 1981, when he questioned the way Chicano scholars and activists in the 1960s and 1970s tried to represent themselves through the single prism of ethnic identity:

> I try to stay away from terms that rely on ethnicity. I use terms that represent what people do for a living—*occupation* is a much more meaningful term. Academics at UCLA have worked on this theme. In Arizona and in New Mexico there is a great deal of scholarly interest in this problem of choice of terminology. I don't think it leads very far, because if you look at these terms—you'll find people who are called Chicanos in San Jose; they're called Chicanos in Imperial Valley; they're called Chicanos in San Francisco. But if you know those people, the occupational differences are more important, to me, anyway. It may be because I have a certain bias against ethnic identity. I don't think people should be handled that way . . . should be catalogued . . . because it's not a permanent characteristic other than to those who believe in very strong racial, ethnic characteristics—and I don't. (Galarza 1982, n.p.)

The Chicano studies project would eventually catch up to Galarza's formulation and embrace his understanding of social constructivism. However, the discipline retains a certain ambivalence regarding the utility of Galarza's cautiously expressed class analysis (one informed more by Weber than by Marx).

Does the bureaucratic imperative to defend Chicano studies in some of the same institutions Galarza mentioned more than four decades ago still trick us into a scholarship that imbues Chicano identity with a transcendent quality, one that defies the historical flux that transforms all others? Do we harbor a deeply buried assimilationist wish when we expect new Latino immigrants to act as Chicanos-in-the-making, a vast transitional population reliving the traumas and joys of inventing a bicultural-bilingual citizenship? Discovering the common experiences with which different immigrant communities have reclaimed their humanity in a system that denies it is indeed valuable. But do lingering notions of identity politics freeze us in a neoliberal status quo that acknowledges diversity while preventing us from facing the brutal economic reality of our time? Will celebrating diversity challenge the state in its current embattled corporate configuration to countenance the continued naturalization of millions of immigrants? Does not the current depth of the crisis require that we rethink what a "Chicano" politics can mean in an economy that will stagnate for decades to come, in which even the most modest, most humane immigration reforms, such as the "Dream Act," will require massive, broad-based national mobilizations to implement? It would seem that the manner in which Galarza's work slowly disappeared from the curriculum has answered these questions. His were not interesting questions.

But an ideological debate that erupted in the 1970s, outside the academy, on L.A.'s picket lines, in its sweatshops, and in INS detention facilities, would revive Galarza's line of questioning. Laura Pulido's *Black, Brown, Yellow, and Left: Radical Activism in Los Angeles* (2006) touched that nerve when she credited the Marxist-Leninist cadres of that decade for pushing the movement in a more radical and ultimately more fruitful direction. Pulido, who does not ignore the failures of Bert Corona and L.A.'s Centro de Acción Social Autónomo (CASA), nevertheless recognizes their undeniable impact on the city's present political landscape: "Former members of CASA had not only created a network of like-minded people but seeds of resistance within the 'old' labor movement that would blossom with advent of greater institutional support" (2006, 221). That cadre's most important discovery was to recognize the likely impact of the emergence of a majority immigrant Latino workforce on all other class and power relations in the city, a realization they obfuscated when they tried to replace Chicano cultural nationalism with Mexican nationalism as a means of achieving a new working-class solidarity. But even the seeming half-measure of representing CASA as the Marxist-Leninist vanguard of workers unified by a crudely constructed theory of nationalist loyalty had the benefit of loosening up the ways Chicano academics and activists had represented class relations and self-awareness until that time, and of recognizing the possibilities of Latin American worker solidarity. The seeds they had sown would bear fruit in the 1990s, when the former CASA members assumed pivotal positions of leadership within the local and national labor movement, within the legal arm of the immigrant rights movement, and within the political class that began to reshape the city's entire political culture. Their emancipatory intentions, moreover, did not simply respond to that decade's material conditions; their practice would create the conditions of another struggle, the one that reappeared to fill the streets of Los Angeles and other major cities in 2006.

But the relative silence with which the Chicano studies standard-bearers have received the work of Pulido and her urban studies colleagues underscores the subtle rift in the discipline's ethnically focused bureaucratic project. The edge of that rift reappears each time Latino students treat the glories of the 1960s with more reverence than the mass immigrant mobilizations that have occurred since the 1990s, a nostalgic gaze that prevents them from recognizing the radical possibilities of the present. That is what made Bert Corona so remarkable. If he were with us today, would he gently coax those students and faculty to overcome their fears and tell them that the present is the best time and place to struggle and that the scale of the immigrant-led labor movement he helped create dwarfs anything the Chicano movement achieved?

We must also acknowledge the limits Pulido imposed on herself. Her understandable focus on the field from which the three ideological configurations of L.A.'s ethnic Left emerged necessarily gave less attention to Bert Corona's biography. Nor did she have the space to adequately address the subtle ways these revived "Lefts" owed their successes to L.A.'s early and mid-twentieth-century leftist radicals. Perhaps we should put the responsibility for that silence at the feet of a prior generation of scholars and journalists who succeeded in distancing Corona from the early twentieth-century Left that formed him and made him a recurring target of Red-baiting. Perhaps we should also question those efforts to remake Bert as a wholesome ethnic leader of generic progressive tendencies and only the slightest "socialist" sympathies (Munoz 1994, 4). These revisions illustrate the ways the ghosts of the Left still haunt the Chicano movement's ideological project, a squeamishness Bert understood and patiently tolerated but ignored when it came time to take the courageous political gamble of challenging the early Chicano movement to embrace the cause of undocumented Mexican and Central and South American immigrant workers.

The effect of Bert's strategic choices, and his consistent critique of corporate capitalism, still cause some Chicano academics to agonize over whether they should embrace the immigrant workers who demonstrate a willingness to put their class loyalties before ethnic, racial, or national allegiances. That ambivalence persists when Chicano and Latino scholars look past the 1970s, that crucial decade in which the organizational and discursive foundations of today's Latino immigrant mass mobilizations began to appear as a complicated, largely urban response to brutal worker exploitation, the government's policies of immigration terror, and the limitations of the previous decade's Chicano radical discourse. It was in that decade that the first women and gay artists began to express their dissatisfaction with constraints of Chicano cultural nationalism, and Chicano activists confronted the immigrant and political refugees who would alter the demographic composition and social relations that characterized what they had once understood as a predominantly Mexican American "community." Not only would Mexican and other Latin American immigrants soon emerge as the barrio's new majority, they would eventually emerge as urban America's working class, a realization that obliged the more farsighted to see the sweatshop or factory floor as the crucial arena of struggle.

The ideological effects of travel to Cuba, Mexico, Central America, and other destinations in Latin America, as well as China, undertaken in the late 1960s and continuing through the 1970s and 1980s, provoked another series of discussions that would further erode the movement's insularity. Those Chicano activists, intellectuals, and artists who traveled and exposed themselves to a variety of Marxist and socialist critiques and debates centered on U.S. capitalism and imperialism would acquire more nuanced understandings of how they fit into a larger anti-imperialist front, as well as of the Left's failures and defeats. The pace of these conversations increased in the 1970s when brutal military repression from Mexico, Chile, and Argentina sent Latin American refugees and intellectuals to the United States. These conversations continued in the late seventies and eighties with the arrival of Central America's political and economic refugees who escaped U.S.-funded terror and counter-revolution.

These intellectuals often arrived with their books, given the popularity of Latin American literature experienced during the "boom" years, a reception enhanced by university courses that assigned them and Spanish-language print media that covered and interpreted them. Whether they passed through as touring performers or as lesser-known artists, writers, or professors who came to stay, young Chicano and Latino intellectuals found it easier to stay abreast of Latin America's political and cultural debates when they socialized with their Latin American cousins, dialogues that pushed that generation into a deeper exploration of their movement's pre-Chicano radical revolutionary roots.

These subversive influences and contradictory tendencies shared a geographic constant: they had converged in the major cities of the United States. The acknowledged centrality of the urban experience, as David Harvey's recent work suggests, therefore underlies the future study of the formation of Latino subjectivity. The recent studies that contextualize José Martí's New York, the city that witnessed Puerto Rican Bernardo Vega's political formation two decades later, represent a sample from that small number of postcolonial works that explore the U.S. city's role in coauthoring a transnational, hemispheric Latino intellectual legacy. We would expect Chicago to have exerted a comparable effect upon Lucy Gonzales Parsons, a possibility only marginally appreciated by the identity-based projects of recent African American and Chicano scholarship. Where else but in that brutal cauldron of industrial exploitation and anarchist protest would the former emancipated and fluently bilingual *mestiza* slave be able to reinvent herself into a radical labor activist who would convince Martí in 1887 of the possibilities of a Latina feminism? Laura Lomas, in her indispensable *Translating Empire: José Martí, Migrant Latino Subjects, and American Modernities* (2008), helps us see that other Lucy, the one the poet witnessed, through his emerging postcolonial gaze, in New York when she spoke in defense of the Haymarket Martyrs. Her oratorical art, because it equaled his, forced him to question his *macho* prejudices of women made mannish because they dared speak in the public sphere, and to recognize her as the unexpected female incarnation of the *mestizo* revolutionary he had begun to envision in *"Nuestra America."* The following passage further illustrates the transformative spell she cast on Martí:

> There were moments when not a sound could be heard in the assembly except her inspired voice, which flowed slowly from her mouth, like spheres of fire, and the gasping of those who had stopped breathing momentarily in order to hear the sob in her throat. When this Indian and Mexican *mestiza* stopped speaking, all the heads were inclined, as if in prayer upon the benches in church, and the room seemed to fill, like a field of wheat bending in the wind. . . . Everything in her appears an invitation to believe and to rise up. Her speech, in its total sincerity, is literary. Her doctrines wave like a flag; she does not ask for mercy for those condemned to death, for her own husband, but denounces the causes and the accomplices to the misery that leads men to desperation. (qtd. in Lomas 2008, 252-53)

Lucy's performance, however, embodied not only a glorious beauty but also the necessity and possibility of a revolutionary, anticapitalist politics rooted in the hemisphere's indigenous soil, and thus the seed of an organic, autochthonous society for which Martí still searched. There was one important realization Lucy's anarchism seemed to lack, one that Martí possessed but did not live long enough to share: that the existence of modern capitalism depended upon the discourse of "race" refined in the conquest of the Americas, a cultural technology readapted to that brutal task of dehumanizing, dividing, and subordinating late nineteenth-century workers.

The asking and answering of these questions, when contextualized in the cultural political economy of the urban scene, not only will provide a way of revitalizing the institutional purpose of Chicano studies but will suggest the role an urban Latino studies agenda can play in transforming progressive national politics, what Mike Davis famously called a "magical urbanism." These interventions can articulate new forms of critique and struggle through which laboring Latino classes, including the fragile first-generation middle class, might go beyond the limits imposed upon them by the logic of market capitalism to propose a Latino power of constructive and lasting effects, one through which a class teaches itself to think about capital while acting against it.

NOTES

1 Our use of the term *cultural political economy* is especially indebted to the work of Bob Jessop and his colleagues in the Cultural Political Economy Research Centre (CPERC) at Lancaster University in the United Kingdom. In this respect, CPERC promotes cultural political economy both as a principal theoretical orientation and method of analysis and as a valuable adjunct to other theories and methods that examines the relations among semiosis, imaginaries, political economy broadly conceived, and issues of governance, government, and governmentality.

REFERENCES

Chacón, Justin Akers, and Mike Davis. 2006. *No One Is Illegal: Fighting Racism and State Violence on the U.S.-Mexico Border.* Chicago: Haymarket Books.

Davis, Mike. 2000. *Magical Urbanism: Latinos Reinvent the US Big City.* London: Verso.

Diaz, David. 2005. *Barrio Urbanism: Chicanos, Planning and American Cities.* New York: Routledge.

Diaz, Jesse, and Javier Rodriguez. 2007. "A Movement of Movements?—22: Jesse Diaz and Javier Rodriguez, Undocumented in America." *New Left Review* 47: 93-106.

Estrada, William David. 2008. *The Los Angeles Plaza: Sacred and Contested Space.* Austin: University of Texas Press.

Foucault, Michel. [1978] 1991. "Governmentality." In *The Foucault Effect: Studies in Governmentality, with Two Lectures by and an Interview with Michel Foucault*, edited by Graham Burcell, Colin Gordon, and Peter Miller, 87-104. Chicago: University of Chicago Press.

Frug, Gerald E. 1999. *Citymaking: Building Communities without Building Walls*. Princeton: Princeton University Press.

Galarza, Ernesto. 1982. "The Burning Light: Action and Organizing in the Mexican Community in California." Interviews by Gabrielle Morris and Timothy Beard, 1977, 1978, and 1981. Transcript. Regional Oral History Office, Bancroft Library, University of California. www.archive.org/stream/burninglightactioogalarich/burninglightactioogalarich_djvu.txt.

Gonzalez, Gilbert G. 2007. *Guest Workers or Colonized Labor? Mexican Labor Migration to the United States*. Boulder, CO: Paradigm.

Hart, Ian. 2006. *Paying with Our Health: The Real Cost of Freight Transportation in California*. Oakland, CA: Pacific Institute.

Jamieson, Dave. 2011. "The New Blue Collar: Temporary Work, Lasting Poverty and the American Warehouse." *Huffington Post*, December 12.

Jessop, Bob, and Stijn Oosterlynck. 2008. "Cultural Political Economy: On Making the Cultural Turn without Falling into Soft Economic Sociology." *Geoforum* 39:1155-69.

Lefebvre, Henri. 2007. *Everyday Life in the Modern World*. New Brunswick, NJ: Transaction.

Lifsher, Marc. 2012. "State Fines Warehouse Companies for Safety Violations." *Los Angeles Times*, January 18.

Lomas, Laura. 2008. *Translating Empire: José Martí, Migrant Latino Subjects, and American Modernities*. Durham: Duke University Press.

Lopez-Calvo, Ignacio. 2011. *Latino Los Angeles in Film and Fiction: The Cultural Production of Social Anxiety*. Tucson: University of Arizona Press.

Lydersen, Kari. 2011. "California Workers Take Walmart's Warehouses to Court." *In These Times*, October 21.

Mao Tse-tung. 1939. "To Be Attacked by the Enemy Is Not a Bad Thing but a Good Thing." Speech, May 26. www.marxists.org/reference/archive/mao/selected-works/volume-6/mswv6_32.htm.

Marx, Karl. 1990. *Capital, Volume 1*. Harmondsworth: Penguin.

Monahan, Torin. 2002. "Los Angeles Studies: The Emergence of a Specialty Field." *City and Society* 14 (2): 155-84.

Munoz, Sergio. 1994. "Guided by a Vision: How Bert Corona Met the Challenges of Latino Leadership. *Memories of Chicano History: The Life and Narrative of Bert Corona*, by Mario T. Garcia." *Los Angeles Times*, October 9, 4.

Pulido, Laura. 2006. *Black, Brown, Yellow, and Left: Radical Activism in Los Angeles*. Berkeley: University of California Press.

Ribera-Fumaz, Ramon. 2009. "From Urban Political Economy to Cultural Political Economy: Rethinking Culture and the Economy in and beyond the Urban." *Progress in Human Geography* 33 (4): 447-65.

Soldatenko, Michael. 2009. *Chicano Studies: The Genesis of a Discipline*. Tucson: University of Arizona Press.

Valle, Victor M. 2009. *City of Industry: Genealogies of Power in Southern California.* New Brunswick: Rutgers University Press.

Valle, Victor M., and Rodolfo D. Torres. 2000. *Latino Metropolis.* Minneapolis: University of Minnesota Press.

Villa, Raul Homero. 2000. *Barrio-Logos: Space and Place in Urban Chicano Literature and Culture.* Austin: University of Texas Press.

Woodman, Spencer. 2012. "Labor Takes Aim at Walmart—Again." *Nation,* January 4.

Zizek, Slavoj. 2009. "Why Populism Is (Sometimes) Good Enough in Practice, but Not in Theory." In *In Defense of Lost Causes,* 264-333. London: Verso.

About the Contributors

DAVID R. DIAZ is Professor of Chicano Studies at California State University, Los Angeles, and author of *Barrio Urbanism: Chicanos, Planning, and American Cities*

SILVIA DOMÍNGUEZ is Assistant Professor of Sociology and Human Services at Northeastern University and author of *Getting Ahead: Social Mobility, Public Housing and Immigrant Networks* (New York University Press, 2011). Domínguez has also published in journals like *Social Problems, Community Psychology,* and *Family Relations* and has received a Ford Foundation Post Doctoral Fellowship.

JOSÉ L. S. GÁMEZ is Associate Professor of Architecture and Urban Design and the Coordinator of the Design + Society Research Center in the School of Architecture at the University of North Carolina at Charlotte. He is also a member of the Latin American Studies faculty and has been a Research Fellow with the Institute for Social Capital and a Faculty Fellow with the Urban Institute at UNC Charlotte.

JOHANA LONDOÑO is a PhD candidate in the American Studies Program, Department of Social and Cultural Analysis, New York University. Her research interests include urban social theory and policy, aesthetics and visual culture, and Latina/o studies. She has published in *Identities: Global Studies in Power and Culture* and is finalizing her dissertation on the cultural politics of late twentieth-century Latino place-making and urban design across the United States.

BENJAMIN MARQUEZ is Professor of Political Science at the University of Wisconsin, Madison. His research interests include social movements, urban politics, and minority politics. His published work examines the relationship between race, political power, social identities, and public and political incorporation. He is the author of *Power and Politics in a Chicano Barrio: A Study of Mobilization Efforts and Community Power in El Paso* (University Press of America, 1985), *LULAC: The Evolution of a Mexican American Political Organization* (University of Texas Press, 1993), and *Mexican-American Political Organizations: Choosing Issues, Taking Sides* (University of Texas Press, 2003), which won the 2004 Best Book Award in the Race, Ethnicity and Politics (REP) Section of the American Political Science Association.

NESTOR RODRIGUEZ is Professor of Sociology at the University of Texas at Austin. His topics of research include international migration, race and ethnic relations, and political sociology.

RODOLFO D. TORRES is Professor of Urban Planning, Chicano Studies, and Political Science at the University of California Irvine, and co-author of *After Race: Racism after Multiculturalism*

VICTOR VALLE is Professor of Ethnic Studies at California Polytechnic State University, San Luis Obispo. He is coauthor of *Latino Metropolis* (University of Minnesota Press, 2000), author of *City of Industry: Genealogies of Power in Southern California* (Rutgers University Press, 2009), and a Radcliffe Fellow.

KEE WARNER is Associate Vice Chancellor for Diversity and Inclusiveness and Professor of Sociology at the University of Colorado, Colorado Springs. His published research, which focuses on the areas of urban sustainability and environmental justice, includes a coauthored book, *Building Rules: How Local Controls Shape Community Economies and Environments* (Westview Press, 2000), as well as articles in sociological and interdisciplinary journals in the United States and abroad.

Index

CRA. *See* Community Reinvestment Act
of 1977
Crusade for Justice, 7, 33
Cruz, Celia, 58
Cuban Refugee Program, 50, 51, 62n1
Cubans: business owners, 58; Catholic
Church and, 62n1; in Miami, 62n2;
population in U.S., 1; racist attitudes
of older, 51; SBA and inclusion of,
50–51; in Union City, 49–52
Cultural community, 4, 23, 24–25
Cultural political economy: alternative futures for, 181–201; Arizona
answered with, 188–99; with city as
narrative observatory, 185–88; explanation of, 181–85, 199n1; genealogy
with, 188; immigration policy protests and, 1, 192
Cultural Political Economy Research
Centre (CPERC), 199n1
Culture: everyday life and barrio, 23–28;
as performative expression, 126;
planning and SUV, 30–32; as social
occupation, 126–27
Cuomo, Mario, 144

Dávila, Arlene, 54, 59
Davis, Mike, 8–9, 35, 54, 111, 115, 193, 199
Dear, Michael J., 54
De Léon, Arnoldo, 105n5
Delinquency, 75
Demographic changes, 145
Demolition, home, 26
Densification, 24, 28, 40–41, 52
Department of Education, U.S., 81
Department of Housing and Urban
Development (HUD), 71, 73, 81–82,
97, 143–44
Development: housing's link to, 78–80.
See also Redevelopment
Diaz, David, 12, 193
Diaz, Jesse, 192
Discrimination, housing, 71, 135, 141, 144.
See also Racism
Diversity, with public housing, 135

Domínguez, Silvia, 15
Donovan, Shaun, 82
Drug Elimination Grants, 154
Duarte, Juan Pablo, 59
Dumb Growth, 21
Dumping, illegal, 16, 168–69

East Boston, MA: Italian Americans in,
16, 135–36, 141; as receiving zone for
immigrants, 141; white population
in, 145. *See also* Boston, MA
East Los Angeles, CA: Boyle Heights in,
115–17; as modern-day Atzlán, 113;
Mothers of, 169, 171–72; population
of Latinas/os in, 114. *See also* Los
Angeles, CA
Economic restructuring: families influ-
enced by, 2; L.A. school and, 35
Economy: cultural political, 181–201;
Latin American women and im-
proved, 135, 147, 152
Education, 81; Chicano studies, 106n11;
Cubans with high school, 51; integra-
tion in, 142; for Latinas/os youth, 67;
minorities in planning, 2–3, 9
Electronics Industry Good Neighbor
Campaign, 170–71, 174
El Pueblo, Inc., 130n8
El Paso, TX, 6, 32, 33
El Salvador, 52, 145
Eminent domain, 8, 11, 33–34, 76
Environmental justice movement:
beginnings, 16; dual agenda with,
169–71; Electronics Industry Good
Neighbor Campaign in, 170–71, 174;
ethnic split within, 164–65; future
of Mexican American, 171–76; lead
poisoning and, 169, 174; MELA in,
169, 171–72; Mexican Americans and,
163–80; origins of Mexican American, 167–69; PODER in, 167–68, 169,
171, 172; racism and, 163–64, 173; settlement agreements, 176n2; SNEEJ
in, 164–67, 171, 172, 174–76; SWOP in,
164, 167, 170–71; TCE in, 168–69

61

RESIDENTIAL APARTEID

PAST LAWS → FHA
SUNSET LAW → ARREST OF
ETHNIC MINORITY
FOR BEING IN WHITE
NEIGHBORHOOD AFTER
SUNSET

STRUCTURAL
UNDERDEVELOPMENT
PRIVATE SECTOR DID NOT INVEST
IN ETH. NEIGHBORHOODS → ACTUALLY
PUBLIC SECTOR → DOES NOT ALLOCATE
$ $ INTO URBAN CITY